LOCATING
ATONEMENT

PROCEEDINGS OF THE LOS ANGELES THEOLOGY CONFERENCE

This is the third volume in a series published by Zondervan Academic. It is the proceedings of the Los Angeles Theology Conference held under the auspices of the Torrey Honors Institute at Biola University, with the support of Fuller Theological Seminary, in January 2015. The conference is an attempt to do several things. First, it provides a regional forum in which scholars, students, and clergy can come together to discuss and reflect upon central doctrinal claims of the Christian faith. It is also an ecumenical endeavor. Bringing together theologians from a number of different schools and confessions, the LATC seeks to foster serious engagement with Scripture and tradition in a spirit of collegial dialogue (and disagreement), looking to retrieve the best of the Christian past in order to forge theology for the future. Finally, each volume in the series focuses on a central topic in dogmatic theology. It is hoped that this endeavor will continue to fructify contemporary systematic theology and foster a greater understanding of the historic Christian faith among the members of its different communions.

LOCATING ATONEMENT
EXPLORATIONS IN CONSTRUCTIVE DOGMATICS
Oliver D. Crisp and Fred Sanders
General Editors

Oliver D. Crisp and Fred Sanders, Editors

LOCATING ATONEMENT

Explorations in
CONSTRUCTIVE DOGMATICS

CONTRIBUTORS

Bruce McCormack • Michael Horton
Matthew Levering • Eleonore Stump • Benjamin Myers

 ZONDERVAN®

LOS ANGELES
THEOLOGY
CONFERENCE

ZONDERVAN

Locating Atonement
Copyright © 2015 by Oliver D. Crisp and Fred Sanders

This title is also available as a Zondervan ebook. Visit www.zondervan.com/ebooks.

Requests for information should be addressed to:

Zondervan, 3900 *Sparks Drive SE, Grand Rapids, Michigan 49546*

Library of Congress Cataloging-in-Publication Data

Locating atonement : explorations in constructive dogmatics / Oliver D. Crisp and Fred
    Sanders, general editors.
        p. cm.
    Includes bibliographical references and index.
    ISBN 978-0-310-52116-7 (softcover)
        1. Atonement—Congresses. I. Crisp, Oliver, editor.
    BT265.3.L63 2015   2015
    232'.3—dc23   2015021605

Cover design: Tammy Johnson
Cover photo: © Peter Barritt/Superstock.com
Interior design: Matthew Van Zomeren and Ben Fetterley

Printed in the United States of America

HB 08.29.2017

To Kevin Vanhoozer,
Theologian of the Drama of Salvation

CONTENTS

ACKNOWLEDGMENTS

THE EDITORS WOULD LIKE TO THANK Dr. Paul Spears, Director of the Torrey Honors Institute at Biola University, and the staff and faculty of Biola for their assistance with and support for the third Los Angeles Theology Conference (LATC) in January of 2015, out of which these published proceedings grew. Sophia Wetzig was of great help in the administration of the conference. We are grateful to her. Thanks too to Fuller Theological Seminary for its ongoing support of LATC. This is now the third time that we are able to record grateful thanks to our editor and colleague, Katya Covrett, for her invaluable assistance without which this volume would not be in your hands, dear reader. Thanks too to the Zondervan Team (aka "The Z Team") — Stan Gundry as editor-in-chief, Jesse Hillman, Jim Ruark, Kari Moore, and Josh Kessler.

The atonement is an important feature of much contemporary systematic theology. Of the many Christian thinkers who have contributed to that recent resurgence of interest, Kevin Vanhoozer is certainly one of the most creative. We dedicate this third LATC volume to him as a token of our gratitude and respect.

CONTRIBUTORS

Stephen T. Davis — is professor at Claremont McKenna College, in Claremont, CA. He holds a BA from Whitworth University, an MDiv from Princeton Theological Seminary, a PhD from Claremont Graduate University, and the LHD (doctor of humane letters) from Whitworth University.

Daniel J. Hill — is lecturer in philosophy at Liverpool University, UK. He holds a BA from Oxford University and an MA and PhD from King's College, University of London.

Michael Horton — is professor of theology at Westminster Theological Seminary, Escondido, CA. He has a BA from Biola University, an MA from Westminster Theological Seminary in Escondido, and a PhD from Wycliffe Hall, Oxford, and Coventry University, UK.

Joseph Jedwab — is assistant professor of philosophy, Kutztown University, PA. His BA is from King's College, London, and his MPhil and DPhil are from Oxford University.

Adam J. Johnson — is assistant professor in the Torrey Honors Institute, Biola University. He received his BA from Biola University, his MA from Talbot Theological Seminary at Biola University, his MDiv from Princeton Theological Seminary, and his PhD from Trinity Evangelical Divinity School.

Matthew Levering — is the James and Mary D. Perry Jr. Professor of Theology at Mundelein Seminary, Chicago. He has a BA from the University of North Carolina, Chapel Hill, an MTS from Duke University, and a PhD from Boston College.

T. Mark McConnell — is lecturer in the School of Theology, Laidlaw College, Auckland, New Zealand. He earned his BSc degree from Glasgow Caledonian University, his LLB and MEd degrees from the University of Aberdeen, an MDiv from Regent College, Vancouver, BC, and a PhD from London School of Theology.

Bruce L. McCormack — is Charles Hodge Professor of Theology, Princeton Theological Seminary. He received his BA from Point Loma Nazarene University, his MDiv from Nazarene Theological Seminary, and his PhD from Princeton Theological Seminary.

Benjamin Myers — is lecturer in systematic theology at the School of Theology, Charles Stuart University, in Sydney, Australia. He has a BA and PhD from James Cook University.

R. Lucas Stamps — is assistant professor of Christian studies at California Baptist University, Riverside, CA. He holds a BA from Auburn University. His MDiv and PhD degrees are from the Southern Baptist Theological Seminary.

Kyle C. Strobel — is assistant professor at Biola University and research associate at the University of the Free State, Bloemfontein, South Africa. He holds a BA from Judson University, two MA degrees in New Testament and philosophy of religion and ethics from Talbot School of Theology at Biola University, and a PhD from the University of Aberdeen.

Eleonore Stump — is Robert J. Henle Professor of Philosophy at St. Louis University. She received a BA in classical languages from Grinnell College, an MA in biblical studies from Harvard University, and an MA and PhD in medieval studies from Cornell University.

Jeremy R. Treat — is a Pastor for Preaching and Vision at Reality LA, a church in Los Angeles, and adjunct professor of theology at Biola University. He received his PhD in theology from Wheaton College.

Adonis Vidu — is associate professor of theology, Gordon-Conwell Theological Seminary, Wenham, MA. He has a BA from Emmanuel Bible Institute, an MPhil from Babes-Bolyai University, and a PhD in theology from the University of Nottingham, UK.

Eric T. Yang — is visiting assistant professor at Claremont McKenna College, Claremont, CA. He received his PhD in philosophy from the University of California, Santa Barbara.

ABBREVIATIONS

CD	*Church Dogmatics* (by Karl Barth)
HTR	*Harvard Theological Review*
IJST	*International Journal of Systematic Theology*
LCC	Library of Christian Classics
LXX	Septuagint
MTh	*Modern Theology*
NPNF1	*Nicene and Post-Nicene Fathers*, series 1
NPNF2	*Nicene and Post-Nicene Fathers*, series 2
PG	Patrologia graeca
PS	Penal substitution
PSA	Penal substitution atonement
RS	*Religious Studies*
ST	*Summa theological* (by Aquinas)

BIBLE VERSIONS

INTRODUCTION

IN THE LAST DECADE there has been a renewed interest in the doctrine of the atonement. Weighty tomes have rolled off the presses, and there appears to be no sign of this abating. Whereas the historic literature on the doctrine has tended to produce particular models or accounts of the doctrine, much of the modern literature has been directed toward denying that there is any single account or model of the atonement that proffers a complete or even an adequate account of this aspect of Christ's work taken in isolation. Instead, many modern writers aver, there is a range of atonement models.

For a number of those writing on the topic today, the way of proceeding is to map out the various atonement models in a typology and then weave together some synthetic understanding of the doctrine from elements of the various extant models, showing how no one approach can do all the work of giving an account of this facet of Christ's work. This we might call the *egalitarian approach to atonement doctrine*. On this way of thinking, no single model of atonement subsumes the others or is superior in its explanatory power. In fact, each has its own particular contribution to make, though none has a monopoly on the truth of the matter. The theological task, so this way of thinking goes, is to pick the right combination of conceptual elements from existing models, recombining them into something both constructive and useful for the church and academy today.

In addition to this egalitarian approach, there has been a decided turn away from those traditional accounts of atonement that privilege notions of satisfaction and penal substitution. Here the influence of certain feminist critics of such models has been widely felt, alongside the philosophical objections to key aspects of such models suggested by the work of philosophers like René Girard. Those influenced by this way of thinking maintain that God the Father cannot be wroth with God the Son, punishing him for our sin in our place as our substitute. That would constitute a sort of cosmic child abuse, the misuse of divine power on an almost unimaginable scale.

Such worries have led a number of contemporary theologians to abandon satisfaction and penal substitutionary accounts of atonement for alternatives that do not appear to suffer from the same debilitating drawbacks. One widely canvassed family of alternatives has to do with so-called nonviolent approaches to the atonement, according to which Christ's work on the cross is part of a much larger work in the incarnation. This larger work has to do with the healing of fallen human natures by means of Christ's victory over sin, death, and the Devil, not with the satisfaction of divine wrath or the exercise of divine retribution.

The debate about which typology of atonement models is most adequate, as well as about which combination of atonement motifs is most appropriate to a contemporary synthetic understanding of the atonement—even whether there is such a thing as an adequate combination of atonement motifs—continues to rage. No doubt this is an important feature of contemporary theological work on the topic. Nevertheless, this volume is not a contribution to that trajectory in the atonement literature. Instead, speakers at the third Los Angeles Theology Conference were asked to address a rather different question. This has to do with the relationship between the doctrine of atonement (however that is conceived) and other related topics in Christian theology.

Suppose the doctrine of atonement is placed beside, say, the doctrine of the external works of the Trinity, or the doctrine of creation, or the image of God, or the notion of human suffering witnessed to in Scripture, or whatever (take your pick of the central topics in Christian theology). What would be the result of such an exercise? How does the redemptive work of Christ relate to other load-bearing structures in dogmatic theology? This is an important task, though one not attended to with the same zeal in the recent literature as mapping out atonement typologies and placing a constructive view within such typologies.

No doubt theologians should focus on giving a proper account of particular doctrines, their shape, their dogmatic function, and so forth. But theologians should also pay attention to the relationship between different doctrines in the wider scheme of Christian theology. Surely that is what it is to be a truly *systematic* theologian. Focusing on a particular doctrine presents its own challenges, and rigorous work still needs to be done on analyzing and explicating the atonement, and the work of Christ more generally. However, exercising a judgment about how one central Christian doctrine relates to another—how, say, atonement relates to the ascension or the Eucharist—these are matters that are in some respects much harder to address in an adequate manner. At least part of the reason for this is just that there are more moving parts, more issues and concepts to attend to, as well as a larger picture of the scope and cohesion of theology that must be considered.

Suppose someone decides to paint a portrait of Christ. Getting the color, shape, form, and relations between different elements of the figure will be important. In portraiture, the relations between parts (e.g., parts of the face to the whole face) and the whole (face and figure in relation to the parts and to the surroundings in which the figure is placed) are vital. Getting these details just right is a matter of fine work and careful aesthetic judgments. Now consider someone who is not just painting a portrait of Christ, but painting a portrait of Christ at the Last Supper. Now there are actually thirteen portraits to worry about — not just Christ but also his twelve apostles: thirteen postures, thirteen figures with complex inter-relationships, as well as the matter of the context and surroundings in which they are placed by the artist, the light that falls upon the scene, the colors chosen, and so on. These two examples pick out relevant differences between theological work on a given doctrine (akin to painting a single portrait) and research on the relation between one doctrine and another in the wider framework of Christian belief encapsulated in systematic theology (akin to painting the Last Supper scene).

Although the comparative, synthetic work of examining one doctrine in light of another is demanding, it also often throws new light on how we regard the doctrine with which we began. In a similar fashion, the artist who begins by painting a portrait of Christ, and then broadens out to paint the other figures in the Last Supper tableaux, finds that at the end of her task she sees her initial work on the Christ-portrait rather differently. It is now part of a larger, more complex whole in which it is situated. Or, more precisely, its relationships to the larger, complex whole are more evident. In painting the whole with all its complex parts, working out the particular relations of those parts to one another and to the whole, the artist is left with a different view of the portrait with which she began.

So it is with synthetic theological work in systematic theology. Relating the part to the whole, the one doctrine to other doctrines, gives us a different vantage, one in which the part with which we began (the particular doctrine), is now revealed as one element in a larger context. The particular portrait no longer dominates, but its place relative to the other parts of the whole produces something beautiful; the parts and their relations to one another and to the totality of Christian doctrine reveal a greater, more harmonious whole. Or at least, that is how it ought to be.

The eighteenth-century New England divine, Jonathan Edwards, once wrote about how the parts of a complex whole might be so related to one another that the overall aesthetic quality of the whole was greater than the sum of its parts.[1] Such complex wholes were, he maintained, instances of "excellency," with God being the supremely excellent being. It may be going a little too far to suggest that the essays contained in this volume all demonstrate the truth of Edwards's maxim, but they do provide windows onto the task of giving an account of this central aspect of God's redemptive work in Christ that sets it in a broader theological context. If the results are not necessarily always instances of Edwardsian "excellency," they do nevertheless exemplify the great theological benefits of approaching the atonement by means of situating it within the larger scheme of Christian doctrine.

Once we see the atonement as one part, or aspect, of the larger scheme of salvation, and once we see more clearly the relation of the parts to the whole of Christian doctrine, our grasp of these parts, and the whole that they comprise, should be *enlarged*. That is surely a good thing, for such enlargement of vision helps fend off the unhappy obsession with doctrinal minutiae at the expense of the larger theological canvas. It also helps us to understand that Christian doctrine is a complex whole in which the various parts relate to one another. Altering one element of that whole has implications for other parts and for the shape of Christian doctrine taken as a whole. What we think about the atonement and how we conceive it will have implications for what we think about other aspects of theology (e.g., the incarnation, the order of salvation, glorification) irrespective of whether we trace those implications out.

The essays in this volume might be thought of as a collection of studies that do attempt to trace out some of the theological implications of the atonement. They also contribute to our understanding of the doctrine, of course. But at least as important as enlarging that aspect of our theological knowledge is the broadening out of our theological vision. It is this larger task at which many of the essays take aim.

OVERVIEW OF THE CHAPTERS

The chapters are ordered topically, as they would appear in a textbook of systematic theology. In the first chapter, Adonis Vidu carries forward a con-

---

1.   See Jonathan Edwards, "The Mind," in *The Works of Jonathan Edwards*, vol. 6, *Scientific and Philosophical Writings*, ed. Wallace E. Anderson (New Haven: Yale University Press, 1980).

structive theological project on the atonement that he began in his recent monograph, *Atonement, Law, and Justice*.[2] In his chapter he addresses the relationship between atonement and the external works of the Trinity in creation, the so-called *opera trinitatis ad extra*. He argues that placing the atonement within the broader context of the external works of God helps to make sense of the way in which this aspect of God's redemptive task is bound up with the eternal decision of the whole Trinity, though it terminates in a particular manner upon the second person of the Trinity incarnate.

In the second chapter, Matthew Levering focuses on the redemptive work of Christ in relation to the created order more directly. Taking as his point of departure the magisterial work of St. Thomas Aquinas, Levering offers a critical but sympathetic reading of several recent proposals on creation before offering his own constructive account at the end of his essay.

In chapter 3, Australian theologian Benjamin Myers presents a rereading of patristic accounts of the atonement in relation to the idea of the image of God. He argues that the influential reading of the patristic approach to atonement popularized by Gustav Aulén is, in fact, a misunderstanding of the patristic witness.[3] His paper goes a considerable way towards providing a corrective to those who have followed Aulén's lead. In it Myers outlines a constructive account of the doctrine in relation to theological anthropology that places the views of several important patristic writers in a different light from a number of recent treatments of the same material.

In the fourth chapter entitled, "Atoning Wisdom: The Wisdom of God in the Way of Salvation," Biola theologians Adam J. Johnson and Kyle Strobel seek to bring the concept of divine wisdom (which has a rich cluster of biblical and traditional connotations) into "dialogue" with the notion of atonement. The result is an instance of just the sort of comparative analysis between atonement and another doctrine (in this case, divine wisdom) that motivated the production of this volume.

In the fifth chapter, pastor-theologian Jeremy Treat tackles the relationship between the doctrine of atonement and the concept of covenant, building on themes showcased in his recent monograph on the subject.[4]

Lucas Stamps turns to the relationship between the atonement and the incarnation in the sixth chapter. He tackles the way in which the ancient

2. Adonis Vidu, *Atonement, Law, and Justice: The Cross in Historical and Cultural Contexts* (Grand Rapids: Baker, 2014).

3. Gustaf Aulén, *Christus Victor: An Historical Study of the Three Main Types of the Idea of the Atonement*, trans. A. G. Herbert (London: SPCK, 1931).

4. Jeremy R. Treat, *The Crucified King: Atonement and Kingdom in Biblical and Systematic Theology* (Grand Rapids: Zondervan, 2014).

doctrine of dyothelitism, which is the claim that Christ had two wills, one human and the other divine, helps make sense of what is happening in the work of Christ on the cross, using the biblical scene of Christ's agony in the garden of Gethsemane as his frame of reference.

There follow two chapters on matters pertaining to divine punishment, retribution, and wrath that are more philosophical in flavor. Chapter 7 offers the beginnings of a rehabilitation of models of atonement that have penal and substitutionary components. Daniel Hill and Joseph Jedwab attempt to locate the atonement in broader theories of punishment and retribution, arguing that there is a plausible way of construing the atonement that draws upon these ways of thinking about what the work of Christ entails. Then in chapter 8, Eric Yang and Stephen Davis focus on the relationship between the doctrine of atonement and divine wrath. In the course of their argument they reason that it is appropriate to think of the atonement in terms of the assuaging or satisfaction of divine wrath, contrary to influential naysayers in the recent atonement debate.

Scottish theologian Mark McConnell focuses on a rather different angle in the ninth chapter. Instead of thinking about atonement in terms of guilt and punishment, he considers the reconciliation of Christ in terms of relational rupture and shame, drawing on work in the social sciences, particularly psychology, in order to flesh out an account of the atonement as a response to shame.

Bruce McCormack is best known for his seminal contributions to the study of the twentieth-century Swiss theologian, Karl Barth. But more recently he has turned his attention to a constructive post-Barthian theological project. This does not leave Barth behind so much as it builds upon elements of Barth's thought, taking it in new, constructive directions. In the tenth chapter, McCormack considers the fraught relationship between the doctrine of atonement and human suffering as part of this newer theological project.

Eleonore Stump's work on medieval philosophy and theology, as well as in contemporary philosophy of religion and philosophical theology, is also well-known. In chapter 11, she considers the relationship between atonement and Eucharist, offering a particular view of Christ's work in the process that owes much to the work of medieval philosopher and theologian Peter Abelard, as well as to the Angelic Doctor, St. Thomas Aquinas.

It is fitting that in the final chapter of this volume, Reformed theologian Michael Horton takes up the task of relating the atonement to the ascension of Christ. Paying particular attention to the work of the

French Reformer, John Calvin, as well as to recent work retrieving Calvin's understanding of participation in the work of theologians like Julie Canlis and Todd Billings, Horton presents his readers with a compelling account of the importance of atonement for ascension and participation in the divine life. In this way Horton's essay in this volume echoes themes in his Covenant series of theological studies,[5] as well as his magisterial systematic theology, *The Christian Faith*.[6]

May these essays extend discussion of the doctrine of atonement and its place among the other central topics of Christian theology, *ad maiorem dei gloriam*.

Oliver D. Crisp and Fred Sanders, February 2015

---

5.   See, e.g., his introduction to the topic developed in his Covenant series of monographs in Michael Horton, *God of Promise: Introducing Covenant Theology* (Grand Rapids: Baker Books, 2005).
6.   Michael Horton, *The Christian Faith: A Systematic Theology for Pilgrims on the Way* (Grand Rapids: Zondervan, 2011).

CHAPTER 1

THE PLACE OF THE CROSS AMONG THE INSEPARABLE OPERATIONS OF THE TRINITY

ADONIS VIDU

THE CONFERENCE TITLE invites us to "locate atonement" within a broader theological framework.[1] In response to this challenge, I wish to explore the integration between the work of Christ at the cross and the classic doctrine of inseparable trinitarian operations. While I will not be defending a specific theory of the atonement, the theses that follow could be taken as a set of trinitarian constraints on any such theory. In particular, such constraints will affect the understanding of "divine punishment" in certain atonement models.

I will first attempt to unpack the logic of inseparable operations. While I am convinced that theology is still searching for an adequate conceptual model of trinitarian economic agency, the patristic grammar of the concept rules out certain misconceptions of what this inseparability entails.

---

1. I would like to acknowledge some very helpful comments by Derek Rishmawy, Jeremy Treat, Oliver Crisp, and students in my Gordon-Conwell seminar on Attributes of the Trinitarian God.

Next, I discuss certain problems in the recent application of the principle to the work of Christ by Kathryn Tanner and Bruce McCormack. In light of these perceived weaknesses, the third section turns to an exploration of the doctrine of the trinitarian missions, with the assistance of Aquinas and Bernard Lonergan. At this point, three theses will be made in relation to our topic. The final section will then outline the significance of these theses for penal substitutionary atonement specifically.

THE LOGIC OF INSEPARABILITY

Since the doctrine of inseparable operations is well engrained in the fabric of Reformational theology, and in particular among defenders of penal substitution (PS), I will not be defending it here. However, *lax construals* of this principle abound. In particular, this unity is often defined as a unity of intention and purpose. The tradition, however, is rather scrupulous about how this unity is to be construed. I will focus mainly on the Cappadocians and Augustine. This is not to say that other important statements of the doctrine are not to be found; however, the Cappadocians and Augustine crystalize some of these scruples, often neglected today.

That the Cappadocians affirm this principle is noncontroversial. Basil affirms it in relation to understanding the work of the Spirit: "The Holy Spirit is inseparable and wholly incapable of being parted from the Father and the Son ... in every operation."[2] For Nyssen, the unity of operations is not a statement merely to the effect that the Father, Son, and Spirit do the same things independently of one another. Rather, because they do the same actions, they share the same power. The action of cleansing from sin, for example, is attributed to both the Spirit (Rom 8:2,13) and to Christ (1 Jn 1:9). Clearly, this is not simply the Spirit cleansing some and Christ others, but both being active in the very same action. For Gregory's argument against Eunomius to work, then, it is not enough to say that the two work in common, both with the intention of achieving an eventual end. Rather, they must each be involved in each other's activities.

Thus, writes Nyssen,

> since among men the action of each in the same pursuits is discriminated, they are properly called many since each of them is separated from the

---

2. Basil the Great, "The Holy Spirit" in *Nicene and Post-Nicene Fathers*, Second series, vol. 8, eds. Phillip Schaff and Henry Wace (Peabody, MA: Hendrickson, 1999), ch. XVI, sect. 37; see also ch. VI, sect. 15.

others within his own environment, according to the special character of his operation. But in the case of the Divine nature we do not similarly learn that the Father does anything by Himself in which the Son does not work conjointly, or again that the Son has any special operation apart from the Holy Spirit; but every operation which extends from God to creation, and is *named according to our variable conceptions of it*, has its origin from the Father, and proceeds through the Son, and is perfected in the Holy Spirit.... For this reason the *name derived from the operation is not divided* with regard to the number of those who fulfil it, because *the action of each concerning anything is not separate and peculiar*, but whatever comes to pass, in reference either to the acts of His providence for us, or to the government or constitution of the universe, comes to pass by the action of the Three, yet what does come to pass *is not three things*.[3]

The above excerpt is extremely careful in the distinctions it is making. They bear directly on my thesis. Nyssen insists that, unlike the operations of man, which although similar and related are nevertheless ascribed to different agents (I read "the name derived from the operation" as a way of talking about ascriptions of agency), the actions of God bear a common agency of the three persons together. Gregory feels compelled to say this because he is concerned with preventing tritheism.

Gregory makes a second distinction between our perception of distinction and multiplicity, and the ultimate and transcendent unity of divine action. What appears to us are "three things," whereas the action of God is really one and indivisible. Human actions are indeed "separate and peculiar," whereas Triune action is indivisible and unified.

The lack of distinction between what the persons bring about is an essential part of the grammar of the Cappadocian concept. It serves Nyssen's ultimate purpose of safeguarding the unity and simplicity of the divine essence as opposed to the division of human nature. And it is precisely "the unity existing in the action [which] prevents plural enumeration."[4] Lack of distinction also implies lack of temporal distinction:

Every good thing and every good name, depending on the power and purpose which is without beginning, is brought to perfection in the power of the Spirit through the Only-begotten God, *without mark of time*

---

3. Gregory of Nyssa, *On 'Not Three Gods'* in *Gregory of Nyssa, Dogmatic Treatises*, vol. 5, *Nicene and Post-Nicene Fathers*, eds. Philip Schaff and Henry Wace (New York: Cosimo Classics), 334, my emphasis.

4. Gregory, *On 'Not Three Gods,'* 335.

or distinction (there is no delay, existent or conceived, in the motion of the divine will from the Father, through the Son, to the Spirit).[5]

Thus, the Cappadocian construal of the unity of external operations is sufficiently precise to caution against construals of such a unity merely in terms of a common intention. The actions of Father, Son, and Spirit must be mutually involved in each other, such that the common action of the Trinity cannot be broken into simpler constituent actions. Basil is quite explicit on this latter point: "The operation of the Father who worketh all in all is not imperfect, neither is the creating work of the Son incomplete if not perfected by the Spirit."[6]

Augustine regards the inseparability principle as something inherited from orthodox tradition: "The catholic faith has it, that the works of the Father and the Son are not separable."[7] It is part of the very grammar of trinitarian monotheism to argue that "just as the Father and Son and Holy Spirit are inseparable, so they work inseparably."[8] This means that in the context of economy, "Father and Son have but one will and are indivisible in their working."[9] Or again, "with reference to creation, Father and Son and Holy Spirit are one origin, just as they are one creator, and one Lord."[10]

Commenting on John's statement that "the Son can do nothing of his own accord, but only what he sees the father doing" (Jn 5:19),[11] Augustine clarifies that this is

> not the Father and the Son doing each his particular works, but the Father doing every work whatsoever by the Son; so that not any works are done by the Father without the Son, or by the Son without the Father; because "all things were made by him and without him was nothing made."[12]

The temporal separation between the components of a possible collective action is rejected in favor of the mutual inter-penetration of the works of the three:

---

5. Ibid.
6. Basil, *On the Holy Spirit*, ch. XVI, sect. 38.
7. Augustine, Tractate 18.6 in *Nicene and Post-Nicene Fathers: First Series,* vol. 7, *St. Augustine: Gospel of John, First Epistle of John, and Soliloquies,* trans. John Gibb and James Innes (New York: Cosimo, 2007), 119; cf. also Tractate 20.3.
8. Augustine, *The Trinity*, trans. Edmund Hill, ed. John E. Rotelle (New York: New City Press, 1991), 1.7, 70–71.
9. Ibid., 2.9, 103.
10. Ibid., 5.15, 202.
11. John finds the same pattern in the operation of the Spirit (John 16:8, 13).
12. Tractate 18.6.

He [the Son, Jesus] meant for us to understand that the Father doeth, not some work which the Son may see, and Son doeth other works after he has seen the Father doing; but that both Father and Son do the very same works.... Not after the Father hath done works, doeth the Son other works in like manner.[13]

Thus, a particular kind of collective agency is implicitly rejected by Augustine as not adequately preserving the unity of divine nature.

Brian Leftow puts this consensus in the more technical language of the philosophy of action: "Any act-token which is the Father's is equally and fully the Son's and Spirit's, without overdetermination, partial contribution, etc."[14] The caveats "without overdetermination, partial contribution" intimate that the trinitarian persons do not simply mirror each other's actions, neither are their actions simply components of larger collective actions. The unity of operations is not undifferentiated, while it remains simple.

TANNER'S CHRIST THE KEY

A common objection against the classical understanding of the inseparability principle is that it leads to a "cloaking" of the immanent Trinity and its relations, stripping us of any genuine way of deriving those relations from the notional (personal) divine acts in the economy. Kathryn Tanner argues in *Christ the Key*[15] that this is not the case. In fact, failure to discern the inseparability of action leads to undesirable Arian consequences.

There is a "pattern of trinitarian relationships" that is the subject of the gospel stories; "information about these relationships can be drawn directly from the way they are narrated in the storyline and does [not?][16] have to be inferred from what Jesus says."[17] This pattern of relationships reveals an intra-trinitarian taxis, the way in which the persons are ordered to one another.

Tanner writes, "Because Jesus' human life exhibits the Word's relationships with the other members of the trinity, one can use it ... to uncover their general pattern."[18] Such a statement of identity between economic and immanent trinities would please Rahner and LaCugna.

---

13. Tractate 18.8, commenting on the same text in John 5:19.
14. Brian Leftow, "Anti-Social Trinitarianism," in *The Trinity: An Interdisciplinary Symposium on the Trinity*, eds. Stephen T. Davis, Daniel Kendall, and Gerald O'Collins (Oxford: Oxford University Press, 1999), 239.
15. Kathryn Tanner, *Christ the Key* (Cambridge: Cambridge University Press, 2010).
16. Tanner's text appears to contain a typo here.
17. Ibid., 158.
18. Ibid., 147.

Atonement, then, is located in a trinitarian framework by the axiom that the pattern of intra-trinitarian relationships is mirrored in the economic relations between the Father and the Son. For Tanner this is essential, because "this sharing in trinitarian life from the first in Jesus' life by way of the incarnation is what brings about the redemption of the human as his life proceeds."[19] Atonement turns precisely on the unrestricted and genuine presence of God in the midst of the human circumstances of Jesus' life, especially including his death.

I will return to the redemptive significance of this, but for now we must dwell for a moment on this "trinitarian mirroring" of the immanent into the economic. It is both the distinction as well as the unity that is so mirrored. Tanner writes, "The Word that becomes flesh in Jesus is taken to be clearly distinct from the Father and Spirit because in the gospel stories Jesus talks to the former and sends the latter."[20] While here the distinction between trinitarian persons is observed, their unity is evident in an "equivalence of power and value among the three."[21]

"The whole story of the gospel is taken, moreover, to be their working a single action of salvation together, through equivalently divine capacities; they each act but always jointly by the very same powers for the very same end."[22] The three accomplish the very same thing, through the very same power "but in different, non-interchangeable manners of fashions."[23]

The missions of the Son and Spirit are also described in ways which uphold a very classic account of inseparability. Tanner denies that the missions are "two separable and sequential acts."[24] Again, remember that for her the economic relationships mirror the immanent relationships. Thus, the processions of the persons are mirrored by the economic missions.

However, there is a wrinkle in the story at this point, related to the ancient dichotomy between the immanent and economic trinities. Tanner explains:

> Even if the very same relations are simply being extended into the mission they undertake for us, when they incorporate the human in a situation of sin and death through the Word's incarnation, the relations that the members of the trinity have with one another come to reflect that fact.

19. Ibid., 145.
20. Ibid., 149.
21. Ibid., 150.
22. Ibid., 152.
23. Ibid., 154.
24. Ibid., 162.

In such a case, to continue the visual analogies, the trinitarian light is not so much reflected (as in a mirror), but rather refracted, as through a blurred medium. "Not everything, therefore, about the relations among the persons of the trinity in their mission for us also holds for their relations simply among themselves."[25]

Tanner goes on to highlight two aspects of this "deforming." The first bears on temporally indexed acts; the second on the issue of obedience/subordination. I will consider each in turn.

While eternally the mission of the Son is simultaneous with the mission of the Spirit, economically they are temporally indexed and sequential events. There is a "spreading out over time in the mission of movements that coincide in eternity." In the economy, "perfect return is delayed, hampered by the sin and death in human life that the Son and Spirit face in the course of the mission." While eternally the Son and the Spirit proceed from the Father "in interwoven, mutually dependent fashion," in the economy this takes time.[26]

Note Tanner's position here: "The Son can send the Spirit—specifically to us—only because he has already received the Spirit and felt the effects of its working within his own human life." Now, all of this takes time. Remember, though, that this is crucial for Tanner's argument: "The very life of God itself ... must be directly *mixed up* with suffering, conflict, death, and disease in the saving action of Christ."[27] The question is, obviously, in what way *can* the life of God be *mixed up* with these? One potential difficulty for Tanner's position can be noted at this point.

In making the Son's sending of the Spirit conditional upon his being first Spirit-filled, Tanner is making the human nature of Jesus a causal (or constitutive) condition not only of the sending of the Spirit, but of the very ability to send it. If this is the case, then it can no longer be asserted, as Tanner would want, that the Son and the Father act jointly by the very same power for the very same end. The Son's power to send the Spirit seems to have an additional constitutive condition. As I will show in my discussion of Thomas's doctrine of trinitarian missions, it is problematic to make Christ's human nature into anything more than just a "consequent condition" of his sending the Spirit to us.

Let me address the second aspect of the "economic refraction" identified by Tanner. The subordination of Jesus to the Father is something to

---

25. Ibid., 180.
26. Ibid., 181.
27. Ibid., 157, emphasis added.

be explained on account of his human nature. However, the Son's human obedience to the Father is indicative of something about the personal identity of the eternal Son:

> There is something in the relations between Father and Son that corresponds to the suggestion of inferiority in Jesus' relation with the Father. There must be, since Jesus is the Word and behaving as himself in his relations with the Father. It is just that what corresponds to it is not properly characterized as a relationship of superiority and subordination.[28]

Tanner is perfectly right to appeal at this point to two staples of the classic inseparability doctrine: (a) The economic relationships between the persons are constituted by their relationships of origin. Thus, it is fitting that the Son be obedient to the Father, because he proceeds from the Father and not vice versa. (b) The Son is obedient to the Father by virtue of their common will. The Son does not obey an external will. Rather, the Son shares the same will as the Father. In this case, the language of "obedience" almost entirely misfires when applied to the eternal relations between the persons.

All of this is consequential for the doctrine of redemption. If the economic relationships between the trinitarian persons reflect/refract eternal relationships of origin and therefore eternal personal identities, and moreover, if even economically distorted relations such as "obedience" reflect something about personal identities, then might it be the case that statements such as "It was the LORD's will to crush him" (Isa. 53:10 NIV) also have their constitution (to speak "Lonerganian") in the personal identities of the Father and the Son? In other words, is there any trinitarian ground for the claim that there is a direct divine punishment of Jesus? Of the Son by the Father? Bruce McCormack can get us started on this reflection.

McCormack on the Trinitarian Constitution of the Cross

Like Tanner, McCormack[29] applies the classic doctrine of inseparable operations to the paschal events. His primary insistence is on the uniqueness of the subject of Jesus' actions, which is the Logos, "in his divine-human unity" (as he often puts it—*passim*). He feels that the post-Chalcedonian

---

28. Ibid., 183.
29. Bruce McCormack, 'The Ontological Presuppositions of Barth's Doctrine of the Atonement,' in *The Glory of the Atonement: Biblical, Historical, and Practical Perspectives*, eds. Frank A. James III and Charles Hill (Downers Grove, IL: InterVarsity, 2004).

tradition has betrayed the spirit of the council by apportioning certain acts—like suffering, submission, ignorance of the last days, and dying itself—to the human nature of Jesus, and certain other acts—omniscience, miracles, etc.—to the divine nature. "Where this occurred," McCormack comments, "the 'natures' were made 'subjects' in their own right. The singularity of the subject of these natures was lost to view—and with that, the unity of the work."[30]

Like Tanner, McCormack is concerned to rescue the doctrine of penal substitution from a legalistic exchange framework, where God rewards the obedience unto death of Jesus Christ by dispensing his grace. Moreover, he thinks that such a failure of nerve means that "the human nature is reduced to the status of a passive instrument in the hands of the Logos; it is the object upon which the Logos acts."[31] It is not surprising that such a treatment invites critiques of PS along the lines of "divine child abuse." PS appears to condition divine favor upon the punishment either of the divine Son or of an innocent human being.

The remedy to this line of thinking is to take the human nature of Jesus as constitutive of the very being of God, such that the Son suffers in his divine-human unity, not in a human nature that remains external to him.

While this does indeed seem to preserve the unity of subject in the God-Man, it raises issues about divine immutability. How can the human nature of Jesus be truly taken into the divine being without the divine nature being changed? McCormack's response is to reject a substantialist metaphysic in favor of what he takes to be a Barthian understanding of divine actualism.

Conversely, God chooses to be God only in the covenant of grace. Contained in this decision is the determination for incarnation and the outpouring of the Spirit. The human nature of Jesus is part of the very essence of God, because it is how God determines to be Godself. Thus, the inclusion of the human nature of Jesus into the essence of God poses no special problem for immutability: "When, in time, he does that which he determined for himself in eternity, no change is brought in him on an ontological level. To God's being-in-act in eternity there corresponds a being-in-act in time; the two are identical in content."[32]

The payout is significant in terms of the doctrine of redemption. The human nature of Jesus, with everything it undergoes, truly belongs to the

---

30. Ibid., 354.
31. Ibid., 352.
32. Ibid., 357.

Logos. Thus, the Logos truly experiences everything, including death, in his divine-human unity. Thus, "death is a human experience that is taken into the divine life and does not remain sealed off from it."[33]

Tipping his hat to Barth again, McCormack appeals to the principle of inseparability: "The force of the axiom is to say that if one member of the Trinity does something, they all do it."[34] The appeal to the *opera ad extra* principle sheds light on the way in which divine persons can be thought to be acting upon one another in the economy. I will allow McCormack to speak here at length:

> First, an economic relation is never merely economic. If the economic Trinity corresponds perfectly to the immanent Trinity, then the relation of the first "person" of the Trinity to the second "person" must be structured in the same way in both. An action by the first person upon the second, then, is not an action of the Father upon the "eternal Son" (conceived along the lines of a Logos simpliciter); nor is it an action of the Father upon a mere human being. It is an action directed toward the Logos as human (the God-human in his divine-human unity).... But secondly, the Trinitarian axiom *opera trinitatis ad extra sunt indivisa* adds to this the thought that if the Father does anything, then all members of the Trinity do it.[35]

The significance of the inseparability principle for McCormack is as follows: If the immanent trinity and the economic trinity are one and the same, it follows that the Son (*simpliciter*) cannot be the object of the Father's economic actions. However, inasmuch as the Logos in his divine-human unity is the object of divine action, then such an action has to be understood as the action of all trinitarian persons. McCormack writes, "An action of the eternal Father upon the eternal Son (seen in abstraction from the assumed humanity) would require a degree of individuation between the two such that the 'separation' needed for an action of the one upon the other becomes thinkable."[36]

McCormack does not hesitate to draw the conclusion: "The subject who delivers Jesus Christ up to death is not the Father alone. For the trinitarian axiom *opera trinitatis ad extra sunt indivisa* means that if one does it, they all do it. So it is the triune God (Father, Son, and Holy Spirit) who

---

33. Ibid., 361.
34. Ibid., 364.
35. Ibid., 365.
36. Ibid.

gives himself over to this experience."[37] The "Father is not doing something to someone other than himself. The triune God pours his wrath out upon himself in and through the human nature that he has made his own in his second mode of his being—that is the ontological significance of penal substitution."[38]

I suggest that McCormack's proposal illustrates a fundamental impasse in conceiving the relation between the immanent and the economic trinity. The difficulty seems to be that of maintaining a strong immanent/economic identity thesis (like Tanner and McCormack both wish), yet without making immanent trinitarian relations and identities depend upon economic relationships.

McCormack, more than Tanner, seems to run this particular risk. He implies that what God does, "whether in eternity, or in time,"[39] is in some sense constitutive of what God is. McCormack is prepared to speak about God's choosing his own identity—presumably as Father, Son, and Holy Spirit—only in the covenant of grace. This is his way of solving the immutability puzzle. But at what cost?

There are two related critical issues here. First, if God truly gives himself to the experience of death, then by what is death overcome? McCormack somewhat negligently applies the inseparability doctrine to say that if one does it, they all do it. Thus, if one dies, they all do. But that seems to imply that God truly submitted himself to a mortal risk. Unless we say that it was a real possibility for God to be overcome by the experience of death, or for the Father never to recover from his loss of his Son, we haven't truly predicated the experience of death—as we have it—to God himself. So for this type of theology to truly provide the resources it promises, it may have to risk too much: a God who risks himself too much. If God truly does experience a genuinely threatening death, in virtue of what does he overcome it? The first possibility is that there is nothing "in virtue of which" God overcomes this death. His victory is not guaranteed by any capacity of his being. In this case, it remains possible that, while he did overcome this particular death, God might eventually be defeated by other encounters with death and suffering. The prospect is very real that divine empathy with human plight might eventually become too much even for God. The second possibility is that there is something about God which guarantees that he will emerge

---

victorious from a genuine experience of death and suffering. In this case, we seem to be faced again with the prospect of a God behind God—precisely the alternative McCormack wishes to avoid.

The second related issue has to do with how the identities of the trinitarian persons depend on their economic relations. If the identity of the divine persons depends on their contingent economic relations, it follows that these identities are themselves contingent. If, as McCormack (and Barth?) argue, God chooses to be this particular God in relation to salvific actions, it follows that the identity of God is constituted by contingent realities which need not have occurred (creation, the fall, redemption, etc.). According to Marshall,[40]

> When we take this alternative, the Son comes forth from God not by nature, but by will (as the Arians once held, for their own reasons), indeed by the same free act in which God contingently constitutes himself as Father. If we take our lead from the contingency of a free agent's acts, it is just as contingent that God is the Father, the Son, and the Holy Spirit as that God creates, or redeems, a world. Each depends alike, or they all depend together, on a free decision of God, which could have been otherwise.[41]

Marshall continues, echoing the critical point above, that we are still left to wonder, Who is this God who just happens to choose this way?

ONTOLOGY OF TRINITARIAN MISSIONS

The following section will modestly summarize some Thomistic insights about the trinitarian missions. The doctrine of penal substitution, with which we are largely (though not exclusively) concerned, is steeped in a Reformational theology that is heavily indebted to this Thomistic reflection on inseparable operations and missions. To the extent that Tanner and McCormack depart from this tradition in these significant respects, they become vulnerable to deficient accounts of God's relation to the world.

CREATED EFFECTS

For Thomas and this tradition, the concept of mission is a way of speaking about the very continuity between the immanent and economic trinities. Mission does not denote a change in the immanent Trinity, as it were, but

---

40. Bruce D. Marshall, "The Dereliction of Christ and the Impassibility of God," in *Divine Impassibility and the Mystery of Human Suffering*, eds. James F. Keating and Thomas Joseph White (Grand Rapids: Eerdmans, 2009), 246–98.

41. Ibid., 287.

rather a new mode of presence of one of the trinitarian persons in creation. As Thomas puts it: "Even as the divine person sent does not begin to be present where he before was not, so he does not cease to be present where he was."[42] In the missions, then, the Trinity itself assumes a new mode of presence in relation to creation, since the persons that are sent (Son and Spirit) do not "take leave," as it were, of their trinitarian home.

Missions are analyzable into two dimensions. First, there is the procession of the person sent. Since a mission is the very life of the Trinity, not some substitute, and what constitutes the identity of the trinitarian persons are precisely the processions, then the mission itself is in fact a procession. The second dimension of mission, however, is a relation to a created effect.

Because mission includes the eternal procession, Giles Emery writes,

> This eliminates the possibility of anthropomorphism: when one says a divine person is "sent," this sending is not that of a minion carrying out his boss's orders, nor is it about receiving instructions from a higher intelligence, and nor is the sending a displacement, spatially separating the sender from the one sent.[43]

Two points merit highlighting here: (a) the person who is sent does not assume a different mode of being than the one he has within the immanent life of the Trinity. Contrary to received opinion, Thomas's account of missions demonstrates the strong continuity between the two 'trinities'; (b) although the person sent is more easily individuated in his being sent, this is not on account of any real separation that takes place.

Turning now to the second dimension of the ontology of mission, Thomas points out that a mission contains, in addition to a relation of origin, a relation to a created effect. For this tradition, however, the relation with this created effect is not constitutive of the identity of the person sent. This would make his identity depend on contingent realities.

The created effect, to which the person sent has a new relation, is in fact the work of the whole of the Trinity, again for this tradition. This is a crucial bit of the puzzle here. McCormack has already picked up on it when speaking about the whole Trinity delivering Jesus up to death. Let me flesh this out. According to the inseparability principle, every work of the Trinity in the economy is common to the three persons. Remember

---

42. Thomas Aquinas, *The Summa Theologica of St. Thomas Aquinas*, trans. Fathers of the English Dominican Province (Westminster, MD: Christian Classics, 1981), I, q. 43, a. 1, ad. 2.

43. Giles Emery, *The Trinitarian Theology of St. Thomas Aquinas*, trans. Francesca A. Murphy (New York: Oxford University Press, 2010), 365.

that a mission contains two parts, or, better, dimensions: a relationship of origin (which solidly grounds the mission in the Trinity itself) and a relation to a created reality. But this created reality is the work of all the persons together (in different manners, to be sure).

Further observe that the relation of origin is necessary and eternal, whereas the created effect is contingent and temporal. So, insofar as the mission is regarded from the perspective of its created effect, this effect is brought about by the whole Trinity, although appropriated by one of the persons, usually the one sent, though not always. The mission itself is not an appropriation, but is proper to one of the persons.

In talking about a mission, we are in effect making a contingent predication about one of the persons of the Trinity. This is where I wish to turn to Lonergan's explanation: "Contingent truths, whether predicated of the divine persons commonly or properly, have their constitution in God but their term in creatures."[44] However, "the necessary external term is not a constitutive cause but only a condition, and indeed a condition that is not prior or simultaneous, but consequent."[45] The reason he gives should be familiar by now: "It is not an antecedent or a simultaneous, but a consequent condition, because the divine persons are absolutely independent with respect to all created things."[46]

One may further distinguish between the "divine efficient causality," which is the origin of every created reality in the common work of the three persons, and "immanent constitution" of the respective created reality. While every created reality is brought into being by the common work of the Trinity, it is done so in a differentiated way. There is a trinitarian constitution of each of these realities in such a way that they mediate the whole Trinity to us.

To conclude, the human nature of Jesus is the created effect through which the Son is present to us in a new way. It is precisely the Son who is present to us, through the medium of his human nature. This human nature is not the proper work of the Son but of all trinitarian persons. However, it is precisely the Son who is given to us in this human nature, and the works which the Son does in virtue of his human nature are properly his (in virtue of this human nature).[47] Moreover, the "immanent

44. Bernard Lonergan, *The Triune God: Systematics*, eds. Robert M. Doran and H. Daniel Monsour, trans. Michael Shields (Toronto: University of Toronto Press, 2007), 439.

45. Ibid., 441.

46. Ibid., 443.

47. See Lonergan, *The Triune God*, 491. Lonergan insists that since the Spirit has not assumed a human nature, the spiritual works are appropriated to the Spirit.

constitution" of this human nature is such that the immanent relationships of the Trinity are mediated to us. Indeed, as Tanner demonstrates, Jesus' humanity is constituted by the Spirit, not by the Son alone. However, where Tanner errs is in making this human nature of Jesus a constitutive condition of the Son's ability to send the Spirit, when in fact it can only be a consequent condition. In making this move, Tanner risks differentiating between the powers on the basis of which the persons are sent, by including Christ's human nature among those powers. The classic tradition, on the contrary, insists that the persons are sent strictly on the basis of their relationships of origin.

I take the foregoing to have established the following thesis:

> (1) Economic relations between trinitarian persons are grounded in the immanent Trinity. Actions in virtue of the human nature of the Son, directed either to the Father or to the Spirit, are proper to the person of the Son in virtue of his having a human nature, which is nonetheless the product of the whole Trinity and a consequent condition of the act. On the other hand, divine actions that terminate in the human nature of Jesus are grounded in the relationships of origin, but they are accomplished by all trinitarian persons.

TEMPORAL INDEXING

Tanner rightly denies a particular kind of sequentiality between the acts of God. In this she is firmly planted in the classic tradition which insists on a version of divine eternity. This is where the inseparability principle meets the doctrine of divine simplicity. While I would hold that these two are analytical to each other, I will not be able to address the latter here, except tangentially.

Emery writes that

> when we acknowledge many divine actions on behalf of the creature, we are not introducing a real differentiation into God himself: within the divine persons, such diverse actions only present a distinction "of reason," not a real distinction. But on the part of the creaturely beneficiaries of God's action, that is, within the divine actions' "effects," the distinction is thoroughly real.[48]

I pointed out that this lack of sequentiality is a characteristic of patristic accounts of inseparable operations. The action of God is one, and that is

---

48. Emery, *Trinitarian Theology of Aquinas*, 373.

to be Godself. However, as this action is "refracted" in the medium of human history, it fans out, so to speak; it is stretched and *appears* to be composed of a variety of divine actions. It is tempting, yet a mistake, to take this sequentiality as basic.

To use the language of the previous section, the divine action in history has its ontological constitution in God's eternal pure act. The diverse temporal actions, in that they include created effects, only serve as *consequent conditions*. Tanner's mistake is to have made a temporally indexed action (the time-consuming filling up of Jesus' human nature by the Spirit) into a constituent condition of his ability to send the Spirit.

Reformed orthodoxy discusses this theme under the rubric of the *consilium Dei*, based on Ephesians 1:11. The divine counsel is an "inward essential act" of the Trinity.[49] Lacking the anthropomorphic hints at deliberation and discussion, the divine counsel represents the eternal will of God to save. Johannes Wollebius writes, "'In itself God's decree is *unicum et simplicissimum*, nor is any *prius* or *posterius* to be found in it. But as regards the things decreed the distinction is that God is said to have decreed their eventuation in the order in which they do eventuate.' "[50]

We are here very much in the same frame of mind as the earlier Thomas, Augustine, and the Cappadocians. The sequentiality is not a dogmatically certain instance of revelation, to use Rahner's terminology. I am now in position to formulate a thesis:

> (2) The economic works of God originate in an eternal unity of intention and execution in the "divine counsel." Their temporal ordering to one another is a "consequent condition" of their "externalization" in time and is in no way part of their "immanent constitution."

SUBJECT AND OBJECT WITHIN TRINITARIAN MODES OF ACTION

As the earliest tradition on inseparable operations indicates, we are not to think about the actions of the divine persons as exhibiting simply a unity of intention or of purpose. They are not executing some sort of collective action together. They act together and inseparably.

Within each essential (as opposed to proper) act of God, therefore, one has to affirm a threefold manner of operation. Again, Reformed ortho-

49. Johannes Wollebius, as quoted in Heinrich Heppe, *Reformed Dogmatics*, ed. Ernst Bizer, trans. G. T. Thomson (Eugene, OR: Wipf and Stock, 2007), 134.
50. Heppe, *Reformed Dogmatics*, 140.

doxy consolidates the Thomistic inheritance by distinguishing between the principle of the operation, which is the same: the trinitarian persons possess common deity, will, and power; their inception and operation are also common; yet their mode of operating is peculiar and distinct.[51] Heppe finds the same consensus: "The works are common to all in an undivided way (*operationes communes*). Yet in the manner of being executed the activity of each separate person is a special one."[52]

Aquinas explains that different dimensions of the realities which God accomplishes in us are to be ascribed to the activity of different persons:

> The "word of wisdom" (cf. Dan. 1:20) by which we know God, and which God sends into us, is properly representative of the Son. And in like fashion the love by which we love God is properly representative of the Holy Spirit. And thus the charity which is in us, although it is an effect of the Father, the Son, and the Holy Spirit, is nonetheless for a special sort of reason said to be in us through the Holy Spirit.[53]

Let me now return to the question of how the trinitarian persons are co-present in the economy. In an otherwise excellent piece on penal substitution, Garry Williams makes the following claim: "No one can deny that the Father acts on the Son, provided we are clear that the Son also wills the action."[54] The dogmatic question is, with what will does the Son "also" will the action? Since there is a single will in God, this cannot be a will that is somehow conjoined with that of the Father.

Williams has to explain how his proposal succeeds in avoiding tritheism with the obvious implication of different wills. Certainly, from the perspective of the human nature Christ has adopted, his acts, including his relation to the Father, are properly his own and need to be taken seriously. As Lonergan explains,[55] it is precisely because the Son has assumed a human nature that, through that nature, he does works that are proper to himself. But on that same account, speaking strictly about the economy, neither the Father nor the Spirit do any works proper to themselves (works are not to be confused with missions!).

51. So Martin Heidegger, cf. R. Muller, *Post-Reformation Reformed Dogmatics: The Rise and Development of Reformed Orthodoxy, ca. 1520 to ca. 1725, vol. 4, The Triunity of God* (Grand Rapids: Baker, 2003), 264.

52. Heppe, *Reformed Dogmatics*, 118.

53. Aquinas, *Summa Contra Gentiles*, trans. Charles J. O'Neil (Notre Dame: University of Notre Dame Press, 1989), book IV, ch. 21, para. 2.

54. Garry J. Williams, "Penal Substitution: A Response to Recent Criticisms," *Journal of the Evangelical Theological Society* 50/1 (March 2007): 71–86, 78.

55. Lonergan, *The Triune God*, Q. 39, 485.

However, this undercuts claims that the Father punishes the Son, or that the Father abandons the Son, etc. If the principle that whatever effects are being brought about in the economy are the common work of the trinitarian persons, then Jesus' human nature and everything which this human nature "suffers" (not necessarily in a negative way, but in the way of *passio*) is brought about by the Trinity as a whole, as McCormack understood.

The interpersonal relationality, strictly speaking, is to be predicated exclusively of the Son in his human nature. As Lonergan puts it in *The Ontological and Psychological Constitution of Christ*, "The person of the Word can speak and actually does speak in accordance with his human nature. But in his divine nature the person of the Word neither can nor does speak but is only spoken."[56]

A full engagement with these points would require me to enter the controversy over social trinitarianism. I beg the reader's understanding that this paper is written precisely from the standpoint of Latin trinitarianism, for all of its weaknesses. Moreover, the doctrine of penal substitution historically emerged on the backdrop of this trinitarian framework. It is my claim that it needs to be more explicitly connected to this framework and that doing so would censor certain of its versions. I am less concerned about the immanent trinitarian relations (*filioque*, relationality, etc.) than about the economic relations, either between the trinitarian persons or between these persons and created realities as such. The thesis that has crystallized about these relations is the following:

> (3) There can be no thought of an action by the Father upon the Son in his human nature in which the Son himself is passive. Since any action of God terminating in a created effect is the action of all divine persons, the Son in his human nature cannot be a mere object of the Father.

As Doran points out, "The inherited tradition of theological doctrines informs us that the only way in which opposites can be predicated of the divine persons is in terms of the relations of origin immanent in the triune God."[57] Hence, oppositional relations such as "Father doing X to the incarnate Son" are ruled out. If anyone divine does X to the incarnate Son,

56. Bernard Lonergan, *The Collected Works of Bernard Lonergan*, vol. 7, *The Ontological and Psychological Constitution of Christ*, trans. Michael G. Shields (Toronto: University of Toronto Press, 2002), 225.

57. Robert M. Doran, *The Trinity in History: A Theology of the Divine Missions*, vol. 1, *Missions and Processions* (Toronto: University of Toronto Press, 2012), 50.

it must be all of them. Were such oppositional relations to hold, such as in "sending" and "being sent," they would refer to immanent relationships.

ATONEMENT AND INSEPARABLE OPERATIONS

Plenty of conceptual clarification and modeling still needs to be done in relation to the *opera ad extra* doctrine. In particular, the notion of "manner of operation" still remains somewhat opaque. Theologians have yet to draw in a systematic way on the conceptuality of the philosophy of action in order to improve the intelligibility of some of our constructs. In respect to the atonement, an appeal to inseparable operations still underdetermines the particular model adopted. Indeed, Tanner and McCormack each explain redemption in different ways.

Foregrounding such trinitarian clarifications, though, can substantially qualify the way in which each atonement model is formulated. I believe this to be the case with respect to penal substitution. In concluding this paper I will try to make explicit some of these implications. The reader will be left to assess whether these qualify as improvements to the doctrine or not.

First, the cross needs to be integrated into a broader unified (and single) action of the trinitarian God. One may think of the cross as an aspect of this unified redemptive action. This makes the cross unintelligible without the incarnation, resurrection, Pentecost, indeed, without the gift of grace dispensed by the Spirit.

Certain PS proponents do indeed wish to do that, but they often make the cross a component of a sequential and causal structure. There, the punishment of Christ plays a part in a mechanism of exchange. God is said to dispense grace *in response* to the work of Christ. The difficulty from the standpoint of inseparable operations is that it orders divine economic operations as causal to one another and therefore obscures their unity of intention and execution in the divine counsel.

It is possible to order what seem to us as being divine actions as simply being dimensions of the same action of God, simply identified in terms of its various effects.[58] An illustration might help. Take the following "actions": I flip the switch, I turn the light on, I illuminate the room, I get ready to read a book, I alert the burglar, I startle Mrs. Smith. In one respectable tradition in action philosophy, all these are descriptions of a

---

58. Stump and Kretzmann, "Absolute Simplicity," *Faith and Philosophy* 2/4 (1985): 353–91; also Joel Feinberg, "Action and Responsibility," in *The Philosophy of Action*, ed. Alan R. White (Oxford: Oxford University Press, 1968).

single action, identified in light of a variety of effects. Similarly, the divine action is simple and eternal, though it unfolds in time and produces a variety of effects. For temporal human actions, the series of effects proceeding from an action are often causally related to one another, and thus I can say that "my flipping the switch" *enables* "my illuminating the room."

However, in the case of divine action this is not the case. "The Father's surrendering Jesus over to death" and "Jesus' being obedient unto the cross" are not *causal conditions* of "God's reconciling the world to himself." The reason for this is that created effects are only consequent conditions of statements about divine missions and works (Thesis 1). What is at stake here for the classical tradition I have been invoking is nothing less than the freedom of God. God wills everything and accomplishes everything in one act of will.

Similar considerations warn us about ascribing to the Father a direct punishment of Jesus. I believe two possibilities are ruled out. The Father does not (unilaterally) punish the incarnate Word, since this involves an action of God terminating in a created effect (the human nature of Jesus). But any such action of God, save actions by a divine person acting through an assumed *esse secundarium*, must be actions common to the three. The second possibility is that the Father punishes the eternal Son, but this would entail (a) a rift in the Father-Son relationship that would be destructive of either of their identities, and therefore of the divine nature itself; and (b) an oppositional relation between divine persons in the economy, of the form "Father does X to the Son" and "Son is Xed by the Father," such as can only obtain within the immanent Trinity. To conclude, the Father can no more punish the eternal Son than he can unilaterally punish the Son in his human nature. Both options have dire trinitarian implications.

I regard the penal sufferings of Jesus (in his human nature) as a created effect of the mission of the Son. As a created effect, they do not go into the ontological constitution of the work of redemption itself, but are a consequent condition. The basic act of God is a particular kind of unitive action. What turns redemption's wheel, so to speak, is the incarnation itself.

Two theologians express this beautifully. Herbert McCabe writes, "That the Trinity looks like a story of (is a story of) rejection, torture, and murder but also of reconciliation is because it is projected on, lived out on, our rubbish tip; it is because of the sin of the world."[59] God does

---

59. Herbert McCabe, *God Matters* (London: Chapman, 1987), 49.

not "punish Jesus" as a causal condition of his redemption. Rather, Jesus' penal suffering is a dimension, an aspect of the redeeming love of God. This is how divine love is refracted through the prism of humanity's God-forsakenness and sin.

P. T. Forsyth also chimes in a similar tune:

> View punishment as an indirect and collateral necessity, like the surgical pains that make room for nature's curing power. You will then find nothing morally repulsive in the idea of judgment effected in and on Christ, anymore than in the thought that the kingdom was set up in him.[60]

The punishment is indeed taken on by God himself, insofar as God steps into a human condition bearing the penal consequences of sin.

It might look as if I am returning to a view of redemption which weakens the centrality of the penal suffering of Christ. What I am suggesting, however, is a careful integration of the notion that Christ dies a death representing divine condemnation into a trinitarian framework closely constrained by the inseparability principle. One implication of this trinitarian framework is that divine action in history is sovereign and unified in such a way that it does not require created components except as consequent conditions. Once God has elected to be present in the human condition as a redeemer—as opposed to a judge, for example—then the Son's penal suffering in his human nature is a consequence of this election. God might have conceivably elected to become incarnate for non-redemptive reasons.

Thus, in my proposal, the incarnation as such is not by itself redemptive. It is God's decree to become one with us as Savior that is the fundamental act of God. But what that act entails is that he will be one with us in our God-forsaken condition, bearing everything that we are destined to bear. Yet the necessity of the suffering is not a necessity of the means, so to speak. God did not need to be *enabled* to be united to us redemptively by anything done from the human side. What happens on the human side of the divine action are the consequences of an eternal act, not the conditions for the possibility of the act. To return to Forsyth's example, the surgeon is not enabled to heal by the pain inflicted on the patient. The pain itself is a consequent condition of the healing act itself, not what causes it.[61]

---

60. P. T. Forsyth, *The Work of Christ* (Eugene, OR: Wipf and Stock, 1938), 135–36.

61. Lonergan's distinction between a consequent condition and a causal condition may be illustrated rather simply. What enables me (causal condition) to purchase apples from the grocer is a payment. There are several consequent conditions of this action, however, such as my influencing the grocer's tax returns, my contributing to the economy, etc. However, it is not *by* influencing the tax returns, or *by* contributing to the economy, that I purchase apples.

To sum up, it was necessary that Christ should die given that God elected to be united to humanity in a redemptive way. An entailment of that union is that Christ would bear our death in God-forsakenness. Yet it is not his penal death which enables God to be with us redemptively as such. Moreover, the whole Trinity is active in the death of Jesus, not just the Father punishing the Son. The whole Trinity is present to us in a new way in the human nature of the Son, taking upon itself, in this human nature, our penal death.

CHAPTER 2

CREATION AND ATONEMENT

MATTHEW LEVERING

IS THERE A RELATIONSHIP between the doctrine of creation, understood as "an understanding of reality as perceived from within the context of a dynamic, personal and existential relationship with the living God," and the doctrine of atonement?[1] I think that there is, and that it is an important one. In order to make this case, I begin with Nicholas Wolterstorff's recent challenge to Anselmian doctrines of the atonement. I then turn to Thomas Aquinas's broadly Anselmian doctrine of how Jesus' cross accomplishes our salvation by way of "satisfaction." I argue that when one appreciates its relationship to the doctrine of creation, Aquinas's account of satisfaction stands up to Wolterstorff's critique of Anselmian approaches.

Indeed, satisfaction theories of atonement can only be understood in light of the doctrine of creation. By perceiving the interpersonal web of justice that characterizes creation, we come to appreciate more fully Christ's saving work as a restoration of justice that entails, in Scot McKnight's words, "a life of relational love for God, self, others, and the world," since true justice "is *altogether and unabashedly relational*."[2]

---

1.   Graham McFarlane, "Atonement, Creation and Trinity," *The Atonement Debate: Papers from the London Symposium on the Theology of Atonement*, eds. Derek Tidball, David Hilborn, and Justin Thacker (Grand Rapids: Zondervan, 2008), 192–207, at 192.

2.   Scot McKnight, *A Community Called Atonement* (Nashville: Abingdon Press, 2007), 126, 133.

To be clear from the outset, I should note that the atonement or sat-isfaction in view here is not *required* or *needed* by God, nor is it God pun-ishing Jesus, nor is it an individualistic transaction.[3] On the contrary, it is God's free gift to the entire human race, healing and elevating humans (if we do not reject it) into a just relationship with God, self, neighbor, and world in the Spirit-filled incarnate Son, who has freely borne our penalty out of supreme love. I should also note that in treating satisfaction, I am treating only one aspect of Aquinas's much broader theology of Jesus' sav-ing work.[4]

My focus on satisfaction's relationship to the doctrine of creation pre-cludes showing how satisfaction relates, via love, to the entirety of Jesus' life as well as to his resurrection and ascension and to the covenantal history of Israel. I hope nonetheless that by attending to the doctrine of creation, my essay serves to ratify, even if inevitably only from one angle, the contention of Adam Johnson that

> it is of the utmost significance that our theological account of this event [the atonement] appropriate from the outset the broadest and most com-prehensive framework for understanding the work of God in the life, death, and resurrection of Jesus Christ.[5]

I. NICHOLAS WOLTERSTORFF'S *JUSTICE IN LOVE:* A CRITIQUE OF SATISFACTION THEORIES

Nicholas Wolterstorff argues that while it is a mistake to read Jesus' Ser-mon on the Mount as advocating pacifism, nonetheless Jesus made a crucial ethical advance by rejecting the "reciprocity code" as a standard for justice.[6] What is the reciprocity code? Jesus finds it in God's com-

---

3. Thus, in his *Atonement, Law, and Justice: The Cross in Historical and Cultural Contexts* (Grand Rapids: Baker, 2014), Adonis Vidu retains the language of punishment but with crucial clarifica-tions: "While the death Jesus died has the quality of punishment, we have no reason to think of this punishment as being directly inflicted by God on Christ" (261).

4. For the breadth of Aquinas's theology of Christ's saving work, see my *Christ's Fulfillment of Torah and Temple: Salvation according to Thomas Aquinas* (Notre Dame: University of Notre Dame Press, 2002).

5. Adam J. Johnson, *God's Being in Reconciliation: The Theological Basis of the Unity and Diversity of the Atonement in the Theology of Karl Barth* (London: Bloomsbury, 2012), 1.

6. Adonis Vidu challenges Wolterstorff's view of the distinctiveness of Jesus' contribution. Drawing upon Homer, Aeschylus, Plato, Aristotle, and Roman law, Vidu argues that "pagan antiq-uity did not exclusively favor retribution, as Wolterstorff argues, but ... alongside retribution there was precisely the idea of a (divine) gratuitous forgiveness, precisely in the name of peace and order (and thus justice).... [T]he undeniable fact is that the idea of divine forgiveness that is both uncondi-tional and just (Rom. 3:26) was not at all foreign to ancient culture" (*Atonement, Law, and Justice*, 3).

mandments in the Torah. For example, God gave the following command through Moses regarding permanent injuries caused to innocent parties during a conflict: "If any harm follows, then you shall give life for life, eye for eye, tooth for tooth, hand for hand, foot for foot, burn for burn, wound for wound, stripe for stripe" (Ex 21:23–25 NKJV). A similar divine commandment is found in Leviticus 24:19–21:

> When a man causes a disfigurement in his neighbor, as he has done it shall be done to him, fracture for fracture, eye for eye, tooth for tooth; as he has disfigured a man, he shall be disfigured. He who kills a beast shall make it good; and he who kills a man shall be put to death.

Such laws conceive of justice in terms of reciprocity: when someone has caused permanent harm to an innocent party, the guilty perpetrator shall receive as punishment the same permanent harm. Justice here is conceived to involve retribution so as to restore, as much as possible, the balance of the scales: if I have harmed someone, retributive justice mandates that I suffer the same harm in order to restore a just balance between me and the person whom I have harmed (and in order to avoid an escalating cycle of violence). This understanding of retributive justice prevails throughout the Torah. Thus in Deuteronomy, Moses teaches that if a person has borne false witness in a court of law, "then you shall do to him as he had meant to do to his brother" (Deut 19:19). Moses goes on to underscore the gravity of this commandment: "Your eye shall not pity; it shall be life for life, eye for eye, tooth for tooth, hand for hand, foot for foot" (Deut 19:21).

As Wolterstorff points out, Jesus rejected this in a fundamental way. The key passage is Jesus' teaching in Matthew 5:38–40, part of his Sermon on the Mount:

> "You have heard that it was said, 'An eye for an eye and a tooth for a tooth.' But I say to you, Do not resist one who is evil. But if any one strikes you on the right cheek, turn to him the other also; and if any one would sue you and take your coat, let him have your cloak as well."

Far from retributive justice rooted in reciprocity, Jesus here teaches us to respond to evil with good. When someone harms us or threatens us with harm, we are to seek no retribution, no reciprocal harm to that person. We are certainly not to seek vengeance. Instead, we are to do good to the one who has harmed us, and not harm the evildoer in any way.

Wolterstorff emphasizes that Jesus' teaching is more radical than many commentators realize. According to Wolterstorff, Jesus' logic means that when you discern that underlying the prohibition of blind vengeance is the command to love, then you will realize that not only should you refrain from blind vengeance; you should also refrain from paying back evil with proportionate evil. You should return good for evil. You should reject not only blind vengeance but reciprocity as well.[7]

Jesus is thereby rejecting, rather than merely adjusting or deepening, the Torah's understanding of the justice that members of God's people should pursue. Even more, Jesus is rejecting *positive* reciprocity. As Jesus goes on to say,

Love your enemies and pray for those who persecute you.... For if you love those who love you, what reward have you? Do not even the tax collectors do the same? And if you salute only your brethren, what more are you doing than others? Do not even the Gentiles do the same? (Mt 5:44, 46–47).

For Jesus, we may not favor our friends, and we may not demand retributive justice with respect to our enemies.

Regarding the reciprocity code, Wolterstorff states, "The reciprocity code had two aspects. If someone does you a favor, you owe them an equal favor in return. If someone does you an evil, an equal evil is due them."[8] To underscore Jesus' rejection of this code, Wolterstorff cites Luke 14:12, where Jesus tells the Pharisee who had invited him to dinner, "When you give a dinner or a banquet, do not invite your friends or your brothers or your kinsmen or rich neighbors, lest they also invite you in return, and you be repaid." Commenting on Jesus' command, Wolterstorff remarks, "This is a barbed rejection of that aspect of the reciprocity code which says that favors must be answered with favors."[9] Followers of Jesus must go to some lengths to avoid reciprocity, since love is tested and made meritorious by going beyond reciprocity. We must become like our "Father who is in heaven; for he makes his sun rise on the evil and on the good, and sends rain on the just and on the unjust" (Mt 5:45).

It seems right to say, as Wolterstorff does, that Jesus rejects "the reciprocity code in favor of the ethic of love," despite the presence of the reciprocity code in the Torah.[10] But I would add that Jesus has not thereby rejected the reciprocity code tout court. The reciprocity code still func-

---

7. Nicholas Wolterstorff, *Justice in Love* (Grand Rapids: Eerdmans, 2011), 122.
8. Ibid., 123.
9. Ibid., 126.
10. Ibid.

tions with respect to God's repayment of our acts of love. Thus Jesus adds to his commandment regarding dinner invitations: "You will be repaid at the resurrection of the just" (Lk 14:13–14). Rather than seeking reciprocal justice from humans, in other words, we should now seek it from God; the good that we hope to obtain is something that can only come from God.

Indeed, although Wolterstorff does not mention it, the reciprocity code is on full display in Jesus' depiction of the final judgment in his parable about the sheep and the goats. The "sheep," or righteous, will receive the reward of "the kingdom prepared for you from the foundation of the world" (Mt 25:34). This reward will take them by surprise, because they cared for others without realizing that they were thereby caring for Jesus. In response to Jesus' praise for the good deeds that they did to those who could not repay them, the righteous say, " 'Lord, when did we see thee hungry and feed thee, or thirsty and give thee drink?...' And the King will answer them, 'Truly, I say to you, as you did it to one of the least of these my brethren, you did it to me' " (Mt 25:37–40). God will reward those who in this life show love for others who cannot repay them; and God will repay, with retributive justice, those who in this life fail to love others in this way (see Mt 25:41–43).

Admittedly, the reward goes beyond pure reciprocity, but it is clearly retributive justice that we see on display in this parable. To underscore the point that there will be both a reciprocal reward and retributive punishment, Jesus concludes his parable by stating, "And they will go away into eternal punishment, but the righteous into eternal life" (Mt 25:46).

Wolterstorff focuses solely on Jesus' rejection of the reciprocity code for his followers with respect to seeking to punish or be recompensed by *other humans*. As Wolterstorff rightly observes, this form of the rejection of the reciprocity code is found not only in the Gospels but also in the Epistles. He cites one representative passage from Peter and two from Paul. In 1 Peter, in the midst of a discussion of how Christians should live together, we find a statement reminiscent of Jesus' words in the Sermon on the Mount: "Do not return evil for evil or reviling for reviling; but on the contrary bless, for to this you have been called, that you may obtain a blessing" (1 Pet 3:9). I note that the blessing we are to seek (a reciprocal reward) will come solely from God.

To obtain this blessing, we must imitate Jesus, who died for the sins of those who rejected and reviled him. Since we have been healed by Jesus, we must love others as he loved us. He loved us when we deserved retributive punishment and when we could repay him in no manner. Earlier in

47

1 Peter, this is made explicit: "Christ also suffered for you, leaving you an example, that you should follow in his steps.... When he was reviled, he did not revile in return; when he suffered, he did not threaten; but he trusted to him who judges justly. He himself bore our sins in his body on the tree, that we might die to sin and live to righteousness. By his wounds you have been healed" (1 Pet 2:21, 23–24).

The two passages that Wolterstorff quotes from Paul come from 1 Thessalonians and Romans. Like 1 Peter 3:9, 1 Thessalonians 5 has to do with the behavior of the Christian community toward each other, and we find the same rejection of reciprocity: "See that none of you repays evil for evil, but always seek to do good to one another and to all" (1 Thess 5:15). Yet Wolterstorff neglects the fact that 1 Thessalonians 5 also envisions a future "wrath" (1 Thess 5:9), or divine judgment. First Thessalonians contains a clear notion of retributive punishment, since it warns against immorality and pleads "that no man transgress, and wrong his brother in this matter, because the Lord is an avenger in all these things, as we solemnly forewarned you" (1 Thess 4:6).

In the passage that Wolterstorff quotes from Romans, Paul states, "Repay no one evil for evil, but take thought for what is noble in the sight of all.... Beloved, never avenge yourselves, but leave it to the wrath of God; for it is written, 'Vengeance is mine, I will repay, says the Lord'" (Rom 12:17, 19). Wolterstorff concentrates here upon the rejection of reciprocity. It is also clear from this passage, however, that God retains reciprocal or retributive justice, since the "wrath of God" will "repay" at the final judgment.

If God will take vengeance at the end of time, why can we not exact retributive justice now? We are to bear witness to Christ's absolute mercy toward us, not least because by so doing we may be able to convert some of our enemies before the final judgment. The latter point—the power of mercy for turning enemies into friends—accords well with Old Testament teaching. Thus, in Romans 12:20, Paul quotes Proverbs 25:21–22: "If your enemy is hungry, give him bread to eat; and if he is thirsty, give him water to drink; for you will heap coals of fire on his head, and the Lord will reward you." Paul understands this proverb to indicate that our good deeds may result in the conversion of our enemy. As Paul emphasizes, much like Jesus, "Do not be overcome by evil, but overcome evil with good" (Rom 12:21). Earlier in the same chapter, Paul offers a version of Jesus' admonition to love our enemies: "Bless those who persecute you; bless and do not curse them" (Rom 12:14).

Thus, while Wolterstorff rightly underscores the ways in which Jesus rejects the reciprocity code, he exaggerates when he argues that Jesus' "rejection of the negative side of the reciprocity code implies opposition to retributive punishment in general."[11] On the contrary, Jesus consistently looks toward a retributive punishment that will be applied by God, in the final judgment, to those who reject God's offer of mercy in Jesus. Wolterstorff is of course aware of this, but he does not give it sufficient attention. He states, "If redressing injury (harm, evil) has any place at all in the moral order, God will do it. Leave it to God."[12] But if the Gospels and Epistles are any evidence, there is no "if" about whether "redressing injury" has a place in God's moral order.

Even so, Wolterstorff is right that with regard to how Christians should behave in this life, "Jesus forbids retribution. Injury imposed on the wrongdoer must be justified by some greater good that it brings about, not by the fact that the wrongdoer imposed an injury."[13]

However, is retributive punishment on the part of governments also forbidden? Wolterstorff interprets Romans 13, which presents authorities as "instituted by God" (Rom 13:1), as not being about retributive punishment. According to Wolterstorff, Paul considers that government authorities "encourage those who do good; and by imposing punishment on wrongdoers, they express anger (*orgē*) against wrongdoing and serve as a terror (*phobos*) to such conduct. Nothing is said about retribution, about getting even, about reciprocating evil with evil, about redress, about vengeance."[14] But it seems to me that retributive justice is indeed envisioned here by Paul, since otherwise he would hardly say that "if you do wrong, be afraid, for he [the government authority] does not bear the sword in vain; he is the servant of God to execute his wrath on the wrongdoer" (Rom 13:4). Why mention "the sword" and "wrath" if retributive justice is not in play here, especially since it surely would have been in Roman courts?

Indeed, although it is clear that Jesus and Paul command Christians to do without retributive punishment when we are personally harmed, it seems wise to avoid imposing a hard-and-fast rule even with regard to personal harm. Thus, Jesus and Paul cursed their enemies when they deemed such a curse to be appropriate, despite their general injunctions against cursing others. In the gospel of Matthew, Jesus formally curses the scribes

---

11. Ibid., 129.
12. Ibid., 128.
13. Ibid.
14. Ibid.

and Pharisees of his time as "hypocrites," "blind guides," and "blind fool" (Mt 23:15–17), despite the fact that he earlier warns that "whoever insults his brother shall be liable to the council, and whoever says, 'You fool!' shall be liable to the hell of fire" (Mt 5:22). Similarly, Paul commands us not to curse our enemies but instead to bless them, and yet—at least according to Acts—Paul responds to the high priest Ananias, "God shall strike you, you whitewashed wall! Are you sitting to judge me according to the law, and yet contrary to the law you order me to be struck?" (Acts 23:3).

This does not take away from the fact that personal forgiveness, rather than retribution, is what Jesus and Paul require from us in response to those who harm us. Citing Hannah Arendt's remark that "the discoverer of the role of forgiveness in the realm of human affairs was Jesus of Nazareth,"[15] Wolterstorff adds that the Old Testament frequently refers to God's forgiveness of humans. But human forgiveness of other humans rarely appears in the Old Testament, and God in the Old Testament never commands humans to forgive those who harm them. So far as I can tell, Wolterstorff is justified in noting the newness of Jesus' teaching to his disciples that "if your brother sins, rebuke him, and if he repents, forgive him; and if he sins against you seven times in the day, and turns to you seven times, and says, 'I repent,' you must forgive him" (Lk 17:3–4). In the gospel of Matthew, Jesus intensifies this in response to a question from Peter: " 'Lord, how often shall my brother sin against me, and I forgive him? As many as seven times?' Jesus said to him, 'I do not say to you seven times, but seventy times seven' " (Mt 18:21–22).[16] The God who forgives his people expects us to forgive.

In Wolterstorff's view, Anselm's satisfaction theory of how Christ's cross reconciles us to God assumes that forgiveness must involve retributive justice, and in fact *reverts back* to the reciprocity code as the standard of justice, just as if Jesus had never taught the opposite.[17] Wolterstorff notes

15. See Hannah Arendt, *The Human Condition* (Garden City, NY: Doubleday, 1959), 214–15.
16. See Wolterstorff, *Justice in Love*, 162–63.
17. See ibid., 163–65. In *Cur Deus homo* I.12, Anselm teaches that "it is not fitting for God to forgive a sin without punishment," because if a sin "is not punished, it is forgiven without its having been regulated." Anselm, *Why God Became Man*, trans. Janet Fairweather, in Anselm of Canterbury, *The Major Works*, ed. Brian Davies and G. R. Evans (Oxford: Oxford University Press, 1998), 260–356, at 284). His interlocutor Boso raises an objection similar to Wolterstorff's: "[W]hen God teaches us to forgive those who sin against us, he seems to be being contradictory—in teaching us to do something which is not fitting for him to do himself" (I.12, p. 285). Anselm replies to Boso, "There is no contradiction in this, because God is giving us this teaching in order that we should not presume to do something which belongs to God alone. For it belongs to no one to take vengeance, except him who is Lord of all" (Ibid.). Boso then raises another crucial objection: "[S]ince God

that Anselm assumes that forgiveness and justice are in tension; justice cannot be served without retribution, that is to say, without the fulfillment of the reciprocity code. Why did Anselm arrive at this position? Wolterstorff observes, "Anselm knew Scripture well and took it as authoritative. He would have known that Jesus enjoined rejection of the reciprocity code. He would have known that Jesus taught that we are not to repay evil with evil but always to seek the good of self and neighbor, even of those who are one's enemies."[18] Yet, despite this knowledge, Anselm still associated justice with retribution in the case of sinners. As Wolterstorff points out, in making this assumption, "Anselm was in line with the majority opinion in the Christian tradition," a majority opinion that leaves Wolterstorff surprised and confounded, given Jesus' clear rejection of the reciprocity code.[19]

The result of Anselm's view, a result particularly clearly expressed in *Cur Deus Homo*, is a theory "of the atonement according to which Christ, in allowing himself to be crucified, suffered on our behalf, thereby satisfying the requirements of retributive justice."[20] In this view, Christ on the cross freely "undergoes the hard treatment that God assigned as our punishment"; he thereby satisfies for our sins by restoring the order of justice between us and God.[21] Justice is restored by the greatest injustice (namely, the acts of Jesus' killers, who in fact include all of us) precisely because Jesus' love, in offering up his life for us, was by far the greatest act of justice—an act of justice that the triune God also wills, insofar as what God wills is (Jesus') love.

Wolterstorff considers this atonement theory to be a terrible distortion of Christianity. He affirms of course that Christ suffered for us, since such a teaching is found clearly in the New Testament. But he argues that "vicarious punishment" not only does not produce forgiveness—since punishment is punishment, not forgiveness—but also goes against Jesus' central teachings. How could Jesus have taught so firmly against

---

is so free that he is subject to no law and no judgment, and is so benevolent that nothing can be conceived of more benevolent than he, and since there is nothing right or proper except what he wishes, it does seem surprising that we should be saying that he is in no way willing to forgive an injury to himself, or that it is not permissible for him to do so, whereas we are in the habit of seeking forgiveness from him even for things we do to other people" (Ibid.). Anselm responds that God can will nothing unjust, because God is justice itself. On this basis, Anselm concludes that "it does not belong to his freedom or benevolence or will to release unpunished a sinner who has not repaid to God what he has taken away from him" (Ibid., 286). Like Aquinas, I disagree with Anselm here, as I discuss further on.

18. Wolterstorff, *Justice in Love*, 192.
19. Ibid.
20. Ibid.
21. Ibid.

retributive justice in Matthew 5 and elsewhere, only to endure God's retributive justice with respect to us? If we must not partake in retributive justice, then surely God should not partake in retributive justice either. If we need not "return evil for evil," an eye for an eye, then surely God, too, does not need to punish us—let alone allow Jesus to suffer for us—in order to establish justice between us and God.

Wolterstorff asks with some acerbity,

> Why has the declaration that God does not punish the repentant sinner but forgives him, and the injunction that we are to do likewise, not jolted Christian theologians and ethicists into concluding that justice does not require punishment? Why has it instead led them into calling vicarious punishment of the wrongdoer, *forgiveness* of the wrongdoer?[22]

For Wolterstorff, it is clear both that retributive punishment is not needed for justice and that *vicarious* retributive punishment, whatever it might supposedly accomplish, cannot cause the forgiveness of the persons for whom the vicarious punishment is endured.

Wolterstorff does not thereby intend to reject all punishment. While rejecting vicarious punishment, he thinks that punishment has a symbolic significance that is beneficial for both the wrongdoer and society. With regard to the wrongdoer, "the imposition of hard treatment on him counts as condemning *him for his deed*, and it is a way of expressing resentment of *the deed done* and anger at *him* for doing it."[23] Wolterstorff calls his theory of punishment "reprobative" rather than "retributive." He distinguishes *reprobative* punishment from the goals of "rehabilitation, deterrence, or protection," since punishment properly looks backward to the deed done, not forward to a future good. Reprobative punishment expresses "a judgment of condemnation and an expression of negative feelings toward deed and doer," and shows that "society does not condone what was done."[24]

Must a victim demand reprobative punishment (not retributive punishment) in order for justice to be fulfilled and forgiveness to be possible? Wolterstorff argues that the answer is no. It is possible to offer full and complete forgiveness even without exacting punishment. Here Wolterstorff responds not only to Anselm but also to Immanuel Kant, who holds that "failure to punish wrongdoers is a double violation of justice."[25] The

---

22. Ibid., 193.
23. Ibid., 196.
24. Ibid., 196–97.
25. Ibid., 201. See Kant, *The Metaphysical Elements of Justice*, trans. John Ladd (Indianapolis: Bobbs-Merrill, 1965), 102.

key question for Wolterstorff is whether foregoing punishment sends a message to the wrongdoer and to society that one condones evil acts. Wolterstorff concludes that it does not; rather, it sends a message of mercy, just as Jesus commanded.

What about the numerous passages in the New Testament that connect Jesus' work of atonement with his spilling of his blood (for example, Mk 14:24 and parallels; Jn 12:31–33; Rom 3:23–25; 5:9; 1 Cor 11:25; Phil 2:6–8; Eph 1:7; 2:13; Col 1:20; Heb 9:26–28; 10:12; 13:20; 1 Peter 1:18–19; Rev 1:5; 5:9)? His spilling of his blood reconciles humans to God, makes peace between humans and God, takes away and expiates sin, pays the ransom owed by sinners, and establishes the new covenant. His death restores us to justice in relation to God: "While we were yet sinners Christ died for us," so that "we are now justified by his blood" (Rom 5:8–9).[26]

Wolterstorff does not address these passages in his account of Jesus' rejection of the reciprocity code or in his critique of theories of atonement centered upon satisfaction for sin (so as to restore justice). Wolterstorff grants only that "Paul held that God justifies sinners on account of the fidelity of Jesus; Christ died *for us*."[27] Since his focus is on "the justice of God's love" and on "the fidelity of Jesus," Wolterstorff thinks that he does not need to spell out the significance of Jesus' dying for us, although he recognizes that the fact that Jesus died *for us* "is an extremely important part of Paul's thought."[28] This seems to me to be an understatement, and I think that Wolterstorff makes a key mistake by not addressing these passages.

In my view, the above biblical texts about Jesus' cross make clear that the justice that Jesus fulfilled on the cross—as part of his mission to accomplish the restoration of Israel and to inaugurate the kingdom of God—was *retributive* justice, as makes sense given the truth that the penalty of sin is death (Gen 2:17; 3:2; 3:19; Rom 5:12; 6:23; Js 1:15). As I noted above, the New Testament also teaches that those who are being configured to Jesus' love by the Holy Spirit will receive an everlasting

---

26. I agree with Scot McKnight when he writes: "I don't know how to read elements of (especially) Paul without explaining his soteriology as penal" (*A Community Called Atonement* [Nashville: Abingdon, 2007], 43; cf. 64–66). McKnight also points out that Jesus' choosing to give up his life during Passover (in light of his Last Supper), and Jesus' statement in Mark 10:45 that "the Son of man also came ... to give his life as a ransom for many," indicate Jesus' intention to take upon himself God's judgment against sin and to liberate us from sin.

27. Wolterstorff, *Justice in Love*, 280.

28. Ibid., 280–81.

reward due in reciprocal justice (though the reward will go beyond any merely human reciprocity), while those who freely reject Jesus' love will receive retributive punishment. Jesus tells those who are fasting that they should strive to be seen "by your Father who is in secret; and your Father who sees in secret will reward you" (Mt 6:16–18), and he promises that good works will be rewarded: "Lay up for yourselves treasures in heaven" (Mt 6:20; cf. Mt 10:41–42 and Lk 6:35).

Retributive justice will be enacted at the final judgment toward those who freely reject God's love (see Mt 25:41–46; Rev 20:14), though we should keep in view that retributive justice has *already* been fulfilled on the cross and that God's desire is to "have mercy upon all" (Rom 11:32). There is another crucial issue, however, that receives insufficient attention from Wolterstorff. Namely, from where does the code of reciprocity come? For Wolterstorff, the code of reciprocity seems to be essentially a cultural prejudice. He states that

> the reciprocity code, and the idea of punishment as retribution that goes along with it, have had such a tight grip on human thought and imagination that not even Jesus' rejection of the code and his injunction to forgive rather than punish have been sufficient to loosen that grip, not even on those who take his words as authoritative.[29]

But why does the code of reciprocity have such a "tight grip on human thought and imagination"? Some might suppose that the reason is a survival-driven sense of equity. Perhaps this is what Wolterstorff has in mind when he comments, "All about us people talk about getting even, giving malefactors what they have coming to them; it's hard to resist thinking the same way."[30] In my view, the reason for the reciprocity code is more profound than the urge to even things up with malefactors or the desire to prevent malefactors from getting away with harming us and our loved ones. I think that the reason for the enduring power of the reciprocity code is that this code is inscribed in the order of creation.

The remainder of this essay offers an account of reciprocal justice as grounded in the created order, in hopes of exhibiting the Anselmian (and patristic) links between creation and atonement. I do so by drawing upon the theology of Thomas Aquinas, since he is well known for his Anselmian insistence that given God's will to free us from sin, it was in a certain

---

29. Ibid., 193.
30. Ibid.

sense "necessary that God should become incarnate for the restoration of human nature"—a restoration that was accomplished "by Christ satisfying for us" and that restored our (and the entire creation's) just ordering to God.[31] The perspective that informs Aquinas's theology of the cross has been articulated well, without reference to Aquinas, by the contemporary evangelical theologian Graham McFarlane: "The cross signifies that our human actions carry with them real consequences, that within creation there is an inbuilt penalty clause for relational unfaithfulness, and that this lies at the very heart of the created order."[32]

II. CREATION AND ATONEMENT: THOMAS AQUINAS'S CONTRIBUTION

IS THERE JUSTICE IN GOD?

The question of whether reciprocal justice is inscribed in the created order depends in part upon whether there is justice in the Creator, since the perfections of creatures participate in a finite mode in the infinite perfections of God. In the question that Aquinas devotes in the *Summa Theologiae* to the justice of God, an objection observes that "the act of justice is to pay what is due. But God is no man's debtor. Therefore justice does not belong to God."[33] Why is God not a debtor? The key scriptural passage that Aquinas cites is Romans 11:35: "[W]ho has given a gift to him, that he might be repaid?" The next verse adds a doxology: "For from him and through him and to him are all things" (Rom 11:36). All things are from God; all things, insofar as they have being and goodness, are his gifts.

The created order and everything in it is sheer divine gift. Interestingly, in Romans 11:35 Paul is paraphrasing Job 35. Elihu criticizes Job for claiming something as "my right before God" (Job 35:2). Elihu tries to bring Job back to reality so that Job will not cry out against God. Thus Elihu asks Job, "If you are righteous, what do you give to him; or what does he receive from your hand?" (Job 35:7). Elihu's point is that the gift is all on God's side. Elihu is not a spokesman for God, and yet God later affirms something of what Elihu says. Speaking directly to Job, God asks rhetorically, "Who has given to me, that I should repay him? Whatever is under the whole heaven is mine" (Job 41:11). If everything is a gift, it

---

31. Thomas Aquinas, *The Summa Theologica of St. Thomas Aquinas*, trans. Fathers of the English Dominican Province (Westminster, MD: Christian Classics, 1981), I, q. 1, a. 2.
32. McFarlane, "Atonement, Creation and Trinity," *Atonement Debate*, 201.
33. Aquinas, *Summa Theologica*, I, q. 21, a. 1, obj. 3.

seems that claims to justice on the side of the creature make no sense, since no one has a right to a gift. God is sheer giver, and creatures cannot make claims of justice as though God owed creatures something, since everything that creatures have and are is God's gift.

Aquinas, however, argues that God possesses justice vis-à-vis creatures, since, as Psalm 11:8 says, "The Lord is just, and has loved justice."[34] In defending this scriptural claim, Aquinas makes use of Aristotle's distinction between commutative and distributive justice. Commutative justice does not apply to God, because God is the giver of all things, and he receives nothing in return because he is infinitely actual and because creatures are finite participations of his infinite actuality. God is an utterly free giver, not one who gives out of a neediness or a hoped-for return. God gives because of his infinite goodness; he loves finite things into being and sustains them in being by his love. Whatever goodness creatures have, is the gift of his causal love. But once commutative justice is ruled out (as Paul and Job confirm it must be), distributive justice remains. Every good ruler or steward, Aquinas observes, must be just in the sense of distributive justice, in giving to each what each deserves. Distributive justice means that "the order of the universe, which is seen both in effects of nature and in effects of will, shows forth the justice of God."[35]

To explain this point further, Aquinas cites Dionysius's *The Divine Names* on God's justice as exemplified in creation. Dionysius urges that people who reject the justice of the existing order of things need to "see that God is truly just, in seeing how He gives to all existing things what is proper to the condition of each; and preserves the nature of each one in the order and with the powers that properly belong to it."[36] Each thing that God creates has a nature, and God gives it the powers that belong to its nature and that enable its flourishing as the kind of thing that it is. Aquinas adds that God's justice is always founded upon his mercy, because it is an act of mercy, flowing from "the abundance of his

34. Aquinas cites Psalm 11:8 (10:8 in his version of the Bible) in the *sed contra* of *Summa Theologica*, I, q. 21, a. 1. The Latin is: *"Iustus Dominus, et iustitias dilexit."* The RSV translates the verse with essentially the same meaning, substituting righteousness for justice: "For the Lord is righteous, he loves righteous deeds."
35. Aquinas, *Summa Theologica*, I, q. 21, a. 1.
36. This is the English translation of Aquinas's Latin version of Pseudo-Dionysius's work; for a contemporary translation, see Pseudo-Dionysius, *The Divine Names*, VIII.7 (896B), in Pseudo-Dionysius, *The Complete Works*, trans. Colm Luibheid with Paul Rorem (New York: Paulist Press, 1987), 49–131, at 113: "What they really should know is that the righteousness of God is truly righteousness in that it gives the appropriate and deserved qualities to everything and that it preserves the nature of each being in its due order and power."

goodness," for God to create things from nothing.[37] As a divine attribute, justice is infinite, and like the other divine attributes, justice is the simple divine essence (though our finite mode of understanding requires many names for God, predicated analogously).[38] Thus, the justice of God belongs equally to each person of the Trinity and is exhibited in the divine work of creation, with regard to which Aquinas consistently holds together the twin truths that "all things caused are the common work of the whole Godhead" and that "God the Father made the creature through his Word, which is his Son; and through his Love, which is the Holy Spirit."[39]

Does God's distributive justice imply that God is not free in his relations to creatures, or that God is bound to "an impersonal set of rules of the game of the universe"? I think not, once we recognize that every personal relationship should include freely giving what is due. Citing Deuteronomy 32:4, "The Rock, his work is perfect; for all his ways are justice," Aquinas notes that God's distributive justice is apparent in the human body.[40] An objection points out that what is "perfect is what lacks nothing. But the human body lacks more than the body of other animals, for these are provided with covering and natural arms of defence, in which man is lacking. Therefore the human body is very imperfectly disposed."[41] Aquinas responds by comparing God to an artist, who gives to his creatures—his "works of art"—all that pertains to their specific nature and perfection (granted, of course, that through material generation, individuals of the species will possess defects).[42] As Aquinas observes, "Every artist intends to give to his work the best disposition; not absolutely the best, but the best as regards the proposed end."[43]

The divine artist here is hardly an impersonal actor, but rather one who wills good for what he makes. Humans therefore receive the "best disposition" suitable to their end or goal of knowing and loving God. As rational creatures, humans do not need horns, claws, and fur in order to remain alive, and human hands serve as the instruments of human rationality. The

---

37. Aquinas, *Summa Theologica*, I, q. 21, a. 4.

38. See ibid., I, q. 4, a. 2; q. 7, aa. 1–2; q. 13, aa. 2, 4, and 5. God would be just even if there were no creatures toward which to exercise justice, since one can have a just will even if one lacks objects for the exercise of justice.

39. Ibid., I, q. 45, a. 6 (including the *sed contra*).

40. See ibid., I, q. 91, a. 1. The portion of Deuteronomy 32:4 that Aquinas cites (in his Latin translation) reads simply, "God's works are perfect."

41. Ibid., I, q. 91, a. 3, obj. 2.

42. Ibid., I, q. 91, a. 3.

43. Ibid.

human being also has an upright stature and faces forward "in order that by the senses, and chiefly by sight, which is more subtle and penetrates further into the differences of things, he may freely survey the sensible objects around him, both heavenly and earthly, so as to gather intelligible truth from all things."[44] Since God's plan for distributive justice is an infinitely wise plan, it can be rightly termed a "law" of justice without thereby rendering it impersonal.[45] Far from creating in an arbitrary fashion, what God "does according to his will he does justly: as we do justly what we do according to law."[46]

Even so, it seems that the fundamental difficulty with attributing distributive justice to God still needs to be answered. Can it really be said that God *owes* something to any creature? Does God really owe it to humans that, given the end or goal of our rational nature, we should not have (for example) cow bodies? If God is our debtor in distributive justice, then it seems as though the order has become topsy-turvy. A true giver does not *owe* someone a gift. If the gift is owed, it is not really a gift but rather is a payment, an obligation. God has no such obligations to pay. Recall God's words to Job, which Paul takes up and affirms: "Who has given to me, that I should repay him? Whatever is under the whole heaven is mine." How then can there be distributive justice in God the Creator?

Aquinas answers in a twofold way. He affirms that God does indeed owe creatures what pertains to their flourishing, to their ability to achieve the end of their nature. In this regard, with particular reference to human nature (and aware that in material things there will be defects in individual instances), he states that it is "due to a created thing that it should possess what is ordered to it; thus it is due to man to have hands."[47] But before making this affirmation, he argues that the primary debt God owes is to himself, to his own goodness. He observes, "It is due to God that there should be fulfilled in creatures what his will and wisdom require, and what manifests his goodness."[48] In giving creatures what he owes in distributive justice, God is primarily giving what he owes to himself as Creator. In ordering creatures to his goodness, God owes them in justice what is due to their natures; but it is the ordering to God, and thus God's debt to his own wisdom and goodness, that is fundamental.

---

44. Ibid., I, q. 91, a. 3, ad 3.
45. Ibid., I, q. 21, a. 1, ad 2.
46. Ibid.
47. Ibid., I, q. 21, a. 1, ad 3.
48. Ibid.

The very same chapter from Anselm that Wolterstorff rejects most strongly is cited here *appreciatively* by Aquinas.[49] Wolterstorff cites two passages from chapter 10 of the *Proslogion*: "You [God] are just not because you give us our due, but because You do what befits You as the supreme good"; and "In sparing the wicked You are just in relation to Yourself and not in relation to us."[50] Aquinas quotes a different passage from chapter 10: "When you [God] punish the wicked, this is just because it accords with their merits; but when you spare the wicked, this is just ... because it is in keeping with your goodness."[51] In Wolterstorff's view, it is doubtful that "relative justice is a coherent concept."[52] He argues that it hardly seems possible for God to be just in relation to God, while being unjust "in relation to us."[53] In Aquinas's view, by contrast, Anselm is simply trying to speak (if rather awkwardly) of justice in God "as the fitting accompaniment of his goodness."[54]

In affirming that God, in giving what is justly *due* to creatures, nonetheless gives freely because God is giving what is due to his own goodness and plan of wisdom, Aquinas shows that creation — the created order — is imbued with justice in two ways: first, insofar as all created things are ordered to God's goodness, and second, insofar as "one created thing is ordered to another, as the parts to the whole, accident to substance, and all things whatsoever to their end."[55] For our purposes, the key point is that the created order is imbued with distributive justice, both in its own interrelationships and in its relation to God. Again, this justice is rooted in God's *goodness*, by which the triune God, not only as creator but also as redeemer, enables creatures to share in the trinitarian life.[56]

It follows that a sharp contrast between a logic of gift/love and a logic of justice is mistaken with respect to creation (and so likewise with respect to redemption). Creation is God's sheer gift, and yet creation is profoundly imbued with structures of justice. Indeed, precisely because creation is God's gift, justice and juridical categories are inseparable from the created

---

49. See ibid., I, q. 21, a. 1, ad 3.
50. See Wolterstorff, *Justice in Love*, 164. I have quoted these passages as they appear in Wolterstorff's book. Wolterstorff cites the translation of the *Proslogion* by M. J. Charlesworth (Notre Dame: University of Notre Dame Press, 1979).
51. Anselm, *Proslogion*, ch. 10, in Anselm, *Monologion and Proslogion with the Replies of Gaunilo and Anselm*, trans. Thomas Williams (Indianapolis: Hackett, 1996), 93–117, at 106.
52. Wolterstorff, *Justice in Love*, 164.
53. Ibid.
54. Aquinas, *Summa Theologica*, I, q. 21, a. 1, ad 3.
55. Ibid.
56. See ibid., III, q. 1, a. 1, including the quotation from John of Damascus in the *sed contra*.

order. An example that Aquinas offers begins with our possession of hands: "To possess hands is due to man on account of his rational soul; and his rational soul is due to him that he may be man; and his being man is on account of the divine goodness."[57] God's justice in creating humans with what is due to them has its source in God's goodness and love. Indeed, Aquinas finds that God's mercy is always deeper than his distributive justice: "In every work of God, viewed at its primary source, there appears mercy," since the giver always bestows not only what is due, but far more than what is due.[58]

CREATURELY INJUSTICE AND RETRIBUTIVE PUNISHMENT

If God is related to creation not only by love and gift but also by justice, can rational creatures rebel against God's goodness in such a way as to fall afoul of justice and to merit punishment in retributive justice? Recall Wolterstorff's criticism of "theories of the atonement according to which Christ, in allowing himself to be crucified, suffered on our behalf, thereby satisfying the requirements of retributive justice."[59] For Wolterstorff, such theories go against Jesus' teaching that "we are to stop thinking in terms of paying back, getting even, evening things up, redressing injury with injury, harm with harm, evil with evil." [60]

As I noted above, Wolterstorff fails to account for a number of New Testament texts that indicate that Christ paid the penalty of sin by his blood, and that make clear that the code of reciprocity continues to hold, although as believers united to Christ we are required to await reward and punishment in the life to come. It should also be clear, however, that Wolterstorff's criticism of atonement theories that involve Christ's "satisfying the requirements of retributive justice" begs the question of whether there is a relationship of justice between rational creatures and the Creator. If there is such a relationship, then the order of justice is indeed likely to be something that the incarnate Son, filled with the Holy Spirit, willed to satisfy for us by restoring the justice of the human race vis-à-vis the triune God.

Aquinas points out that just as the Creator owes a debt to creatures (because of his own goodness), so also rational creatures owe a debt of worship and service to the Creator, since "he made all things, and has

57. Ibid., I, q. 21, a. 4.
58. Ibid.
59. Wolterstorff, *Justice in Love*, 192.
60. Ibid., 193.

supreme dominion over all."[61] Reflecting upon the virtue of piety, Aquinas comments that

> [m]an becomes a debtor to other men in various ways, according to their various excellence and the various benefits received from them. On both counts God holds first place, for he is supremely excellent, and is for us the first principle of being and government.[62]

This debt is both a debt of justice and a debt that rightly calls forth love: the triune God who lovingly creates us has a just claim upon our love. God's infinite goodness, manifested not least in the gift of creation, makes him infinitely lovable. Indeed, if we were able to apprehend how lovable God actually is, we literally could not help but love him.

When humans turn away from this divine love and refuse our debt of justice, humans lack the justice that we were created to have. Aquinas observes that sin "is not a pure privation but an act deprived of its due order."[63] The sinner rebels against the order of justice that exists between rational creatures and God, an interpersonal order that characterizes full human flourishing (virtue). Aquinas describes the resulting disorder as the "debt of punishment [reatus poenae]" that sin produces.[64] Human beings were created for a graced union with the triune God, in God's kingdom, through knowledge and love. Having rejected God's grace and destroyed "the principle of the order whereby man's will is subject to God," humans fall into disorder and slavery to sin.[65] Sin itself, then, is a punishment of sin. As Aquinas says,

> Whatever rises up against an order, is put down by that order or by the principle thereof. And because sin is an inordinate act, it is evident that whoever sins, commits an offense against an order: wherefore he is put down, in consequence, by that same order, which repression is punishment.[66]

The order of creation is such that when we rebel against this order, we disorder ourselves, losing our interior justice and our just relation to God. Aquinas adds that "so long as the disturbance of the order [perversitas ordinis] remains, the debt of punishment [reatus poenae] must needs remain

---

61. Aquinas, Summa Theologica, II–II, q. 81, a. 1, ad 3.
62. Ibid., II–II, q. 101, a. 1.
63. Ibid., I–II, q. 72, a. 1, ad 2.
64. Ibid., I–II, q. 87, a. 1.
65. Ibid., I–II, q. 87, a. 3.
66. Ibid., I–II, q. 87, a. 1.

also."[67] The "disturbance of the order" is that in pride we have turned away from God as our ultimate end and have cut ourselves off from God by the loss of charity. Aquinas notes that this disorder, considered in itself, is "irreparable, although it is possible to repair it by the power of God."[68] Only God can restore our graced charity and draw us into his kingdom.

Is such punishment, wherein God does not actively inflict anything but rather simply permits humans to have their own way in rejecting God, "retributive" punishment? Aquinas explains that "in so far as sin consists in turning away from something, its corresponding punishment is the *pain of loss* [*poena damni*], which also is infinite, because it is the loss of the infinite good, i.e. God."[69] Humans rebel against the order of love, and as punishment, God permits humans to live in this disorder. This is a just punishment and reflects the inability of sinners truly to overthrow the order of justice. God does not *actively* inflict the punishment, but the punishment is retributive, because the punishment consists in a harm that the sinner incurs due to the harm that the sinner has inflicted.

There is more to say about the fallen human condition, however. When a person commits a sin, the sin incurs guilt or debt (*reatus*) because of the harm that it causes, and the sin also stains the will by causing the will to lose holiness. The sinner needs to be freed from both the debt and the stain (*macula*). For this to happen, the repentant sinner must willingly embrace the order of justice inscribed in creation and must freely choose to endure the just retributive punishment. With regard to the debt, the sinner must "pay some sort of penal compensation, which restores him to the equality of justice."[70] With regard to the stain, the sinner must willingly "accept the order of divine justice" either by "[taking] upon himself the punishment of his past sin, or [bearing] patiently the punishment which God inflicts upon him."[71]

Again, punishment will be given to the sinner whether or not the sinner embraces it. Sin carries with it its own punishment due to the disorder that it brings. Thus, removal of the debt of punishment involves the sinner actively embracing and accepting punishment as justly owed to him or her. By embracing the just punishment in love, the sinner turns it into a "satisfactory" punishment, a punishment that heals the disorder rather than simply reflecting the disorder.

67. Ibid., I–II, q. 87, a. 3.
68. Ibid.
69. Ibid., I–II, q. 87, a. 4.
70. Ibid., I–II, q. 87, a. 6.
71. Ibid.

Is Aquinas right to argue that "the equality of justice" is restored "by penal compensation [*per recompensationem poenae*]"?[72] It would seem that "penal compensation" is not needed once the sinner's will has been healed. In this regard, Aquinas recalls the story of David, who has sexual intercourse with Uriah the Hittite's wife and then, in an attempt to conceal the crime, has Uriah the Hittite killed.[73] The prophet Nathan confronts David with his sin, and David repents, saying to Nathan, "I have sinned against the LORD" (2 Sam 12:13). In his sincere repentance, David embraces the order of justice anew; his will is healed. In response, Nathan tells David that "[t]he LORD also has put away your sin" (2 Sam 12:14). Should this suffice, or does David still owe a "penal compensation" for his sin? Scripture suggests the latter: David must endure the death of the child he conceived with Bathsheba.

This story would certainly not persuade Wolterstorff, since he is well aware that the Old Testament endorses retributive punishment and "penal compensation," and he argues that Jesus reverses this teaching. But in Aquinas's view, "when the stain of sin has been removed, there may remain a debt of punishment, not indeed of punishment simply, but of satisfactory punishment."[74] Again, why is this so? If the stain has been removed by the will's return to its holy brightness, which happens when the will embraces the order of justice (which is an order of love), why should a "satisfactory punishment" remain to be paid, let alone a "penal compensation" for the guilt? Aquinas states with respect to the guilt: "Now it is evident that in all actual sins, when the act of sin has ceased, the guilt remains; because the act of sin makes man deserving of punishment, in so far as he transgresses the order of divine justice."[75] In justice, the rational creature owes a debt of worship and service—a debt of love—to the creator God. Sin means that the rational creature turns away from God and refuses unjustly to give the worship and service that the rational creature owes. To restore justice in this situation means not only returning the will to its proper "brightness" (love), but also paying the debt due for failing to give to God what should have been given.

The retributive punishment at work here, both with regard to the debt and the stain, brings about the full restoration of justice between humans and God, which is a hallmark of God's kingdom. Note, however, that although sin places us in radical opposition to the perfect love, justice,

---

72. Ibid., I–II, q. 87, a. 6 and ad 3.
73. See ibid., I–I, q. 87, a. 6, *sed contra*.
74. Ibid., I–II, q. 87, a. 6.
75. Ibid.

and innocence of God—and in this sense the biblical depictions of God's "wrath" against sin are crucially important—God could freely forgive sin without any retributive punishment, since such punishment meets no need of God's, and our crimes are against him.

JESUS' DEATH AS SATISFACTION FOR SIN

Aquinas emphasizes that no "satisfactory punishment" was strictly necessary for salvation. He observes that if God "had willed to free man from sin without any satisfaction, he would not have acted against justice."[76] Rather, since sin "has the formality of fault in that it is committed against himself," God can forgive it "just as anyone else, overlooking a personal trespass, without satisfaction, acts mercifully and not unjustly."[77] If so, however, then why did God send his Son to restore the human race by enduring, with perfect love, the penalty of death, thereby removing both the stain and the debt of human sin? According to Aquinas, God did so because he thereby showed "more copious mercy than if he had forgiven sins without satisfaction."[78] Not only did he show how much he loves us and inspire us to love him in return, but also he greatly dignified humanity by healing its sinful disorder through Jesus as the head of the human race, rather than extrinsically by divine fiat. In this regard, Aquinas underscores that only the incarnate Son could have made condign satisfaction, fully restoring the order of justice between humans and God. This is so both because "the goodness of any person or persons could not make up adequately for the harm done to the whole of the nature; and also because a sin committed against God has a kind of infinity from the infinity of the divine majesty."[79]

Yet, is it really possible to affirm that Jesus' cross satisfies for the huge number of human sins, including the sin of Jesus' executioners? In response, Aquinas emphasizes that as the head of all humans, Jesus is not separated from other humans in such a way that his suffering and death are utterly extrinsic to them, as Wolterstorff seems to suppose in his critique of the notion of vicarious punishment (though insofar as Wolterstorff has

---

76. Ibid., III, q. 46, a. 2, ad 3. Aquinas is implicitly responding to Anselm's *Cur Deus Homo* I.12–13. In a passage approvingly cited here by Aquinas, Augustine comments that in showing that it was fitting for Jesus to die for our sins, "we must also show, *not indeed that no other possible way was available to God, since all things are equally within his power,* but that there neither was nor should have been a more suitable way of curing our unhappy state." Augustine, *The Trinity,* trans. Edmund Hill (Brooklyn: New City Press, 1991), XIII.iv.13, 353, emphasis added).
77. Ibid., III, q. 46, a. 2, ad 3.
78. Ibid., III, q. 46, a. 1, ad 3.
79. Ibid., III, q. 1, a. 2, ad 2.

substitution theories in view, Aquinas would agree with him). As Aquinas states, "The head and members are one mystic person; and therefore Christ's satisfaction belongs to all the faithful as being His members."[80]

Here it is also important to note that God does not punish Jesus as the vicarious victim in the place of all sinners; rather, Jesus pays the penalty of death with such love and such dignity (since his death is the death of the divine Son) that the order of justice is restored between the whole human race and God. Since Jesus' death was that of the incarnate Son, Aquinas concludes that the "penal compensation" that Jesus paid was far more "than was required to compensate for the offense of the whole human race."[81]

But why did Jesus choose to die on a cross for us, if a lesser suffering on his part would have sufficed for condign satisfaction? Aquinas answers this question by reference to human death as caused by original sin. He is well aware that material corruption and the death of plants and animals did not result from original sin. But the human experience of death as a profound rupture, gravely threatening the dignity that we have as rational creatures made for lasting interpersonal communion, does flow from original sin. As the consummation of his covenantal love for his people, the triune God freely willed to assume to the person of the Son a human nature "subject to penalty," so that the incarnate Son could heal our sinful alienation by undergoing death out of humility, obedience, and love, and transforming death itself into the path of life, the path by which we can obtain "the full participation of the divinity, which is the true bliss of man and end of human life."[82]

Reflecting on Romans 5:10, "For if while we were enemies we were reconciled to God by the death of his Son," Aquinas adds an important clarification about this reconciliation. Namely, God's attitude toward us does not change. Aquinas explains,

> Christ is not said to have reconciled us with God, as if God had begun anew to love us, since it is written (Jer 33:3): "I have loved thee with an everlasting love"; but because the source of hatred was taken away by Christ's Passion, both through sin being washed away and through compensation being made in the shape of a more pleasing offering.[83]

---

80. Ibid., III, q. 48, a. 2, ad 1.
81. Ibid., III, q. 48, a. 2; cf. III, q. 48, a. 4.
82. Ibid., III, q. 1, a. 1, ad 4; III, q. 1, a. 2. See also III, q. 14, a. 1.
83. Ibid., III, q. 49, a. 4, ad 2.

God is not our enemy, since God always loves whatever goodness (ontological and moral) we possess, and God loves us even though we turn away from him. It is we who have chosen to be "God's enemies" by committing crimes that God "hates," since our crimes make us lacking in goodness and produce terrible harm in the world.[84] Thus it is we who need healing and changing, not God. Jesus' loving act of satisfaction restores the justice of the human race in relation to God and opens for us, insofar as we are united to Jesus (as the head of the human race) by faith and the sacraments of faith, "the gate of heaven's kingdom," the kingdom of God that is the kingdom of love.[85]

III. CONCLUSION

For Wolterstorff, Jesus' rejection of the code of reciprocity and of retributive justice means that God, despite having approved it in his commandments to his people Israel, must consider the code of reciprocity and retributive justice to be wrong.

I have argued on the contrary that Jesus came to bear our sin and to restore the just order of human beings to God. It is because Jesus has fulfilled retributive justice, through a supreme act of mercy, that the people formed by faith in Jesus do not need to pursue our own retributive justice but must instead be people of mercy. Furthermore, if we imitate him by allowing his Spirit to configure our hearts to his love, we will come to share in his eternal reward. The code of reciprocity is not negated. Rather, it takes on a higher significance insofar as the reward that believers in Jesus strive for, and the punishment that believers seek to avoid, belongs to the world to come and will be given only by God. The reward will be the consummated kingdom marked by the everlasting indwelling of the divine persons in the redeemed (Jn 14:23) and by "face to face" knowledge of God (1 Cor 13:12). Believers already have a foretaste of this eternal reward, as Jesus makes clear in the gospel of John (see Jn 3:36; 4:14).

Wolterstorff's supposition that God could have nothing to do with reciprocal justice fails to make sense of the New Testament's statements about Jesus' cross and about the life to come. But the core of my argument has been that Wolterstorff undervalues retributive justice because he does not attend to its roots in the order of creation. In creation, God bonds

---

84. Ibid., III, q. 49, a. 4 and ad 1.
85. Ibid., III, q. 49, a. 5.

rational creatures to himself through a web of justice. Although creation is pure gift, God can rightly be said to owe creatures something, namely what pertains to the achievement of the end or goal proper to their nature. The logic of gift and the logic of justice, then, are integrally related even on the side of God. Rational creatures, having received the gift of being, must in justice offer love, worship, and service to the creator God. When we turn away from our Creator, we receive punishment in this very turning away, due to our violation of the order of justice. This punishment consists in existential disorder, alienation, and death.

In perfect self-giving love, God sends his Son to undergo freely the retributive punishment due to us so as to restore the order of justice (which is an order of love) between humans and God. God does so not out of a thirst for revenge, let alone out of any need on his part or for the purpose of punishing his Son, but rather because this is such a merciful way of healing and elevating humans. Jesus' free act of supreme love, his suffering and death on the cross, takes away the guilt and stain of all human sin, and it displays for us how much God loves us and what humility really is. It shows us what a sinless human being looks like, as God in creation intended for all of us to be. As the incarnate Son, Jesus is united to all persons as their head, and so his act of satisfaction is by no means extrinsic to those for whom he dies. In light of the gift of creation, with its web of justice, we can properly appreciate the cruciform pattern of Jesus' love and the way in which it establishes the interpersonal communion (or kingdom) of the new creation.

Reflection on the order of creation in order to understand the atonement better does not originate with Aquinas (or Anselm). Thus, when Athanasius treats the mode of our salvation, he states, "We will begin ... with the creation of the world and with God its Maker, for the first fact that you must grasp is this: *the renewal of creation has been wrought by the Self-same Word Who made it in the beginning.*"[86] Athanasius emphasizes that creation, which God accomplishes through his Word, is rooted in the transcendent divine goodness: "For God is good — or rather, of all goodness He is Fountainhead, and it is impossible for one who is good to be mean or grudging about anything."[87]

Having made humans in his own image, with "a share in the rational being of the very Word Himself," God placed them in a "paradise" marked

---

86. Athanasius, *On the Incarnation*, trans. Religious of C.S.M.V. (Yonkers: St. Vladimir's Seminary Press,, 1993), ch. 1, § 1, 26.
87. Ibid., ch. 1, § 3, 28.

by a law, "a single prohibition," which he required the first humans to obey in order to retain "the loveliness of their original innocence" and to enjoy a life free from "sorrow, pain or care, and after it the assurance of immortality in heaven."[88] If the first humans sinned, "they would come under the natural law of death and live no longer in paradise, but, dying outside of it, continue in death and corruption."[89] For Athanasius, this law and punishment are the meaning of Genesis 2:17: "Of the tree of the knowledge of good and evil you shall not eat, for in the day that you eat of it you shall die."

Could God have ignored his own law and promise of punishment when the first humans sinned? For Athanasius, much like Anselm, it is "monstrous and unfitting" that "[t]he law of death, which followed from the Transgression, prevailed upon us," but nonetheless "[i]t would ... have been unthinkable that God should go back upon His word and that man, having transgressed, should not die."[90] Not even the sincere repentance of the first humans could save them, because "repentance would not guard the Divine consistency, for, if death did not hold dominion over men, God would still remain untrue."[91] Furthermore, given the nature of the sin and the punishment, repentance could not save fallen humans, because their loss of grace and the corruption of their rational image meant that they had harmed themselves beyond the power of repentance to heal. Athanasius concludes, therefore, that "there was a debt owing which must needs be paid; for ... all men were due to die.... Death there had to be, and death for all, so that the due of all might be paid."[92]

Precisely because we were created in the rational image of the Word, however, God could hardly leave us to such a dreadful fate: "It was unworthy of the goodness of God that creatures made by Him should be brought to nothing through the deceit wrought upon man by the devil."[93] For this reason, the Word incarnate freely came to die for us and to restore us to a just relationship with God, freed from the corruption of death. Athanasius affirms,

> Thus, taking a body like our own, because all our bodies were liable to the corruption of death, He surrendered His body to death in place of all,

---

88. Ibid., 28–29.
89. Ibid., 29.
90. Ibid., ch. 2, § 6, 32.
91. Ibid., ch. 2, § 7, 33.
92. Ibid., ch. 4, § 20, 49.
93. Ibid., ch. 2, § 6, 32.

and offered it to the Father. This He did out of sheer love for us, so that in His death all might die, and the law of death thereby be abolished.[94]

The key point for my purposes is that Athanasius, like Aquinas (and Anselm), begins with the order of creation, and then reflects upon the just punishment of sin, the superabundant goodness of God, and the incarnate Son's paying of the penalty of death for the whole human race out of supreme love. Not surprisingly, Athanasius's approach also includes elements that are not found, or are developed in a different way, in Aquinas. For instance, Athanasius emphasizes that by turning away from the Word, by turning away from wisdom and rationality, the first humans turned toward death and nonbeing. Similarly, Athanasius insists that God could not have ignored the plight of humanity:

> Surely it would have been better never to have been created at all than, having been created, to be neglected and perish; and besides that, such indifference to the ruin of His own work before His very eyes would argue not goodness in God but limitation.[95]

Athanasius also describes the mechanism of salvation not only in terms of the incarnate Word freely undergoing the punishment of death and thereby paying our debt, but also in terms of an "exchange" in which the incorruptibility of the Word reverses the corruption of bodily death.[96] In this vein he remarks that the Word

> assumed a body capable of death, in order that it, through belonging to the Word Who is above all, might become in dying a sufficient exchange for all, and, itself remaining incorruptible through His indwelling, might thereafter put an end to corruption for all others as well.[97]

Here he envisions the incarnate Word's saving work in light of the "solidarity" of all humans in one nature: "For the solidarity of mankind is such that, by virtue of the Word's indwelling a single human body, the corruption which goes with death has lost its power over all."[98]

Although Aquinas does not take up this way of depicting the incorruptible Word's transformation of human corruptibility, he does echo Athanasius's insistence that God inscribed in the order of creation a just law

---

94. Ibid., ch. 2, § 8, 34.
95. Ibid., ch. 2, § 6, 32.
96. Ibid., ch. 2, § 9, 35.
97. Ibid.
98. Ibid. See Benjamin Myers's superb essay in this volume.

that required that original sin incur the punishment of death, a retributive punishment. Aquinas and Athanasius (and Anselm) fundamentally agree when it comes to viewing Jesus' death in light of the reciprocity code and retributive punishment, even though this is only one of the lenses through which Aquinas and Athanasius interpret Jesus' death.

At the heart of this agreement is the New Testament testimony that, in Paul's words, "we are now justified by his blood" (Rom 5:9). It is in Jesus that "all the fulness of God was pleased to dwell, and through him to reconcile to himself all things, whether on earth or in heaven, making peace by the blood of his cross" (Col 1:19–20); and it is this same Jesus who "is the image of the invisible God, the first-born of all creation; for in him all things were created" (Col 1:15–16). Atonement and creation must be held together.

Graham McFarlane, therefore, rightly emphasizes that "it is proper to locate the drama of redemption within the stage of creation. We do so because our understanding of creation provides the blueprint for redemption and therefore informs what can and cannot be said about the means by which the pathology may be redressed and redeemed."[99] Among the paths for understanding Jesus' merciful death for our sins, a central one is marked by the justice inscribed in the sheer gift of creation.

---

99. McFarlane, "Atonement, Creation and Trinity," 197.

CHAPTER 3

THE PATRISTIC ATONEMENT MODEL

BENJAMIN MYERS

I. NO EXPLANATION?

In his 2014 Annual Analytic Theology Lecture in San Diego, Oliver Crisp left his audience quite exercised after demonstrating that purported atonement theories are often only restatements instead of explanations.[1] They assert *that* the atonement happens without explaining *how*. To that extent they are not really atonement theories at all. They are, one might say, kerygma instead of theology. For something to qualify as a theory, it would have to explain how the thing actually works.

In a 1995 study on the atonement, Michael Winter drew attention to this problem in a withering excursus titled "No Explanation: Agreed."[2] Here he observed that modern theologians, no matter how great their disagreement over the nature of the atonement, are united in their principled refusal to explain how the atonement works. The insistence of F. W. Dillistone is representative of a wider mood: "The 'how' of this operation remains a mystery."[3] In Winter's opinion, modern theologians have been far too easily contented with "restatements" rather than "explanations" of the atonement, an approach that is hard to justify at a time when so many

---

1. Forthcoming as Oliver D. Crisp, "Is Ransom Enough?" *Journal of Analytic Theology* 3 (Spring 2015): 1–11.
2. Michael Winter, *The Atonement* (Collegeville, MN: Liturgical Press, 1995), 30–37.
3. F. W. Dillistone, *The Christian Understanding of the Atonement* (London: Nisbet, 1968), 177; cited in Winter, *The Atonement*, 33.

objections to the atonement have been posed by both secular and religious writers.[4]

Gustaf Aulén has been influential here. The aim of his book, *Christus Victor*, was to show the superiority of the patristic atonement model over later Catholic, evangelical, and liberal Protestant approaches. Aulén praised the patristic model for its lack of clarity and consistency. Unlike its theological competitors, the patristic model has no mechanism. It "defies systematization."[5] It is too rich for rational accounting. Aulén did not only mean that this model was hard to understand. He believed that patristic teaching on the atonement was internally contradictory. It involves, he said, "an antinomy which cannot be resolved by a rational statement."[6]

By contrast, Aulén implied that the Anselmian model is disreputable precisely because it is "in its very structure a rational theory."[7] Aulén's refusal to systematise his patristic *Christus Victor* model has recently led Kathryn Tanner to observe, quite rightly, that "*Christus Victor* is not a model [of atonement] at all in that it fails ... to address the question of the mechanism of the atonement."[8] But this was hardly an oversight on Aulén's part, since one aim of his book was to foster a distrust of atonement mechanisms. His approach, with its underlying northern-European-Lutheran assumptions about the perfidious unreliability of reason, has done much to shape subsequent discussions of the atonement. When it comes to thinking about the death of Christ, precision and intelligibility have come to be regarded as deficits. The best atonement model, apparently, would be the one that is least capable of explanation.

In this paper I wish to present an alternative to Aulén's interpretation of early Christian theology. I will argue that Christian antiquity did indeed develop what could be called (with obvious anachronism) an atonement model. I will try to show that this model is capable of rational explanation: it has its own precise atonement mechanism driven by its own metaphysical gears. This model, I will argue, is not only more coherent than anything described by Aulén; it is also far richer in its christology and its vision of the human condition.

---

4.   Winter, *The Atonement*, 35.
5.   Gustaf Aulén, *Christus Victor: An Historical Study of the Three Main Types of the Idea of the Atonement*, trans. A. G. Hebert (London: SPCK, 1931), 107.
6.   Ibid.
7.   Ibid., 75.
8.   Kathryn Tanner, *Christ the Key* (Cambridge: Cambridge University Press, 2010), 253.

II. THE MODEL

I begin by stating the patristic atonement model in outline. Implied meta-physical assumptions are stated in the form M:

(1) Humanity, created in the image of God, is loved by God.

(M1) There is one human nature. All individual human beings participate in this universal. *(Realism.)*

(2) But human nature has succumbed to the power of death.

(M2) Death is not a positive quality but a privation of being. *(Privation.)*

(3) To rescue humanity from its plight, God needs to retrieve human beings from the state of death.

(4) But God is unable to enter a state of death, i.e., to undergo privation from being.

(M3) The divine nature is infinite life and fullness, incapable of suffering or change. *(Impassibility.)*

(5) What is God to do?

(6) In Christ, God becomes incarnate: the divine nature is united with human nature.

(M4) Exactly how this union occurs is unknowable. *(Hypostatic union.)*

(7) In this union, each nature retains its own distinctiveness while participating in the properties of the other. Christ's human nature (without compromising its humanness) is filled with divine life; and the divine nature (without compromising its impassibility) is able to enter the privation of death.

(8) When Christ's human nature succumbs to death, the fullness of divine life enters the privative state of death. As a result, the privation is filled, i.e., cancelled out. In the death of Christ, death dies. *(The mechanism.)*

(9) Christ's resurrection is the inevitable consequence of his death. The suffering, dying Christ shows the union of the divine nature with a human nature subject to death; the resurrected Christ shows the union of the divine nature with a human nature no longer subject to death.

(10) What happens to human nature in Christ happens to humanity as a whole, because of (M1). *(The universal effect.)*

(11) Human nature is now freed from the power of death and is restored to its created position. This is a Good Thing. *(The solution.)*

(12) Human nature is now united to God and receives benefits far surpassing its created position. This is a Very Good Thing. *(The surplus.)*

Even from this bare outline it will be clear that the metaphysical assumptions are not window dressing. The assumptions of realism (M1) and the nature of death (M2) and divine impassibility (M3) are all essential for the functioning of the model. I will not be exploring (M4) in this paper, but it is important to keep this point in mind because it draws a clear line between the knowable bits of this model and the unknowable bits. Discussions of the atonement can too easily be short-circuited by premature appeals to mystery. At the first sign of difficulty there is always someone ready to throw up their hands and say, "We just don't know how it all happens, and that's that."

There is an admirable clarity in the way patristic thinkers distinguished between the things that *are* knowable and the things that *aren't*. Virtually nobody in Christian antiquity thought it was possible to understand the hypostatic union; but they did believe it was possible to understand the atonement. That is enough about (M4). In the rest of this paper I will consider the other three metaphysical assumptions in reverse order: divine nature as impassible, death as a privation, and human nature as a universal.

III. DIVINE IMPASSIBILITY

One seldom finds patristic writers defending or even explaining the idea of divine impassibility. They take it for granted as something that is entailed in the idea of God. But impassibility is critical to the way they understand the economy of salvation. Divine impassibility is the reason for the incarnation. Athanasius spells out this logic in his treatise *On the Incarnation*. Because of the fall, human beings need to be rescued from their "corruptibility," their tendency toward death and decay (using Paul's term φθορά from 1 Cor 15:42). The Son of God saw that someone would need to die if humanity was to be rescued from death. Yet here the Son encounters the problem of his own impassibility. As Athanasius puts it, "Yet being immortal and the Son of the Father, the Word was not able to die."[9] The solution to this problem was the incarnation. "For this reason he takes to

---

9. Athanasius, *On the Incarnation*, Greek/English edition, trans. John Behr (Yonkers: St. Vladimir's Seminary Press, 2011), §9.

himself a body capable of death."[10] The Son becomes incarnate so that he will be able to die. He dies to snatch humanity back from death.

Cyril of Alexandria develops the same argument, with special attention to the communication of attributes between the two natures of Christ. Because each nature participates in the properties of the other, it is true to say that God undergoes suffering and death, even though the divine nature remains unchanged by the ordeal. Cyril writes:

> This was a matter of the salvation of the whole world. And since on this account [the Son] wished to suffer, even though he was beyond the power of suffering in his nature as God ... he wrapped himself in flesh that was capable of suffering, and revealed it as his very own, so that even the suffering might be said to be his because it was his own body which suffered and no one else's.[11]

And again:

> He made his very own a body capable of tasting death and capable of coming back to life again, so that he himself might remain impassible and yet be said to suffer in his flesh.[12]

The incarnation is not only a solution to the problem of human sin and death. It is a solution to the problem of divine impassibility. It allows God to drink the cup of human suffering to the dregs while still remaining God. God is touched by suffering without being changed by it. Or in Cyril's paradoxical expression, God "suffers human things impassibly" (πάθοι ἀπαθώς).[13]

Death, after all, is harmless to the divine nature. According to Gregory of Nyssa, just as you can easily touch water without harm, so it is easy—in fact, "infinitely easier"—for the divine nature to touch death without suffering harm.[14] The problem is for God to find a way to make contact with death at all, since God cannot simply jump on the slippery slide into nonbeing. God cannot create a rock so heavy that even God cannot lift it, and by the same logic God cannot use the divine power to make the divine nature subject to nonbeing.

---

10. Ibid., §9; cf. §20.
11. Cyril of Alexandria, *On the Unity of Christ*, trans. John Anthony McGuckin (Yonkers: St. Vladimir's Seminary Press, 1995), 118.
12. Ibid., 127.
13. Cyril of Alexandria, *On the Right Faith*, trans. Rowan A. Greer, http://www.yale.edu/adhoc/etexts/cyril.htm.
14. Gregory of Nyssa, *Catechetical Oration*, ed. James Herbert Strawley (Cambridge: Cambridge University Press, 1903), 35; English translation in *Christology of the Later Fathers*, ed. Edward Rochie Hardy (Library of Christian Classics; London: SCM, 1954).

The early Christian tradition would have agreed with Dietrich Bonhoeffer's celebrated saying that "only the suffering God can help."[15] But while modern theologians have used this insight to attack the idea of divine impassibility, patristic theologians used it to defend the incarnation. From the standpoint of early Christian thought, a divine nature capable of suffering would be no help at all, since it would mean (a) that God had not really shared in the *human* plight, but only in some divine version of it; and (b) that God is unable to transform death into life, since God would be subject to death as though to an equal or superior power. Only an incorruptible, life-giving divine nature united to corruptible human nature is able both to share fully in the human plight and to overcome it. Gregory of Nazianzus sounds almost like Bonhoeffer when he exclaims, "We needed a God made flesh and made dead, that we might live."[16] The Son's human nature is the doorway into death, but what steps through that door is the life-giving Word who, by his mere presence, turns death into life.

IV. DEATH AND PRIVATION

This connection between divine impassibility and human corruptibility has brought us into the inner workings of the patristic atonement model. Human mortality is reversed when the life-giving divine nature makes contact with human nature at the point of its collapse into nonbeing. If the slide toward nonbeing is reversed, then death has become life, which is another way of saying that death has died. In the words of Gregory of Nyssa, "When death came into contact with life, darkness with light, corruption with incorruption, the worse of these things disappeared into a state of non-existence."[17] The metaphysical assumption (M1) stated above, that death is a privation of being, is critical to this view of salvation. Nonbeing is cancelled out when it is touched by the life-giving Creator. Death is defeated not in the manner of a combat: you cannot wrestle with a privation. Death ceases in the same way that darkness ceases whenever the light is turned on.

It is true that early Christian teachers, especially in their preaching, like to use vivid mythical language to describe Christ's triumph over the

---

15. Dietrich Bonhoeffer, *Letters and Papers from Prison*, ed. John W. de Gruchy (Minneapolis: Augsburg Fortress, 2010), 479.

16. Gregory of Nazianzus, *Oration* 45.28; translation in *Festal Orations*, trans. Nonna Verna Harrison (Yonkers: St. Vladimir's Seminary Press, 2008).

17. Gregory of Nyssa, *Catechetical Oration*, 26.

power of death and hell. Gustaf Aulén was so far led astray by such mythic language as to conclude that the early church viewed the atonement as a "combat" between God and Satan. It is hard to imagine a more extravagant misunderstanding of early Christian teaching.

Already in the second century, Christian writers had developed complex metaphysical refutations of the ideas that evil exists as a positive entity and that evil could have a spooky ontological status alongside God, so that God would have to combat it. Successive generations of anti-Marcionite, anti-gnostic, and anti-Manichaean polemics hammered home the axiomatic convictions that evil is not a positive thing in its own right but a privation of being, and that this privation occurs among creatures, not on a transcendent plane alongside God. When the early Christians identified the demons as fallen angels, they were making a polemical point. They were not glorifying the demons by comparing them to angels; they were demoting the demons from the quasi-divine status that they enjoyed in Hellenistic culture. Christianity relegated the demons to the lowly office of wayward creatures within God's world.

It is intriguing to notice how many early Christian teachers regarded the demons not with grisly awe but with something closer to sympathy. Augustine's treatment of the demons in the first half of the *City of God* straddles the boundary between pity and contempt, while Origen and Gregory of Nyssa speculated that the fallen angels would probably be saved in the end. They are creatures, after all, so why shouldn't they be redeemed along with the rest of creation?

While early Christian theology had a large and colorful demonology, it was a demonology contained within definite metaphysical limits. The demons do not play a leading role in Christian accounts of creation or redemption. God is not preoccupied with them or engaged in struggle against them. Instead, it is *believers* who have to struggle against the demons. This struggle takes two main forms: the spiritual life of believers is marked by struggle against the demons (a central theme of Christian monastic literature); and the geographical spread of Christianity involves the progressive displacement of the gods of Hellenistic polytheism, understood to be demons (a central theme of apologetic literature).

Athanasius draws attention to the demons in both of these contexts. His *Life of Antony* is filled with demons, but it is Antony, not God, who does battle with them. In his treatise on the incarnation, Athanasius first develops his account of the incarnation and atonement and then offers two proofs that death has been defeated. First, the lives of the Christian martyrs prove that death has lost its power, since the martyrs are not afraid of dying;[18] and second, the spread of Christianity among Hellenistic peoples proves that Christ is alive and that, compared to him, all the gods and demons are nothing.[19]

> The gods and the demons ... fall dead at the advent of Christ, their show being futile and empty; but by the sign of the cross all magic ceases, all witchcraft is brought to nothing, all idols are deserted and abandoned.[20]

The atonement is not a struggle against Satan but a defeat of death, and the visible, tangible proof of death's defeat is the existence of the church with its powerful twin engines of martyrdom and exorcism. In so far as there is a combat, it is strictly an intra-creaturely affair. God is the creator, not a combatant.

Gustaf Aulén was right to note that the ancient Christians often depicted the atonement in striking visual and mythic language. In one sermon, John Chrysostom compares death to a hungry dragon. The dragon swallowed up Christ, not knowing that Christ's mortal body was a poisoned bait. This poison brought on violent stomach cramps, even worse (so Chrysostom assures us) than the agony of a woman in labor. The dragon writhed in pain, then vomited. "He received the body which he could not digest, and so he had to throw it up again."[21] The same food metaphor is used in the famous paschal homily attributed to Chrysostom, where Hades is said to be embittered by the "taste" of Christ's flesh. The point of this metaphor is not to show that Christ defeated the Devil through trickery; it is death, not the Devil, that is personified in the homily. Swallowing a human body, death discovers that it has also swallowed God. Because of the union of natures in Christ, it is possible for the impassible divine nature to enter death and to overcome it from within. The paschal homily makes this quite explicit when it says of hades: "It took a body and discovered God; it took earth and encountered heaven; it took what it saw, but crumbled before what it had not seen."[22]

Probably the best known metaphorical account of the atonement from Christian antiquity is Gregory of Nyssa's fishhook analogy. Most readers

---

18. Athanasius, *On the Incarnation*, 27–29.
19. Ibid., 30–32.
20. Ibid., 31.
21. John Chrysostom, *Homilies on 1 Corinthians*, 24.7; translation in Nicene and Post-Nicene Fathers, first series, vol. 12, ed. Philip Schaff (Peabody, MA: Hendrickson, 1994).
22. "Paschal Homily," in *Patrologia Graeca*, ed. J. P. Migne (Paris: 1857–1886), volume 59, col. 721.

of *Christus Victor* will recall this analogy, if nothing else, since Aulén bases so much of his account on Gregory's fishhook. In Aulén's view, Gregory depicts a conflict between God and Satan; in this conflict, God resorts to guerrilla tactics and overcomes Satan's power through a grand deception. Christ was the hook and Satan took the bait.

I have stated that early Christian teaching sees death, and not the Devil, as the basic human problem from which we have to be redeemed. And I have stated that death was understood as a privation, not as a positive thing in its own right. Both of these claims are supported by the fishhook passage in Gregory's *Catechetical Oration*. The *Christus Victor* interpretation misses both of these critical points. Here is the passage in question:

> The opposing power could not, by its nature, come into immediate contact with God's presence and endure the unveiled sight of him. Hence it was that God, in order to make himself easily accessible to him who sought the ransom for us, veiled himself in our nature. In that way, as it is with greedy fish, he might swallow the Godhead like a fishhook along with the flesh, which was the bait. Thus, when life came to dwell with death and light shone upon darkness, their contraries might vanish away. For it is not in the nature of darkness to endure the presence of light, nor can death exist where life is active.[23]

Aulén is right to note that the *Catechetical Oration* develops an elaborate mythic picture of a ransom paid to the Devil. But when Gregory comes down to explaining what his mythic picture is all about, two things become clear: first, that the real problem is not Satan but death; and second, that death is not a rival that God has to contend with, but only a privation of life. In fact, one of Gregory's major preoccupations in this oration is the privation theory of evil—an irony, given the way the fishhook passage has been used to support Aulén's dualistic picture of a combat between God and the Devil. Toward the beginning of the oration, Gregory explains that evil is nothing but the absence of good, just as darkness is the absence of light. He takes pains to reject any notion of a dualism between good and evil, explaining:

> We must not think of virtue as opposed to vice in the way of two existing phenomena. To illustrate: nonbeing is opposed to being; but we cannot say that the latter is opposed to the former as something existing in its own right. Rather we say that there is a logical opposition between what

---

does not exist and what exists.... Again, we say that blindness is logically opposed to sight. But blindness does not by nature have real existence. On the contrary it is the privation of a former capacity.[24]

Gregory's point could hardly be clearer. Evil is not a reality but a "privation" (στέρησις). It appears in the world "just as a shadow follows the withdrawal of the sun's rays."[25]

In the fishhook passage, Gregory uses an analogy to show that salvation can be understood as the removal of a privation. His point is that the union of natures in Christ allows the divine nature to enter into a state of privation, thus immediately cancelling out that privation. Tellingly, Gregory does not speak here of God's victory over death; he simply says that death "vanishes" in the presence of life.[26] Athanasius had similarly concluded his account of the atonement with the remark that "death has been dissolved."[27] And though he uses Aulén-like language at this point, describing believers' "victory" (νίκη) over death, his point is not that Christ has struggled victoriously against death's power but that believers experience victory now that death has been dissolved. Metaphysically, death is cancelled out in the way that shadows are removed by light; experientially, this is a "victory" for believers.

The language of victory is valid, therefore, as long as it is clear that this is not a *divine* victory. It is not God who engages in combat. Gregory's fishhook analogy was contrived to explain the mechanism by which an impassible, life-giving divine nature enters into the privation of death, so that privation is dispelled by the presence of life. It is an extended metaphor to illustrate the way the union of natures in Christ makes possible the descent of the divine nature into a state of privation. Aulén's mistake was to skip over the explicit metaphysical parts of Gregory's oration and to attach alien metaphysical meanings to the metaphorical parts. The resulting *Christus Victor* model, marked as it is by combat and dualism, is barely recognisable as an interpretation of early Christian teaching.

Combat language, as far as I can tell, figured more prominently in the Syrian tradition than in the Greek or Latin. But Syrian writers and preachers stressed the fact that the language of combat does not apply to God. There can be no combat between the divine nature and anything

---

24. Ibid., 6.
25. Ibid.
26. Ibid., 24.
27. Athanasius, *On the Incarnation*, 27.

else, otherwise the distinction between creator and creation would be meaningless. Perhaps the most extensive use of combat language in all patristic literature is found in Jacob of Sarug's homilies "on our Lord's combat with Satan." The homilies give an extremely warlike depiction of Christ's temptation in the wilderness. Satan is portrayed as the leader of a vast army. The demons engage Christ on the battlefield and he defeats them. But Jacob repeatedly reminds his hearers that it was only Christ's human nature that struggled against Satan:

> He became a human and as a human Son he did battle.
> His contest with Satan was a human one:
>   Let no one say that he was fighting divinely.[28]

Christ recapitulates Adam's temptation; it is as a human being that he overcomes the Devil. He does this as an example for his followers so that they will know how to stand firm against temptation. There is no cosmic battle between God and evil. In fact, even as a human being Christ cannot really be said to be fighting anything. The warlike language in these homilies is used almost exclusively to describe Satan's tactics. It is Satan who gathers an army and prepares his strategies; it is Satan who mounts a campaign against Christ. By contrast, the homilies present Christ as gentle, peaceable, and soft-spoken. He responds to Satan's attacks not with counterattacks but with "humility," "serenity," and "a gentle struggle." "He did not act with strength," Jacob says, but with "wisdom."[29] Satan is full of sound and fury, but Christ responds simply by quoting Scripture "in whispers, not shouts."[30] Paradoxically, the combat language in these homilies is used to show that there is no true combat between Christ and Satan. Only from Satan's deluded perspective does it look like a combat at all. Christ has no need to fight against anything. Even in his human nature, he overcomes evil more in the manner of a light that dispels the shadows simply by shining. Such is the subtle and suggestive use of combat language in early Christian theology. Compared to this, Aulén's notion of a "divine warfare against the evil that holds mankind in bondage"[31] seems not only theologically unsupportable but also a rather crude and heavy-handed use of metaphor.

---

28. Jacob of Sarug, *Mêmrâ* 82.62–64; Syriac and English translation in *Jacob of Sarug's Homilies on Jesus' Temptation*, ed. Adam Carter McCollum (Piscataway, NJ: Gorgias Press, 2014).
29. Ibid., 126.249–53.
30. Ibid., 126.265.
31. Aulén, *Christus Victor*, 163.

The language of hell or hades, so pervasive in Christian antiquity, was also liable to be disciplined by a metaphysical commitment to the privation theory of evil. It is true that Christians tended to describe hades as a place. Such spatial language is hard to avoid, especially given the New Testament's spatial motif of Christ's "descent" to the dead and subsequent "ascension."[32]

But Gregory of Nyssa pointed out that such spatial language is best understood as a metaphorical description of spiritual realities. In the dialogue on the soul and the resurrection, Macrina tells her brother Gregory that although hades is portrayed in Scripture as a place, "it is likely that this hades ... is not intended to signify a place with that name." Instead it refers to "some invisible and incorporeal condition of life, in which the soul lives."[33] Insofar as the soul is stretching out toward God, it is already in heaven, or at least on the way; insofar as the soul turns away from God, it is already dissolving into shadows. If "hades" designates not a quasi-transcendent world but such a state of spiritual privation, then the language of Christ's "victory" over death is likewise metaphorical. Death is not a power against which Christ has to struggle; it is an absence that Christ fills.

V. REALISM AND HUMAN NATURE

The early Christian atonement model also requires certain metaphysical assumptions about human nature. The view that humanity is essentially one — that there is a universal human nature in which individuals participate — is so widely taken for granted in early Christianity that it is seldom discussed or defended. This metaphysical realism has been attributed, like so many other things, to the influence of Platonic philosophy on early Christian thought.

It is true that a Platonic theory of universals had far-reaching influence on Hellenistic and Christian cultures. But Christian thought about human nature was drawn from deeper springs, especially from the Pauline Christ-Adam typology, which crystallised a vision of history around two

---

32. Writing in the second century, Tertullian sets out a geographical view of hell: "We Christians do not consider hell to be an empty cavern or some subterranean sewer of the world, but a profound and vast space hidden away in the deepest interior of the earth." And his proof for this view is the fact that Christ is said to have "descended" and "ascended." See *On the Soul*, 55.1–2; translation in *Apologetical Works and Minucius Felix Octavius* (Fathers of the Church; Washington: Catholic University of America Press, 1950).
33. Gregory of Nyssa, *On the Soul and the Resurrection*, trans. Catharine P. Roth (Yonkers: St. Vladimir's Seminary Press, 1993), 73.

universal articulations of human nature. In 1 Corinthians 15 and Romans 5, St. Paul lumps together the whole human race under two representative heads, Christ and Adam; and in both passages he specifically links the Christ-Adam typology to the universality of death. Few scriptural motifs left such an indelible impression on the imagination of the ancient church.[34]

Christian teachers used a variety of metaphors and analogies to depict Christ's impact on human nature. Irenaeus suggests that the unfolding history of human nature is like a single book, and that Christ is the précis that encompasses the whole story in brief.[35] Athanasius compares humanity to a town; one day the king decides to come and live there, and the whole town is dignified by its new resident. In the same way, the whole of humanity reaps the benefits when the Son of God takes up residence in our nature.[36] The sermons of Gregory of Nazianzus use examples from the kitchen to describe Christ's effect on human nature. Christ is compared to yeast in the dough or to a curdling agent in milk:

> He bears the title "Man" ... with the aim of hallowing humanity through himself, by becoming a sort of yeast for the whole lump. He has united with himself all that lay under condemnation, in order to release it from condemnation. For all our sakes he became all that we are, sin apart — body, soul, mind, all that death pervades.[37]
>
> Yet none is like the wonder of my salvation: a few drops of blood recreate the whole world and become for all human beings like a curdling agent for milk, binding and drawing us together into one.[38]

In another analogy, closer to the language of St. Paul, Gregory of Nyssa compares the human race to a single corpse that Christ brings back to life:

> Our whole nature had to be brought back from death. In consequence he stooped down to our dead body and stretched out a hand, as it were, to one who was prostrate. He approached so near death as to come into contact with it. With his own body he gave our nature the principle of resurrection, by raising our total humanity along with him by his power.[39]

---

34. For one aspect of the influence of the Christ-Adam typology on Christian literature, see Benjamin Myers, "A Tale of Two Gardens: Augustine's Narrative Interpretation of Romans 5," in *Apocalyptic Paul: Cosmos and Anthropos in Romans 5–8*, ed. Beverly Roberts Gaventa (Waco: Baylor University Press, 2013), 39–58.

35. Irenaeus, *Against the Heresies*, trans. Dominic J. Unger (Ancient Christian Writers; New York: Newman Press, 1992–2012), 3.18.

36. Athanasius, *On the Incarnation*, 9.

37. Gregory of Nazianzus, *Oration* 30.21; translation in *On God and Christ: The Five Theological Orations and Two Letters to Cledonius*, trans. Frederick Williams and Lionel Wickham (Yonkers: St. Vladimir's Seminary Press, 2002).

38. Ibid., *Oration* 45.29; translation in *Festal Orations*.

39. Gregory of Nyssa, *Catechetical Oration*, 32.

These passages show how flexibly Christian writers and preachers could *illustrate* the unity of human nature without necessarily trying to *explain* it in metaphysical terms. It was enough to have a working assumption of the essential oneness of human nature.

At times the language of sacrifice was used in the same way. In a frequently quoted passage, Athanasius describes Christ's death as a necessary sacrifice. He writes:

> Since what was required from all still had to be rendered (for, as I said earlier, it was absolutely necessary to die and for this, in particular, he sojourned among us), for this reason … he now offered the sacrifice on behalf of all, delivering his own temple to death in the place of all, in order to make all not liable to and free from the ancient transgression, and to show himself superior to death, displaying his own body as incorruptible, the first-fruits of the universal resurrection.[40]

This is a classic passage in studies of the atonement, since the Athanasius of this passage is generally thought to have paved the way for Anselm and Calvin. He is said to supply all the key ingredients for the later development of penal substitutionary atonement theory. This interpretation assumes that Athanasius is describing the atonement mechanism in sacrificial terms. The problem with this interpretation is to explain how this mechanism, set out in just a few lines, fits with the rest of Athanasius's scheme, which does not seem to require penal or sacrificial concepts. But the passage appears in a very different light if we view it as a statement not of the atonement mechanism but of the universality of human nature.

One of the functions of sacrifice is to represent the relation between the one and the many. In sacrifice, one particular thing is offered on behalf of the many. The oneness of the community is symbolised and enacted in the sacrifice. When Athanasius wants to describe the atonement mechanism, he speaks at great length along the lines that I have been discussing: an impassible divine nature assumes mortal human nature in order to dispel death. But when he wants to describe the universal reach of Christ's death—the way one person affects the whole of human nature—he takes up the language of sacrifice.

In this passage, Athanasius is simply pointing out that Christ's death is for all. The word "all" chimes like a bell through the passage. This is not the part of the treatise that explains *how* the atonement works. It is a

---

40. Athanasius, *On the Incarnation*, 20.

transitional point in the argument, and at this juncture Athanasius simply wants to state that Christ's death affects everyone. What happens in Christ happens to human nature as a whole. Even within this short passage, the language of temple and sacrifice flickers for a moment only to disappear again as soon as it has served its purpose of depicting universality. By the end of the passage Athanasius is back to his usual idiom of death's defeat by an incorruptible divine nature. *That* is the atonement mechanism; the sacrificial language is used to show that the mechanism affects human nature as a whole.

There is a second sacrificial passage in *On the Incarnation*. Again it figures prominently in modern writing on the atonement, and again the sacrificial language is viewed as a step on the way to later theories of penal substitution. But the real function of Athanasius's sacrificial language is even clearer in this context:

> So by offering to death the body he had taken to himself, as an offering holy and free of all spot, he immediately abolished death from all like him, by the offering of a like. For ... by offering his own temple and his bodily instrument as a substitute for all, [the Word] fulfilled in death what was required; and, being united with all human beings by a body like theirs, the incorruptible Son of God consequently clothed all with incorruptibility.[41]

It is remarkable that this passage is so often judged as being proto-Anselmian in spite of the fact that it depicts Christ as a sacrifice offered *to death*, not to God. The assumption that Athanasius is describing an atonement mechanism leads the reader immediately into a thicket of absurdities. How can a sacrifice be offered to death? Do human beings owe a debt to death? Is death a transcendent being that needs to be placated? But as soon as we change perspective and see the passage as a depiction not of the atonement mechanism but of its universal effects, then the difficulties vanish. Christ has come to get rid of death for everyone, to bring about a change to human nature as a whole. His defeat of death affects everybody, just as a sacrifice or a temple benefits the whole group through a single offering.

The question Athanasius is answering is not *how* the atonement works, but *for whom*. That is why the sacrifice passage is immediately followed by another very different analogy: the passage I mentioned earlier, in which

---

41. Ibid., 9.

a whole town is affected when a king takes up residence there. Neither of these analogies—the sacrifice or the town with the king—is meant to be taken too literally, and neither of them is describing a mechanism of how Christ's death saves. They are both used as illustrations to remind the reader that what happens in Christ happens for the benefit of the whole of humanity.

Returning for a moment to my outline of the early Christian atonement model, one can conclude that sacrificial language is used not for (8) (the mechanism proper), but for (10) (the universality of the atonement). This is not to suggest that sacrificial language is unimportant. Such language has a place, as the passages from Athanasius show. The language of sacrifice is used to depict the way humanity as a whole is included in whatever happens to Christ. The sacrificial passages in Athanasius should be a reminder of how easy it is for modern readers to project their Anselmian and Calvinist assumptions back onto early Christian sources. When this happens, the outlines of the patristic model are distorted, and the patristic atonement mechanism tends to vanish completely.

VI. THE SOLUTION AND THE SURPLUS

I have outlined the patristic model in a series of propositions and have tried to elucidate the three metaphysical assumptions that operate like hidden gears within this model. Let me now briefly restate the model in a way that draws attention to its overall shape.

Human beings are the products of love. They are created in God's image for the purpose of reciprocating divine love. Human nature, motivated by an internal principle of desire, tends naturally upward toward God. Since God is the source of all life, to be lovingly moving toward God is to be alive. But to turn away from God, even for one second, is to begin to die: to slide downward, away from life, love, and reality.

Since the beginning of history, the whole human race has been locked in a downward slide toward nothingness. But because of his great love for humanity, the Son of God leapt down from heaven and wrapped himself in our plummeting human nature. Because he was human, he participated fully in our perilous slide toward nothingness. But because he was divine, he was able to arrest our downward movement and to reverse it, initiating an upward movement toward the life, love, and reality of God. In the movement of that one human life, the life of Christ, the whole of human nature has undergone death and resurrection.

One might depict this as a U-shaped drama. Humanity begins at a high point, then plummets down; then in Christ the line reaches its lowest point before curving back up again. But the upward line doesn't terminate at the top. Christ does not merely restore humanity to its original position. The upward line of the curve shoots much higher than its starting point. So far I have been considering only the negative side of the atonement: God's response to the human plight. But there is also a positive side: the upward arc that raises humanity higher than the place from which it fell. My outline of the patristic alludes to this positive side of the atonement when it distinguishes between the solution (11) and the surplus (12). It seems to me that most theological writing on the atonement stops with the solution. But if we think of the atonement only as a solution to a problem, then we are really only getting one half of the picture.

Earlier I quoted Athanasius's statement that the Son of God became incarnate in order to die. He needed to assume a mortal nature so that he could get access to death. That was the solution to the human problem. But Athanasius does not restrict his account to this solution. Later in his argument he explains that God's intention was not only to free human nature from death but also to elevate it to a new status. If Christ had only freed us from death, we would still remain corruptible by nature. We would still be *able* to die even if death had been warded off for the time being. "The principle of bodies," as Athanasius puts it, would still be mortal.[42] So the Son of God goes a step further. He not only removes us from the clutches of death but also allows our nature to participate in his own incorruptible life. He "interweaves" his life with ours.[43]

In a different metaphor, Cyril says that the Son's divine life has been "implanted" as a principle within human nature.[44] This is more than a solution to the human plight. It is a gift that surpasses nature. It elevates, sanctifies, and deifies. In addition to "escaping corruption," Cyril writes, "we rise up to an honor that is above our nature because of Christ."[45] This happens by means of exactly the same atonement mechanism. It is just the communication of attributes working in the other direction. Through the union of natures, the divine nature shares in the experience of death without ceasing to be divine and impassible, while dying human nature is suffused with divine life without ceasing to be human.

---

42. Ibid., 44.
43. Ibid.
44. Cyril, *Unity of Christ*, 125.
45. Cyril of Alexandria, *Commentary on John*, Ancient Christian Texts, vol. 1, trans. David R. Maxwell (Downers Grove, IL: InterVarsity, 2013), 60.

From this perspective, the surplus factor can be seen not as an implication or aftereffect of the atonement, the way sanctification is sometimes understood in Protestant theology. The surplus factor belongs to the atonement model proper. The mechanism works in two directions at the same time, communicating human qualities to the divine nature (so that God can enter death) and divine qualities to human nature (so that humanity is elevated to a new status).

In a sermon on Romans 5, John Chrysostom compared the human plight to a small debt. A man owes a few coins. When he cannot pay the debt, he is cast into prison along with his wife, children, and servants. His only hope is for someone to come and clear the debt. And that is what happens. A benefactor comes along and pays the small debt. The poor man's problems are solved, and he is overjoyed. But there is more. The benefactor is not content only to clear the prisoner's debts. In addition he gives the man ten thousand talents of gold, a vast fortune. And as if that were not enough, he leads him into the royal palace and gives him an introduction to the king. As a result, the man is elevated to the highest status in the land. And never again does the benefactor remind the man of the few coins that he had owed.

In this parable one can see where the real emphasis lies in the patristic understanding of the atonement. There is a solution: the payment of a few coins. And there is a surplus: ten thousand talents of gold and a position of honor in the royal palace. Chrysostom uses the language of debt, so familiar to us now from later atonement models. But his parable is worlds away from the kind of atonement theology that sees Christ's death as nothing more than a necessary payment. Chrysostom concludes: "For Christ paid off much more than we owed—as much more as a limitless ocean compared to a small drop of water."[46]

There is a solution and a surplus, and both are achieved by a single atonement mechanism. The richness of this early Christian model lies not only in its coherence and clarity but also in its refreshing breadth of vision: its sober assessment of human nature as well as its youthful optimism; its devotion to the death of Christ as well as its celebration of the resurrection; an attitude of humble gratitude as well as an audacity and freedom of spirit that come from believing that one is not only saved but also loved, not only debt-free but rich beyond imagining.

---

46. John Chrysostom, *Homilies on Romans*, vol. 1, trans. Panayiotis Papageorgiou (Brookline, MA: Holy Cross Orthodox Press, 2013), 10.17–20.

CHAPTER 4

ATONING WISDOM
The Wisdom of God in the
Way of Salvation

KYLE STROBEL AND ADAM J. JOHNSON

I. INTRODUCTION

The primary dogmatic location of the atonement is the doctrine of God; that is, the doctrines of the Trinity and of the divine attributes form the primary and determinative features of the doctrine of the atonement.[1] They create the room or structure within which other doctrines have their respective dignity, playing their distinct and valuable roles.

In this sense, the atonement is the doctrinal elaboration of the movement and action of God incarnate for us through death into resurrection; it is doctrinal reflection on who God is and how he is for us in the descent and exaltation of Christ. In this sense, the doctrine of the atonement is not as narrow as often understood, dominated by theories addressing the cross in relation to various features of sin.[2] Rather, the atonement names a specific movement of God with an explicit directionality—a *telos* that guides God's economic activity to save what was created *by* him, *through* him, and *for* him—that he might reconcile all things to himself (Col 1:15–20) by

---

1. For a fuller development of this thesis, see Adam J. Johnson, *Atonement: A Guide for the Perplexed* (New York: T&T Clark, 2015); *God's Being in Reconciliation: The Theological Basis of the Unity and Diversity of the Atonement in the Theology of Karl Barth* (New York: T&T Clark, 2012).

2. Consider, for instance, the way that penal substitution emphasizes sin as guilt, and also consider Green and Baker's work to suggest the alternative emphasis on shame in chapter 6 of Mark D. Baker and Joel B. Green, *Recovering the Scandal of the Cross: Atonement in New Testament and Contemporary Contexts* (Downers Grove, IL: InterVarsity, 2003).

sharing himself with all things. And because this reconciling work is an effective work in the midst of many conflicting forces and powers, a work saturated with purpose, intentionality, or *telos*, it is a work of God's wisdom, or, better, a work *by* Wisdom, *of* wisdom, and *for* wisdom, the power of the omnipotent God unleashed for the salvation of the world (1 Cor 1:18).

This paper develops the dogmatic location of the atonement within the doctrine of God by expounding on the atonement from this particular vantage point: atonement as an act of divine wisdom, considering the nature and implications thereof. Considering God's triune life in relation to redemption, therefore, wisdom is the category that addresses both the divine life *in se* as well as wisdom as it has taken on flesh and dwelt among us. Among the benefits of such an approach, we highlight the manner in which exploring the atonement as a work of divine wisdom (1) offers a rich line of inquiry regarding the ethical implications of Christ's work, and (2) offers resources for exploring the scope or range of God's creative purposes brought to completion by the death and resurrection of Jesus Christ.

II. DIVINE WISDOM (ATONEMENT *BY* WISDOM)

To start, it is helpful to understand wisdom in its broadest terms as "expertise in the craft of life enabling us to excel."[3] The book of Proverbs and a host of other biblical, theological, and devotional material guide us along these lines, equipping us to navigate the many realities and forces of life in the hope of living well, partly through shared wisdom in the form of sayings, and partly by guiding us into an understanding of the principles of life.[4] But wisdom is so much more than this, for its basis and power in our own lives derives from its role in the life of God.

Among God's many attributes is the fact that in and of himself, he is wise (Rom 16:27; Dan 2:20; Job 12:13), and from him all wisdom derives its name (linking Eph 3:10 and 3:15), and he alone knows its place and the way to it (Job 28:12–28). God, as the living God, lives well, acting in keeping with and by means of his whole, unified character to bring about the full range of his purposes (Isa 46:11). In God there is no final dilemma, no course of action with unattainable ends in which God is forced to choose one thing and abandon the other, or where he can only retain one aspect of himself at the expense of another. As the God who lives eternally

---

3. Aristotle, *Nicomachean Ethics*, trans. Terence Irwin (Indianapolis: Hackett, 1985), 156.
4. As Aristotle points out, the "wise person must not only know what is derived from the origins of a science, but also grasp the truth about the origins." Ibid., 157.

in the fellowship of Father, Son, and Holy Spirit (John 17:20–26), God lives and acts in the unity of the divine character, bringing his purposes to their fitting end (Eph 2:4–10) by means of that aspect of his character specified as divine wisdom—for that is his goal, to make known his manifold wisdom to the rulers and authorities (Eph 3:10). In and of himself in eternity, and in his manifold relationships with his creatures, God is and always will be the ever-wise God, living a life in which the origin, means, and end of the divine intention and act are equally rooted in the divine life, and therefore deep, meaningful, and effective (Rom 11:33–36).[5] This is so much the case, so core to the divine character, that the second person of the Trinity is himself the divine Wisdom (cf. *De Trin*, 7.1.2).

The death and resurrection of Jesus is thus the work of Wisdom himself, Wisdom incarnate. For if it is the case that God in his being and act is wise, that he himself is wisdom and thereby the source of all that partakes of this name, then surely this central act within his creation will bear the stamp of an act which is *by, of,* and *for* wisdom. But we do well to stop at the first step, noting that this work is done *by* Wisdom. As such, it bears all the characteristics of a wise act, but is simultaneously revelatory of the nature of wisdom itself; binding together reconciliation and self-revelation as wisdom is simultaneously the source, means, and end of our salvation. We are made wise through our redemption from folly by means of an act which was itself the epitome of wisdom. Christian wisdom, therefore, as the wisdom of God, cannot remain an abstract notion, but must trade in the economy of redemption. The wisdom of Christ is the embodied reality of the divine life penetrating the brokenness of the world.

III. ATONING WISDOM (ACT *OF* WISDOM)

As a work done *by* Wisdom, Christ's atonement is a work thoroughly characterized by that reality: a work *of* wisdom.[6] The basic logic of the

---

5. Barth says God's Word is "meaningful in itself, and it shows itself to be meaningful to us who hear it. The wisdom of God is that God not only wills but knows what He wills. And He knows not only what He wills, but why and wherefore He wills it," which is to say that the will and action of God is laden with purpose, meaning, plan, and intention, and because his will is accompanied by his power, he can, in his wisdom, accomplish and bring to fruition this meaning, plan, and intention. Karl Barth, *Church Dogmatics II/2: The Doctrine of God* (Edinburgh: T&T Clark, 1957), 423.

6. According to David Ford, "Christian wisdom is shaped by and in relation to Jesus Christ.... He was seen as both teaching and living out a prophetic wisdom, 'greater than Solomon', 'greater than Jonah', rooted in the reciprocal knowing of himself and his Father. His wisdom was both a discerning of cries and an embodying of them, with his final loud cry from the cross as the central reference point for Christian wisdom. The convergence of Luke and John on key dimensions of this wisdom was explored: it is God-centered, has the whole of creation as its context, is immersed in history and the contemporary

atonement is that in Christ, God took upon himself what was ours in order that we might partake of what is his, in this way bringing completion to God's creative purposes.[7] Filling out this insight by means of the categories of divine wisdom, we affirm that in Jesus the God who is in and of himself wise took upon himself the reality and consequences of human folly unto death, that through the resurrection he might restore us into a life of divine wisdom. That is, the work of Jesus was one of the wise God bringing to completion his plan to share with his creatures a life of wisdom in the face of human folly.

In the face of this folly, God did not rest content with any means of restoring his creatures to the lives of wisdom he originally intended for them: he made Wisdom itself the means of restoring his creatures to wisdom, making the end into the means, and vice-versa, by enacting the divine life and character on our behalf. His work was thus a wise act in that it was properly intended, ordered, and executed to bring about its end(s) or purpose(s).[8] It was an act such as to bring about, in the best possible way, the full range of divine purposes for creation, including the overcoming of our folly and our establishment as creatures remade in the image of God, fit to walk in his ways in lives of wisdom. Jesus is Wisdom incarnate, acting on our behalf, and through him we receive the Spirit of wisdom (Isa 11:2; Acts 2:33), such that the wisdom we receive is the wisdom that is had only through participation in the divine life of Wisdom.

In order to bring about these purposes, God chose to overcome human folly, not by power alone, but by means of an act that would take up and transform our foolishness on its own terms, offering what it above all else perversely sought: wisdom (Gen 3:6). In opposition to our foolishness, God in Christ bore our folly and the death it brings, taking a course of action so unfathomable to sinner and Satan alike that we mistook his wisdom and our folly, labeling Christ as foolishness and a stumbling block (1 Cor 1:23). In opposition to our foolish longing for wisdom (Gen 3:6), Christ hung on the cross of folly, becoming the root of our knowledge of good and evil for those abiding in him.

---

world, interprets the Old and New Testaments in relation to each other, and is constantly sought afresh with others in a community whose basic trust is that the Spirit will lead them into further truth." David F. Ford, *Christian Wisdom: Desiring God and Learning in Love* (Cambridge: Cambridge University Press, 2007), 153. Our analysis follows similar contours to the ones noted here by Ford.

7. Athanasius, *On the Incarnation*, trans. John Behr (Yonkers: St. Vladimir's Seminary Press, 2011), 157.

8. Because this is true, divine wisdom is the foundation for the theological enterprise of "faith seeking understanding."

This penetration of wisdom into our folly forms the reality of Christ's self-giving. The cross is the wisdom of God that cannot be processed as anything other than foolishness, because it unveils the foundation of our sinful autonomy, of wisdom independent of the *divine* life, wisdom, and goodness. This is why James can compare the wisdom that comes from above, which is pure, peaceable, gentle, reasonable, merciful, impartial, and sincere, against the wisdom from below, which he labels earthly, unspiritual, and demonic (Jas 3:13–17). In Christ, God was revealing that the "foolishness of God is wiser than humankind, and the weakness of God is stronger than humankind" (1 Cor 1:25); and in Christ, God bore the full reality of foolish human "wisdom" and its consequences in himself on the cross.

This foolishness is no mere comedic relief in a Shakespearian drama. Sin, affronting the character and will of the wise God, takes the form of folly, tragically mis-taking and disordering in such a way as to unleash hell in the place where wisdom was to bring about beauty, order, and peace.[9] Foolishness and its consequences are no less real, no less tragic, and no less an affront to the will and being of God than guilt, disobedience, murder, or any other aspect of sin.[10] And Christ bears this reality and its consequences. He suffers the fate of human folly. He suffers the disorder and chaos it unleashes. He suffers the physical, relational, political, and ultimately, theological consequences of playing the fool. For like the fool, in the place of the fool, as the fool he is rejected by God and suffers the fate of every admonishing Proverb (vv. 3:35; 10:8; 18:7; 26:3–13).

But this was no act of folly; it was we who labeled it as such, able to see in it nothing more. Rather, this was the way of wisdom, as we see the triumph of God's wisdom in the bodily resurrection of Jesus: a resurrection that reestablishes the way of wisdom in the community of Christ, opens our eyes to the role of wisdom throughout the Scriptures, and shares with us the lifeblood of wisdom, the Spirit of the risen Christ, the Spirit of wisdom (Isa 11:2). The resurrection is the triumph and ascension of Wisdom incarnate, by means of which we, in the Spirit of the risen Lord, are established in lives of wisdom through our participation in Wisdom.

---

9. Cf. Thomas Aquinas, *Summa Theologica*, trans. Fathers of the English Dominican Province (Westminster, MD: Christian Classics, 1981), II-II.46.

10. Dostoevsky's *The Idiot* portrays this powerfully.

IV. SAVED *FOR* WISDOM: THE ETHICS OF THE ATONEMENT

As the Son descends into the human condition, what the Scriptures portray is a peculiar kind of wisdom. The resurrection is the triumph of this wisdom, but it does not undo the death of Christ; we do not rid ourselves of a theology of the cross for a theology of glory.[11] Jesus' life is a particular kind of life—a life unto death for resurrection and ascension, but as such, a fully unified and indivisible life which constitutes a whole and is meaningful only as such. This is the act of wisdom, calling for the reconciliation of all things in Christ, but only as the crucified Lord of glory and the resurrected Lamb.

What the atonement names, therefore, is God's *telos* in the incarnation, not into a generic human nature but into the depths of humanity in death. But the Wisdom of God does not die in death; the Wisdom of God defeats it from within, rising from the dead and ascending to God in our nature as our great high priest (Heb 8–10). This turning point in death to resurrection names the hinge point of Christ's atoning work and establishes the contours of the Christian life. Any talk of the location of the atonement must take this last point seriously. Holy Scripture turns to the atonement for ethical imperatives, establishing the contours of the Christian life in specifically cruciform ways.[12] While not at the center of the doctrine, aesthetics and ethics must not be ignored.[13]

While it is possible for the cross to become doctrinally overbearing, pitting the cross against other informing features of revelation, the opposite can quickly become a problem as well. It is easy to allow the cross to shrink to the point of uselessness when weight is shifted elsewhere (e.g., the incarnation). Paul will have none of it, for the cross is the wisdom of God itself, breaking forth into creation for recreation and reconciliation.

---

11. Jonathan Edwards, using wisdom as the broad location of the atonement, grounds Christ's work in Ephesians 3:10: "To the intent that now unto the principalities and powers in the heavenly places, might be known by the church the manifold wisdom of God." This manifold wisdom of God is on display in Christ's life and death, never for its own sake but for his resurrection and ascension. Resurrection is the great *denoument* in the history of redemption. But the resurrection does not, somehow, overcome the cross—as if the resurrection undoes the revelation inherent in Christ's death.

12. See Michael J. Gorman, *Cruciformity: Paul's Narrative Spirituality of the Cross* (Grand Rapids: Eerdmans, 2001).

13. Exemplarist theories of the atonement thrive when they describe the revelatory nature of the cross. When this inclination overtakes the doctrine, the doctrine itself is in danger of being reduced to simply a feature of Christ's example to his people. This is well-documented. The opposite error is equally troubling: a development of the doctrine of atonement abstracted away from ethics. Rather, as Christ's teachings show, the Christian life is a cruciform life.

In this sense, part of God's wisdom in his work of atonement is to reveal the true wisdom engrained in his reign.[14]

As an act *for* wisdom, the atoning work of Christ unveils how God's character and will—divine wisdom—engages evil.[15] Namely, Wisdom confronts evil directly, but it does so by entering the reality of evil so as to deal with it effectively from within. Wisdom thus gives direction for the economy, holding together the divine attributes in unity, but it also holds together God's self-revelation in Christ unto death with the kind of power Christ opens to his people. Christ's is a power in weakness (2 Cor 12:9)—a bearing-one's-cross kind of power—and as such, the atonement is wisdom breaking forth into reality that is put on display for the powers and principalities to witness (Eph 3:10),[16] as Christ puts "them to open shame, by triumphing over them" (Col 2:15 ESV).

By locating the doctrine of the atonement in the doctrine of God, focused through the lens of wisdom, the place of ethics in relation to the atonement is given specific shape. Regenerate wisdom, therefore, is pushed into the mold of God's self-giving in Christ unto death, such that Paul calls the cross the wisdom of God (1 Cor 1:18–25) and uses the movement of incarnation unto death as the broad contours of our imitation of Christ (Phil 2:5–11). As put by John Webster,

> Regenerate life in Christ is not simply a received and completed condition, but a summons actively to reiterate the death of the old nature and to perform the new, to die and rise again not only once for all but also continually. Evangelical obedience—reverent enactment of the creaturely life which the Gospel manifests—entails mortification and vivification.[17]

Mortification and vivification are traditional categories for framing the Christian life within the self-giving of God in death and resurrection. As a

---

14. Wisdom, as found in the Proverbs, is given new shape by Christ. Christ reveals what the blessed one who finds wisdom and understanding looks like (see Prov 3:13–18). Likewise, "The fear of the LORD is the beginning of wisdom" (Prov 9:10), and therefore, the beginning of regenerate wisdom is the cross. Fear is the reality of being confronted by God's wisdom and being undone by that wisdom which leads to weakness.

15. "Look carefully then how you walk, not as unwise but as wise, making the best use of the time, because the days are evil" (Eph 5:15–16).

16. As the revelation of divine wisdom, Edwards turns to categories of aesthetics to talk about Christ's atoning work and ethics. "The infinite grace of his divine nature—that infinite ocean of love that is in his heart—was never manifested in any other way, in any comparison as it hath been in his coming down from heaven and laying down his life for us." Jonathan Edwards, "Thy Name is as Ointment Poured Forth," in *The Blessings of God: Previously Unpublished Sermons of Jonathan Edwards* edited by Michael D. McMullen, vol. 1 (Nashville: B&H Publishing, 2003), 172.

17. John Webster, "Communion with Christ: Mortification and Vivification" in *Sanctified By Grace: A Theology of the Christian Life* edited by Kent Eilers and Kyle Strobel (London: T&T Clark, 2014), 122.

work *by*, *of*, and *for* wisdom, the incarnation-unto-death-for-resurrection provides the broad features of regenerate existence.[18] This is why bearing one's cross can serve as a helpful overview of discipleship. Or, more broadly, it is why Paul narrates not only the cross but also Christ's self-giving in the incarnation unto death in Philippians 2 as a depiction of the Christian life, as a depiction of the mind of Christ (Phil 2:5).

To reject this "pattern" is to walk as "enemies of the cross" (Phil 3:18), in a similar way as preaching in cleverness of speech makes the cross void (1 Cor 1:17). The cross is a "power" that undermines the system from below, just as it is the foolishness that undermines the wisdom of the world. This wisdom leads Paul to say, "Whenever I am weak, then I am strong" (2 Cor 12:10 NRSV). It is the structural principle behind Jesus' teachings that the first will be last and the last first (Matt 20:16) and that the one who tries to save his life will lose it, but the one who loses his life for Jesus' sake will find it (Matt 16:25).

This movement of God to us in Son and Spirit provides the context for ethics, and therefore, the atonement must be located such that it can speak directly and meaningfully into lived Christian existence. By focusing on models of the atonement that fail to embrace its breadth and depth, the atonement is too often abstracted away from its connection to the Christian life.[19] If a doctrine of atonement fails to speak into the Christian life, helping to establish and form its contours, then this points to a deeper question concerning its doctrinal location. By grounding the atonement in God's wisdom, as we have done here, the Christian life is developed as a

---

18.   There is a purposeful connection made here concerning the incarnation, death, and resurrection of Christ. Our worry is that a single aspect of Christ's life—his death, for instance—is abstracted away and analyzed as an artifact in itself. Rather, all aspects are united in the life of Christ in the incarnation-unto-death-for-resurrection. It is, unfortunately, a clunky phrase, but the purpose is to hold these elements together in one movement of God that must be united.

19.   For example, penal substitution has been criticized for failing to ground the ethical life of the Christian adequately. One such critique denies that penal substitution allows for God's forgiveness and, therefore, calls into question what it may mean for the believer to forgive as God forgives (Col 3:13). Another critique addresses the question of why Christians struggle to be missional—in the sense that Christians often seclude themselves from the world rather than engaging it directly. Using disgust psychology, Richard Beck suggests that penal substitution fails to address the larger scheme of Christ's descent into uncleanness. By missing this feature, he suggests, Christians do not follow Christ's lead but assume that unclean unbelievers will somehow infect them. See Richard Beck, *Unclean: Meditations on Purity, Hospitality and Mortality* (Eugene: OR: Wipf & Stock, 2011). It could prove fruitful to explore how wisdom could reframe this notion of disgust by focusing on the defeat of folly in the descent of wisdom. Wisdom, in this sense, is not "tainted" by foolishness but "puts it to open shame" (Col 2:15). Christ puts the world's foolish wisdom to open shame by ushering in an alternative wisdom, a wisdom that is hidden from the wise but revealed to infants (Luke 10:21). It is telling that Christ rejoices in this reality, triumphing over the wisdom of the age with his "hidden wisdom."

wise life "from the cross out" rather than from general assumptions about the good life. Excelling in the kingdom of God is not the same, it would seem, as excelling in the world.

V. WISDOM AND THE SCOPE OF ATONEMENT

As a work *by*, *of*, and *for* wisdom, the atonement is a broad work with a vast scope. We often experience folly's havoc in our lives, families, institutions, and nations, and for this reason alone, a gospel of wisdom is both welcome and needed. But unpacking wisdom is of greater value still. We have already seen the advantage of looking through the lens of wisdom for Christian ethics; therefore, here we explore the unparalleled perspective afforded by wisdom for grasping the *scope* of the atonement—the breadth of the character of God which is involved, the range of God's purposes entailed in its reconciliation of the Old and New Testaments, and the manner in which it simultaneously reconciles to God and brings to creaturely fruition all things in heaven and earth. Developing the atonement from within the wisdom of God unveils the immense frame of reference for the scope of this reconciling work.

1. THE DIVINE ATTRIBUTES

The divine attributes do not act in opposition or isolation.[20] Much has been made of the union (or conflict) between God's mercy and wrath, for instance. But wisdom has a special and unique role to play in this discussion as it pertains to the atonement, for emphasizing wisdom naturally and necessarily leads to an ordered emphasis of the other divine attributes enacted in the work of Christ. One aspect of wisdom as a divine attribute is the way that it brings about the divine ends by divine means; or, put theologically, wisdom brings about the divine will in keeping with, or by means of, the enacted divine character. This interplay between ends and means, or will and character, is at the very heart of divine (and therefore human) wisdom, necessarily calling attention to the whole divine character and its role in the atonement. A focus on God's redemptive movement in wisdom tightly connects the economic with the immanent, expanding from an emphasis on wisdom to the whole enacted character of God and, therefore, the inconceivable fullness of his united attributes. Wisdom is

---

20. Cf. Jonathan Edwards, "The Wisdom of God Displayed in the Way of Salvation," *The Works of Jonathan Edwards*, eds. Henry Rogers, Sereno Edwards Dwight, and Edward Hickman, (Peabody, MA: Hendrickson, 1998), 144–45.

thus a gateway into the immanent life and character of God, enacted for us in the economic activity of Christ.

Wisdom necessarily brings to mind the interplay between the whole divine character and the end in question amid the impediments in its way, for this is what it means to be wise. And because the atonement is a divine act, an act made by the whole divine character incarnate in Christ, our appreciation of Christ's work is only as full as our understanding of the role of the whole divine character, both unified and in its distinction. What we perceive, therefore, is what Edwards calls "the excellency of Christ."[21] It is the lion who comes as a lamb, the eternal Son born as a child, and the Creator of life hanging on the cross. Within this seeming paradox God is revealing the unity of his life and attributes, calling his people to see the beauty of his life and redemption.

2. THE OLD AND NEW TESTAMENTS

But the divine character is enacted in the making and fulfilling of the divine covenants and promises, for in his wisdom, the course of God's action focuses on the specific people of Israel, that they, through his self-revealing and saving work, might become wise. And the divine wisdom shines here as well, for it opens our eyes to the subtlety and art with which God took up the history of his interactions with humankind and simultaneously repeated and restored them in Christ. The New Testament is thus what Irenaeus calls the recapitulation of the Old, a work of art in which the history of God's dealings with Israel is simultaneously repeated/fulfilled through Christ and his church, and in which the promises and covenants are fulfilled despite our sin. It is in this recapitulation that we find divine wisdom manifested on the cross, where the "form of God" (Phil 2:5–11), the preexistent divine wisdom, is made known in the descent of the incarnation unto death.[22] This is not a new story but the reaping of what had already been sown throughout God's revelation and work to draw a people to himself.

---

21. Jonathan Edwards, "The Excellency of Christ," *Sermons and Discourses, 1734–1738*, in *The Works of Jonathan Edwards*, vol. 19, ed. M. X. Lesser (New Haven: Yale University Press, 2001), 560–95.

22. Michael Gorman discusses this feature of the Philippian hymn. See his *Inhabiting the Cruciform God: Kenosis, Justification, and Theosis in Paul's Narrative Soteriology* (Grand Rapids: Eerdmans, 2009), 14–15, 27. Furthermore, Gorman notes "that Christ crucified is the counterintuitive reality of divine wisdom and power, that the cross is in fact *theophanic*—revelatory of God's essential attributes, known in the reality and the narrative of the crucified Messiah" (ibid., 27). I don't think you have to go as far as Gorman here, concerning the divine attributes, to make the same point.

3. COSMIC SCOPE

The divine purposes for creation extend far beyond the role of Israel, though it is by means of Israel and its Messiah (rather than in addition to it or at its expense) that these purposes are fulfilled. "By wisdom the LORD laid the earth's foundations" (Prov 3:19 NIV), and it is through the completed work of the Messiah that all things in creation are reconciled to God (Col 1:19–20; 2 Cor 5:18–19).

The angels are confirmed in glory and grow in worship through their deeper understanding of their God.[23] Humankind, of course, is brought to its proper end as creatures made whole and wise through their participation in the Wisdom of the Father through his indwelling Spirit. The animals in creation are likewise brought to peace through the installation and revelation of the sons and daughters of God through their wise rule of creation (Isa 11:6), though the manifestation of this awaits the second coming of our Lord (Heb 2:8). The same holds true for the groanings of creation (Rom 8:22), which will give way to their proper song through the righteous rule of the wise creator and ruler of heaven and earth, Jesus Christ. Even the demons, through the wisdom of God, will be brought to participate in God's purposes for them, inasmuch as is possible for a creature resolutely and finally turned against the will of God (Phil 2:10).

This whole range of ends is brought about by means of the work of Wisdom incarnate, who is simultaneously the origin, means, and end of creation, working to bring to completion his whole creation in a single, fitting act.[24] There is no better vantage point from which to appreciate the cosmic scope of Christ's work than the divine wisdom.

VI. CONCLUSION: UNCAGED WISDOM

Because the work of Christ is first and foremost the act of the living God, it is the doctrine of God that provides the primary dogmatic location for the doctrine of the atonement. Accordingly, exploring the interrelationships between various aspects of the doctrines of God and the atonement will provide particularly fruitful lines of inquiry, offering ways past doctrinal stalemates and venues for new lines of dogmatic exploration.

In this essay, we have explored the relationship between atonement and the immanent life of God by means of considering the role of divine

---

23. Edwards, "The Wisdom of God," *Works of Edwards*, 2–3.
24. For a fuller elaboration development of this section, see Johnson, *Atonement: A Guide for the Perplexed*, ch. 6.

wisdom (a wisdom intrinsic to the divine life) within the work of Christ (the enactment or effective imaging of that immanent reality within the economy). The result is a reflection of the atonement in which Wisdom incarnate bears in himself our folly and its consequences, that through the resurrection we might be restored in wisdom through creaturely participation in that divine reality.

The implications of such a theory are significant, for it opens our eyes to the way that the whole character of God brings about the fulfillment of God's will as seen in the united vision of the Old and New Testaments, and in the way that this single act brings all created things to reconciliation with God and one another. At the same time, such a perspective opens us to the rich implications of Christ's work for the Christian life as a life characterized by wisdom.[25]

25. Thank you to Ty Kieser, Rachael Smith, and Daniel St. Clair for editorial and research assistance on this chapter. Adam would like to acknowledge that his work on this chapter benefited from a research fellowship at Biola University's Center for Christian Thought, made possible through the support of a grant from the John Templeton Foundation.

CHAPTER 5

ATONEMENT AND COVENANT

Binding Together Aspects of Christ's Work

JEREMY R. TREAT

INTRODUCTION

The night before Jesus was betrayed, he expressed the meaning of his ensuing death by appealing to the concept of covenant: "This is my blood of the covenant, which is poured out for many for the forgiveness of sins" (Matt 26:28). And yet, despite Jesus, Paul, and the author of Hebrews appealing to covenant as a significant theme for understanding Christ's work (Mark 14:24; Rom 11:27; 1 Cor 11:25; Heb 7–9), the concept of covenant has often been overlooked in atonement theology, a trend that Michael Gorman calls "the absence of the obvious."[1] Fortunately, scholars from various traditions have recently begun to recognize the need for covenant in the church's understanding and explanation of Christ's atoning work.[2]

---

1. Michael J. Gorman, *The Death of the Messiah and the Birth of the New Covenant: A (Not So) New Model of the Atonement* (Eugene, OR: Cascade, 2014), 9. For the neglect of covenant in atonement theology, see ibid., 1–5, 9–11.

2. In other words, Reformed "covenant theologians" are not the only ones appealing to covenant to understand atonement. Scholars who are Methodist, Anabaptist, Catholic, Orthodox, and Jewish have recently called for the importance of covenant in understanding atonement. See, for example, R. Larry Shelton, *Cross and Covenant: Interpreting the Atonement for 21st Century Mission* (Carlisle, UK: Paternoster, 2006); Gorman, *Death of the Messiah*; Scott Hahn, *Kinship by Covenant: A Canonical Approach to the Fulfillment of God's Saving Promises* (New Haven: Yale University Press, 2009), 319; Jon Levenson, *The Death and Resurrection of the Beloved Son: The Transformation of Child Sacrifice in Judaism and Christianity* (New Haven: Yale University Press, 1993), 173–232.

This essay seeks to advance the conversation by further clarifying how covenant informs the doctrine of atonement. I offer three theses:

1. Covenant is indispensable for the context of atonement.
2. Covenant is intrinsic to the definition of atonement.
3. Covenant is integrative in the doctrine of atonement.

Before discussing the role of covenant in the doctrine of atonement, however, I must first give provisional definitions of each respectively.

DEFINING "ATONEMENT"

The word "atonement" is a distinctively English word that has been used since the sixteenth century to describe the at-one-ment of parties formerly alienated. Since Tyndale's use of the word to translate the Hebrew כִּפֶּר (Lev 23:28) and the Greek καταλλαγή (2 Cor 5:18–19), "atonement" has become a technical term in theology that usually refers to the way in which Christ, through all of his work but primarily his death, has dealt with sin and its effects in order to reconcile God and sinners. I offer the following definition of atonement:

> The doctrine of the atonement is the church's understanding of the way in which Christ, through all of his work but primarily his death, has dealt with sin and its effects in order to restore the broken covenant relationship between God and sinners and thereby establish God's redemptive rule over his creation. At its core, the doctrine of the atonement is the attempt to understand the meaning of Christ's death as "for our sins in accordance with the Scriptures" (1 Cor 15:3).

Because atonement discussions are often plagued by different uses of the word "atonement," I offer four further qualifications.[3] First, atonement includes both the outcome of Christ's work (at-one-ment) and the means of Christ's accomplishment (*making* atonement). Second, atonement is centered on Christ's death but includes the spectrum of Christ's work in his life, resurrection, ascension, sending of the Spirit, and second coming. Third, the meaning of atonement is not only the way in which Christ's work affects the vertical relationship between God and humanity but also

---

3. For a more thorough understanding of how I understand and use "atonement," see Jeremy R. Treat, *The Crucified King: Atonement and Kingdom in Biblical and Systematic Theology* (Grand Rapids: Zondervan, 2014), 45–49.

how it impacts the horizontal shape of redemptive history as it moves toward the consummated kingdom of God. Lastly, Christ's atoning work is multifaceted, and its various aspects ought to complement one another and cohere together in an expansive account.

DEFINING "COVENANT"

Although the nature of covenants in Scripture has been debated for centuries, a general consensus has emerged on the basic elements of a definition.[4] I will offer my own summative definition and then briefly explain each component.

A "covenant" is a binding relationship based on obligations and sealed with an oath that makes two parties as close as family.

First, a covenant is a type of *relationship*, a particular way that two parties relate. A covenant is similar to a contract in its legality but exceeds it in relationality. According to Elmer Martens,

The occasion for contract is largely the benefits that each party expects.... The contract is characteristically *thing*-oriented. The covenant is *person*-oriented and, theologically speaking, arises, not with benefits as the chief barter item, but out of a desire for a measure of intimacy.[5]

A covenant is, therefore, fundamentally a relationship. We must then ask: what kind of relationship is it?

Second, a covenant is a *binding* relationship *that makes two parties as close as family*. When God enters into a covenant with a people, he is binding himself to them as family. A covenant is, therefore, a kinship bond, and is based not on natural relations but rather on elected relations, on two parties choosing to be like family.[6] As Scott Hahn has demonstrated, "a 'covenant' is, in its essence, a legal means to establish kinship between two previously unrelated parties."[7] For this reason, a man and a woman who are previously unrelated become family when they enter into a covenant marriage (Mal 2:14; cf. Gen 2:24).[8] Two friends become

---

4.   Scott Hahn surveys this "virtual consensus" among Protestant, Catholic, and Jewish scholars. See "Covenant," in *Catholic Bible Dictionary*, ed. Scott Hahn (New York: Doubleday, 2009), 168.

5.   Elmer A. Martens, *God's Design: A Focus on Old Testament Theology* (Grand Rapids: Baker, 1981), 73.

6.   As Hugenberger says, "A covenant, in its normal sense, is an elected, as opposed to natural, relationship of obligation under oath." See Gordon P. Hugenberger, *Marriage as a Covenant: Biblical Law and Ethics as Developed from Malachi* (Eugene, OR: Wipf & Stock, 1994), 132.

7.   Hahn, "Covenant," 168; Hahn, *Kinship by Covenant*.

8.   Hugenberger, *Marriage as a Covenant*.

like brothers when they enter into a covenant friendship (1 Sam 18:3; 2 Sam 1:26).

Third, a covenant is *based on obligations*, with ensuing curses for the party that breaks the covenant. There are two different types of covenants in Scripture based on whether the obligations are placed on one or both of the parties. A suzerain-vassal treaty is a conditional agreement where both parties assume obligations. A royal grant is an unconditional promise where the initiator alone agrees to obligations.[9] The party that breaks the covenant by not keeping their obligations receives covenant curses. This is where sacrifice often enters into the covenant-making process, representing the curse-bearing that will take place if one of the parties does not keep their obligations.

The role of obligations, curses, and sacrifice can be seen in the different covenants that the LORD makes with Abraham and with Moses. The royal grant covenant with Abraham is a unilateral and unconditional promise where God agrees to bear the curse himself, which is demonstrated through a sacrificial ritual (Gen 15, 17). The suzerain-vassal covenant with Moses is a conditional treaty where both parties agree to obligations, which is ratified through the sacrificial shedding of blood (Ex 24:1–8).[10]

Fourth, a covenant is *sealed with an oath*, which is the declarative commitment to keep the obligations of the covenant. According to Paul Williamson,

> A solemn oath … could well be described as the *sine qua non* of a covenant…. It is now widely acknowledged that an oath was indeed an indispensable aspect in the ratification of a covenant. Thus understood, it is this aspect that constitutes the most important common denominator between the various covenants attested to in Scripture.[11]

Having defined "covenant" and "atonement" respectively, we can proceed to discuss how the former informs the latter.

---

9. For the difference between suzerain-vassal covenants and royal grants, see Moshe Weinfeld, "The Covenant of Grant in the Old Testament and in the Ancient Near East," *Journal of the American Oriental Society*, no. 90 (1970): 184–203.

10. There are, of course, greater complexities to each covenant. Robert Letham helpfully explains the relationship between the Abrahamic and Mosaic covenants: "The Mosaic covenant was added as a custodian for Israel in its minority…. It served a protective function for the people of the Abrahamic covenant until that covenant was fully realized. The two covenants were not competitive but complementary. Grace was constitutive, law regulative." See Letham, *The Work of Christ* (Downers Grove, IL: InterVarsity, 1993), 44.

11. Paul Williamson, *Sealed with an Oath: Covenant in God's Unfolding Purpose*, NSBT (Downers Grove, IL: InterVarsity, 2007), 39.

COVENANT IS INDISPENSABLE FOR THE CONTEXT OF ATONEMENT

Covenant provides indispensable context for atonement in at least two ways: redemptive historical, and relational. Before elaborating, however, I should first clarify the scope of my claim. Covenant is *an* essential aspect of the context of atonement, not *the* context by itself. Covenant fits within a broader story of the kingdom of God coming through the Son of God for the glory of God.[12] Covenant, however, is not merely another piece in the puzzle, another aspect of the story that stacks up next to the others. Rather, the concept of covenant is like glue that holds together the other aspects. Theologically speaking, covenant functions less as a locus and more like a lens—a salient point in the broader aim of "locating atonement." And through this covenant lens, one can see the relational and redemptive historical context of atonement.

REDEMPTIVE HISTORICAL CONTEXT

Within the unfolding story of Scripture, atonement enters in at a stage where God has already bound himself to his people. In other words, the biblical refrain *forgiveness through atonement* (Lev 4:35; 5:10; 6:7) comes within the broader covenant song of *I will be your God and you will be my people* (Ex 6:6–8; Lev 26:12; Rev 21:3). Covenant, therefore, provides redemptive historical context for atonement.[13] As Peter Gentry and Stephen Wellum argue, "Covenants form the backbone of the metanarrative of Scripture," and therefore provide essential context for Christ's atoning work.[14]

Beginning at least with Abraham, covenant provides indispensable context for sacrifice and atonement.[15] Robert Letham explains that in

---

12. My proposal for the role of covenant within the doctrine of atonement is therefore much more modest than Gorman's, who offers a "comprehensive model" based on the new covenant (Gorman, *Death of the Messiah*, 19). I question whether producing new exclusive models or theories is the best approach to begin with, but granting Gorman's aim, it seems to me that covenant (and the new covenant in particular) functions in the New Testament more in the background rather than in the foreground. I see covenant, therefore as *a* (not *the*) key theme that informs atonement.

13. This is a needed feature in the doctrine of atonement, which, as Hans Boersma argues, has often been "de-historicized." *Violence, Hospitality, and the Cross: Reappropriating the Atonement Tradition* (Grand Rapids: Baker, 2004), 168. Covenant can help re-historicize the doctrine of atonement because covenant is necessarily a redemptive-historical concept. The covenant theme unfolds progressively, contains unity and diversity, and finds its ultimate fulfillment through the new covenant in Christ.

14. Peter Gentry and Stephen Wellum, *Kingdom through Covenant: A Biblical-Theological Understanding of the Covenants* (Wheaton, IL: Crossway, 2012), 21.

15. Although I believe the discussion of covenants could begin with Adam, I begin with Abraham because it makes the connection explicitly and it makes the point—that covenant provides context for atonement—with equal weight. I also want to make clear that by appealing to covenant as context for atonement, I am not merely drawing upon federal theology.

Genesis 15, "Yahweh took on himself a self-maledictory oath as he himself passed between the pieces of the divided birds, calling on himself the curses of the covenant should he prove unfaithful to his promises, effectually guaranteeing to Abraham his faithfulness to his covenantal word (Gn. 15:1–21)."[16]

The covenantal context of atonement comes to full fruition in the Mosaic covenant. The sacrificial system, the means of atonement in the Old Testament, is introduced as part of the instructions of the covenant. As J. I. Packer says, "When God brought Israel out of Egypt, he set up as part of the covenant relationship a system of sacrifices that had at its heart the shedding and offering of the blood of unflawed animals 'to make atonement for yourselves' (Lev.17:11)."[17]

The covenantal context of atonement is evident not only in the sweeping narrative of Israel, but also in specific passages. In Ezekiel 16:62–63, for example, the LORD says,

> I will establish my covenant with you, and you shall know that I am the LORD, that you may remember and be confounded, and never open your mouth again because of your shame, when I atone for you for all that you have done, declares the Lord GOD (ESV).

From the perspective of the old covenant, Ezekiel looks forward to God's promise of atoning for sins within the broader framework of God binding himself to his people through a new and everlasting covenant.

In the New Testament, Christ's atoning work is presented not merely as the fulfillment of general promises but rather as the culmination of God's covenants with his people and as the inauguration of the promised new covenant (Jer 31:31; Matt 26:8). As Jeremiah had prophesied, "Behold, the days are coming, says the LORD, when I will make a new covenant with the house of Israel and the house of Judah" (Jer 31:31). It is a covenant in which the law will be written on hearts and sin will be forgiven. Jesus is the mediator of this new covenant accomplishing the forgiveness of sins through his atoning work.

Covenant provides redemptive historical context for atonement not only by showing its background and its fulfillment in Christ but also by pointing forward to its goal in the eschaton. Atonement is never about less than forgiveness of sin, but it is certainly about more. God's unfolding

---

16. Letham, *The Work of Christ*, 48.
17. J. I. Packer, *Concise Theology: A Guide to Historic Christian Beliefs* (Wheaton, IL: Tyndale House, 1993), 135.

purposes rushing headlong toward the eschaton are accomplished through the covenants that God makes and culminate in the New Jerusalem where "they will be his people, and God himself will be with them as their God" (Rev 21:3 ESV). Atonement is aimed at a new covenant with a renewed people in a new creation. Once again, covenant is not *the* redemptive historical context, but it is an essential part of it. As Seyoon Kim says, "Through the atoning and covenant-establishing death, Jesus was to create the people of the new covenant, the people of the kingdom of God."[18]

RELATIONAL CONTEXT

The nature of sin is complex and its implications are many, but perhaps the most basic consequence is that sinners are separated from their Creator (Isa 59:2). From the banishment of Adam from Eden (Gen 3:23–24) to the eternal estrangement from God for all those who are in Adam (2 Thess 1:9), Scripture is a story of overcoming the sin-induced separation between God and his people, within the broader aim of mending the breach between heaven and earth (Rev 21:1–5). But what type of "separation" is implied in this story: ontological, legal, geographical? The answer to this question is significant, for prescribing the remedy depends on rightly describing the ruin.

The covenantal background of atonement reveals that the "separation" between God and sinners is primarily relational, which, far from ruling out the other aspects (e.g., ontological, legal, geographical), actually provides a framework for them.[19] As Colin Gunton says, "Our sinfulness ... is not conceived *mathematically* as the accumulation of wrong acts, but *relationally* as that which universally qualifies human existence in the flesh."[20] Michael Horton rightly argues that in Scripture divine presence and absence are primarily relational rather than ontological categories.[21] Presence is synonymous with God's blessings and salvation. Absence names the judicial curse: not only being apart from the goodness of God but also being under the wrath of God. Horton makes a helpful analogy with marriage:

---

18. Seyoon Kim, *The "Son of Man" as the Son of God*, WUNT 30 (Tübingen: J. C. B. Mohr, 1983), 99.

19. See Michael Horton's arguments for a "covenantal ontology" in *Lord and Servant: A Covenant Christology* (Louisville: Westminster John Knox, 2005), 10–16.

20. Colin Gunton, *Father, Son and Holy Spirit: Toward a Fully Trinitarian Theology* (New York: T&T Clark, 2003), 192.

21. Horton, *Lord and Servant*, 12–13.

We know this form of presence and absence in our own covenantal experience with marriage. Sometimes even when the spouse is physically present, he or she may be said to 'not really be *there*' in the relationship. Desertion happens in the heart. It is this ethical or covenantal form of presence and absence that Scripture employs. Although, ontologically speaking, God is omnipresent, the real question is this: Where is God *for us*?[22]

The greatest need of sinners is to be reconciled to God, to be brought into a covenantal relationship with their Creator. Such a covenantal framework roots sin relationally but also integrates legal, ontological, and geographical aspects.

If relational separation is at the heart of the problem, then at-one-ment between God and sinners will be at the heart of the solution. Christ's atoning work is multifaceted and expansive, but perhaps the most direct aim is reconciliation with God.[23] Yet while Christ died to reconcile sinners into a relationship with their Creator, it is not a generic, undefined relationship. Rather, Christ's atoning work reconciles sinners into a *covenant* relationship with God, a relational bond that makes two parties as close as family. Reconciliation has always been the aim of atonement, but reconciliation in Scripture has a covenantal ring.

In sum, the concept of covenant reveals the relational context of atonement and further specifies the type of relationship toward which reconciliation is aimed. Steven McKenzie's assertion that "covenant is the principal image used in the Bible to express the relationship between God and humans"[24] is certainly true of the restored relationship made possible by Christ's atoning work.

COVENANT IS INTRINSIC TO THE DEFINITION OF ATONEMENT

Context not only provides background, it also informs meaning. It is only natural, therefore, that the previous discussion of the covenantal context of atonement crept toward defining atonement itself. Covenant is not only indispensable context for atonement, but it is also intrinsic to the very definition of atonement. In other words, one cannot rightly understand atonement itself apart from covenant. Jesus is "the mediator of a new cov-

---

22. Ibid.
23. I understand reconciliation to be the most direct aim of atonement, but within the broader aim of a new creation and the ultimate aim of the glory of God.
24. Steven L. McKenzie, *Covenant* (St. Louis: Chalice, 2000), 8.

enant" (Heb 9:15), bringing about a new binding relationship between God and his people through his multifaceted work of atonement. But how precisely does covenant inform the definition of Christ's atoning work, particularly in the various stages of Jesus' ministry?

In the paragraphs below, I will argue that covenant is intrinsic to the definition of atonement by demonstrating that Christ fulfills the covenant obligations with his life, bears the covenant curses through his sacrificial death, and then resurrects and ascends as the high priest of the new covenant—all of which are part of his work of reconciling God and sinners into a covenant relationship. Each aspect of Christ's atoning work is essential, for, as John Webster says, "No one moment of the history can bear the weight of the whole."[25]

THE LIFE OF CHRIST: KEEPING THE COVENANT OBLIGATIONS

The life of Christ has often been neglected in atonement theology, routinely treated as a mere warmup act for the main event and celebrated with the anticlimactic lag that comes between Christmas and Good Friday. It is not enough to merely affirm Christ's sinlessness, as if to say that what he did not do (sin) is ample reason to ignore what he did do in his ministry. What, then, did Jesus accomplish in his ministry? Through his life and ministry, Jesus preached and demonstrated the kingdom of God, fulfilled the law, and kept the covenant as the last Adam and faithful Israel. For the purposes of this essay, I will focus on Christ as the covenant keeper in his life. The concept of covenant fills Christ's life not only with meaning, but also with atoning significance.

The Bible can be told as the story of three sons: Adam, Israel, and Jesus. Adam was created in a covenantal relationship with God (or at least a covenant-like relationship with God) and given the task of extending God's royal blessings from Eden to the ends of the earth (Gen 1:28; 2:15; cf. Ps 8). Adam, however, "transgressed the covenant" (Hos 6:7), and rather than extending God's blessings, he spread the curse instead. Israel was then called into a covenant with God and similarly commissioned to be a "kingdom of priests" (Ex 19:6) and a "light to the nations" (Isa 49:6). As William Dumbrell says, "Israel resumed the role, initially given to

---

25. John Webster, "*Rector et iudex super omnia genera doctrinarum?* The Place of the Doctrine of Justification," in *What Is Justification About? Reformed Contributions to an Ecumenical Theme*, eds. Michael Weinrich and John Burgess (Grand Rapids: Eerdmans, 2009), 41.

Adam, of God's regent in a world that needs order."[26] Yet Israel broke the covenant as a disobedient son, and just as Adam was banished from Eden, Israel was exiled from the Promised Land.

Jesus, the eternal Son of God, came as the last Adam (1 Cor 15:45; Rom 5:12–21) and faithful Israel (Matt 4:1–11), recapitulating their histories in his own life and ministry and keeping the covenant at each point they had broken it. Whereas Adam submitted to the rule of the serpent in the garden, Jesus subdued the serpent at Golgotha. Israel failed the forty-year test in the wilderness; Jesus remained faithful for forty days in the wilderness. Jesus kept the covenant with God and faithfully fulfilled the task of embodying God's redemptive rule in the midst of the sin-shattered creation. As Irenaeus says, Jesus was "procuring for us a comprehensive salvation, that we might recover in Christ Jesus what in Adam we had lost."[27]

Jesus was not merely sinless; he was faithful. And he was not merely faithful; he was faithful to the covenant. The Messiah kept the covenant, fulfilling its precepts and suffering its sanctions on our behalf. If sinners are to be reconciled to God (as opposed to merely receiving a clear slate), this covenant-keeping is absolutely necessary. It is the kingdom-bringing, law-fulfilling, covenant-keeping Messiah who goes to the cross in our place.

THE DEATH OF CHRIST: BEARING THE COVENANT CURSES

Covenant is essential for understanding the atoning significance of Christ's death for at least three reasons. First, Christ's death is not merely any type of sacrifice; it is a covenantal sacrifice.[28] Although not all covenants in Scripture include sacrifice, the covenants with Abraham and Moses both include ritual sacrifices as a way of sealing the covenant and serving to remind the covenant parties of the penalty for breaking the covenant. Furthermore, the sacrifices of the Mosaic covenant serve not only as reminders of covenant curses but actually atone for the sins already committed (at least in a provisional sense; see Heb 10:1–10). Christ's death must be understood in both senses: it is a covenantal sacrifice that reminds the

---

26. William Dumbrell, *The Search for Order: Biblical Eschatology in Focus* (Grand Rapids: Baker, 1994), 9–10.

27. Irenaeus, *Against Heresies*, trans. A. Roberts and W. H. Rambaut, *ANF* 1 (Buffalo: Christian Literature, 1885; reprint, Grand Rapids: Eerdmans, 1975), 3.18.1.

28. According to Williamson, "sacrifice [was] the means by which the central blessing of the covenant—communion between Yahweh and his people—was ensured and maintained" (*Sealed with an Oath*, 111).

partakers of the consequences of breaking the covenant and yet at the same time atones for sins already committed.

Second, in his death, Christ does not merely bear any penalty; rather, he bears the covenant curses, which include refusal of forgiveness and the bestowal of God's anger (Deut 29:20–21). As one who kept the covenant in his life, Christ voluntarily and graciously bears these covenant curses through his substitutionary death on the cross. As the apostle Paul proclaimed, "Christ redeemed us from the curse of the law by becoming a curse for us" (Gal 3:13). Israel broke the covenant at Sinai. Jesus bore the covenant curses on Golgotha.

Third, and cumulatively, by bearing the curses of the covenant through his sacrificial death, Jesus ratifies the new covenant. When Jesus said, "This is my blood of the covenant," on the night before he was betrayed (Matt 26:28), he was drawing upon Exodus 24:8, where Moses ratified the covenant made between God and Israel after the exodus by sacrificing animals and dashing blood on the people. As the old covenant was inaugurated by blood, Christ's sacrificial death seals the new covenant between God and his people (Heb 10:15–22). As Kevin Vanhoozer says, "The cross is the climax of the history of the Son's covenantal mediation."[29]

THE RESURRECTION AND ASCENSION OF CHRIST: CONTINUING AS THE HIGH PRIEST OF THE NEW COVENANT

How does covenant help make sense of the atoning value of Christ's resurrection and ascension? This requires precision, for while many ignore resurrection and ascension altogether in atonement, others place atonement solely in Christ's post-resurrection heavenly offering. Faustus Socinus seems to have separated atonement from Christ's death altogether, interpreting the cross only as an example and locating Christ's sacrificial atonement in his post-resurrection/ascension offering of himself in heaven.[30] Although Socinus's argument has not been adopted due to his largely unorthodox theology, David Moffitt has recently come to a similar conclusion, at least in regards to the book of Hebrews.[31] According to Moffitt,

---

29. Kevin Vanhoozer, "Atonement," in *Mapping Modern Theology: A Thematic and Historical Introduction*, eds. Kelly Kapic and Bruce McCormack (Grand Rapids: Baker, 2012), 201.

30. Faustus Socinus, *De Jesu Christo Servatore: Hoc Est Cur & Qua Ratione Iesus Christus Noster Seruator Sit* (Rakow, Poland: Rodecius, 1594).

31. David Moffitt, *Atonement and the Logic of Resurrection in the Epistle to the Hebrews* (Leiden: Brill, 2011).

atonement is not accomplished on the cross but in the heavenly sanctuary where the resurrected Jesus presents his life (not death) on the altar: "His death sets the sequence into motion. His appearance before God in heaven effects atonement."[32]

Part of the way forward must be rightly understanding Jesus as the high priest of the new covenant. As the true priest toward which every other priest pointed, Jesus offered up a pleasing sacrifice to God and was at the same time the sacrifice himself. The author of Hebrews, however, forcefully reminds the reader that the priesthood of Christ is not limited to his work on the cross: "The former priests were many in number, because they were prevented by death from continuing in office; but he holds his priesthood permanently, because he continues forever" (Heb 7:23–24). Gerald O'Collins and Michael Keenan Jones helpfully unpack the nature of Christ's continuing priesthood:

> The priesthood of Christ continues forever, since he eternally intercedes for the world and blesses the world, offers himself through the Holy Spirit to the Father, continues to pour out the Holy Spirit upon the Church and the world, acts on earth as primary minister in all the Church's preaching and sacramental life, and in heaven remains forever the Mediator through whom the blessed enjoy the vision of God and the risen life of glory.[33]

The atoning value of Christ's offering in the heavenly sanctuary (Heb 9:11–14) need not be set against Christ's atoning accomplishment on the cross; rather, it can show the breadth of Christ's atoning work, and specifically, it can demonstrate that, just as in the Old Testament sacrificial system, atonement was a process.[34] Furthermore, it is the resurrected and ascended Christ who sends his Spirit to continue his work on earth. "*Pentecost belongs to the atonement*," says Thomas Torrance, "for the presence of the Spirit is the actualisation amongst us of the new or redeemed life."[35] As Horton says, "The pouring out of 'the blood of the new covenant' (Matt 26:28) is the presupposition of the pouring out of the Spirit at Pentecost (Acts 2)."[36]

---

32. Ibid., 294.
33. Gerald O'Collins and Michael Keenan Jones, *Jesus Our Priest: A Christian Approach to the Priesthood of Christ* (Oxford: Oxford University Press, 2010), 265.
34. For a constructive proposal of the role of the ascension in Christ's atoning work, see Douglas Farrow, *Ascension Theology* (New York: T&T Clark, 2011), ch. 7, "Ascension and Atonement."
35. Thomas Torrance, *Atonement: The Person and Work of Christ*, ed. Robert Walker (Downers Grove, IL: IVP Academic, 2009), 178, italics his.
36. Horton, *Lord and Servant*, 177.

COVENANT IS INTEGRATIVE IN THE DOCTRINE OF ATONEMENT

Atonement theology has long been plagued by pendulum-swinging reductionism. It would seem, according to many, that Christ *either* satisfied the wrath of God *or* defeated death and Satan *or* provided an example of sacrificial love. This is unfortunate, for Scripture provides a multivalent and fully orbed understanding of Christ's atoning work, one in which the various aspects of Christ's work complement one another in a comprehensive and expansive account.[37] Perhaps covenant can help.

While we have seen what covenant *is* (a binding relationship), I will now make a proposal for what covenant can *do* in atonement theology: namely, bind together various aspects of Christ's atoning work. In other words, a covenant is about God binding himself to his people, but the *concept* of covenant can bind together disparate themes in atonement theology. Vanhoozer aptly summarizes the integrating power of covenant for understanding Christ's work:

> While the sundry conceptualities championed by the various atonement theories do not, strictly speaking, cohere, they are nevertheless compatible thanks to the integrative framework of the covenant—a complex, multilevel reality that combines the judicial and relational aspects of Jesus' death "for us" in a garment as seamless as the one for which the soldiers cast lots.[38]

The integrating power of covenant is especially helpful for the aim of "locating atonement." Covenant does not constitute a mere locus to place atonement within or beside. Rather, covenant has an adhesive function in atonement theology, encouraging integration and upholding coherence. When Jesus quoted Genesis 2:24 to refer to the covenant of marriage, he used the word *kollhqh/setai* (Matt 19:5), which, often translated "hold fast," could also literally be translated "be glued together." The concept of covenant has the ability to function like glue in the doctrine of the

---

37. John Stott is right in saying, " 'Images' of salvation (or of the atonement) ... are not alternative explanations of the cross, providing us with a range to choose from, but complementary to one another, each contributing a vital part to the whole." John Stott, *The Cross of Christ* (Downers Grove, IL: InterVarsity, 1986), 168.

38. Kevin Vanhoozer, *The Drama of Doctrine: A Canonical-Linguistic Approach to Christian Theology* (Louisville: Westminster John Knox, 2005), 387. Others have also discovered the binding power of the concept of covenant. Michael Horton says, "A covenant perspective emphasizes solidarity and therefore resists reduction to individualist theories of atonement" (*Lord and Servant*, 220). Gorman speaks of "covenantal integration" (*Death of the Messiah*, 46). Shelton refers to covenant as "an integrative motif" (*Cross and Covenant*, 5).

atonement, holding many aspects together into a multifaceted yet united understanding of Christ's atoning work.

Covenant as "a bonding agent in the cement that unites Scripture" has the potential to repair many common false dichotomies.[39] For example, through the lens of covenant, theology can embrace both relational and juridical, individual and corporate, and restorative and retributive aspects of atonement.

RELATIONAL AND JURIDICAL

Atonement discussions often experience a tension between the relational and juridical aspects of Christ's work. Scot McKnight, for example, in his attempt to frame atonement with relational/communal categories, sharply critiques the "over-judicialization of atonement imagery" in the Reformed tradition.[40] The concept of covenant, however, should safeguard atonement discussions from veering reductively to either a juridical *or* relational account of Christ's work. Scholars of various stripes have demonstrated that covenants were both intensely relational *and* legal, with the two aspects being intertwined beyond separation. As Hahn says, "A covenant was a *familial bond* established by a *legally binding* oath."[41]

The binding power of covenant in regards to relational and legal categories is still evident today in covenant marriage. The fact that a marriage is a legally binding relationship does not make it any less relational or personal. In fact, the legality of a marriage is, in part, to ensure the personal and relational aspects of the covenant. As Dietrich Bonhoeffer said in one of his letters from prison, "It is not your love that sustains the marriage, but from now on, the marriage that sustains your love."[42] Such a spousal understanding of covenant is fitting for the doctrine of atonement, for marriage itself is a picture of Christ's covenant-keeping love for the church, the bride for which he lays down his life in love (Eph 5:25, 32).

INDIVIDUAL AND CORPORATE

Another pendulum upon which atonement theology has swung is the relationship between individual and corporate aspects of Christ's work. Hans

---

39. Williamson, *Sealed with an Oath*, 13.

40. Scot McKnight, *A Community Called Atonement* (Nashville: Abingdon, 2007), 95. Hans Boersma also traces this trend in the Reformed tradition (*Violence, Hospitality, and the Cross*, 163–69).

41. Hahn, "Covenant," 170; italics added.

42. Dietrich Bonhoeffer, *Letters and Papers from Prison*, ed. Eberhard Bethge (New York: Macmillan, 1967), 28.

Boersma traces individualistic tendencies in atonement theology from Anselm to Abelard and on to American culture. According to Boersma,

> The problem lies with a Western mind-set that has overemphasized the relative importance of the individual. This is not to say that the individual and his or her responsibility are insignificant. But Western thought has suffered from a preoccupation with the individual that goes well beyond a biblical appreciation for individual responsibility.[43]

Many theologians, such as N. T. Wright, have responded to such a trend by trying to emphasize the corporate nature of Christ's atoning work.[44]

The nature of covenants in Scripture, as both individual and corporate, can help overcome what often masquerades as a false dichotomy between the individual and the community. In Scripture, God's covenants are with a people (corporate) but make room for individual and corporate responsibility, individual and corporate guilt, and individual and corporate atonement. Richard Lints rightly captures the dynamic between individual and corporate aspects of the atonement in light of the concept of covenant:

> Salvation concerns individuals-in-community. Covenant language throughout the Scriptures underscores this tension inherent in God's actions of salvation. God's act of restoring us into a covenant relationship with him also puts us into a differently ordered (i.e., covenantal) relationship with all others who are reconciled to God.[45]

Covenant does not do all the work in holding together the individual and corporate (e.g., the concepts of kingdom and family add much to the conversation), but the covenantal nature of Christ's atoning work forbids any polarized perspective on the subject. Christ's atoning death creates a new covenant community, a kingdom of priests.

RESTORATIVE AND RETRIBUTIVE JUSTICE

Atonement theology deals not only with how sinners are forgiven but also with the nature of the God who forgives. Is God just? Is he merciful? Can he be both? Adonis Vidu rightly remarks that "all atonement theories want to affirm that God preserves justice in the process of redemption. But not all

---

43. Boersma, *Violence, Hospitality, and the Cross*, 166–67.
44. See, for example, N. T. Wright, *Jesus and the Victory of God*, Christian Origins and the Question of God (Minneapolis: Fortress, 1996), 561.
45. Richard Lints, "Soteriology," in *Mapping Modern Theology: A Thematic and Historical Introduction*, eds. Kelly Kapic and Bruce McCormack (Grand Rapids: Baker, 2012), 263–64.

theologians operate with the same understandings of justice."[46] Perhaps the sharpest contemporary divide on the nature of justice in atonement theology is regarding whether God's justice is retributive and/or restorative.[47]

Vanhoozer reviews the strongest critiques against retributive justice and responds with the assertion that the covenantal nature of Christ's work provides a holistic defense.[48] Covenant provides the categories not only to defend retributive justice but also to show how it informs Christ's atoning work.

> In the context of God's covenant with Israel, the law served the purpose of regulating relationships, both within the covenant community and between the covenant community and God. Let me therefore suggest that, from a biblical perspective, God's justice is a matter of his preserving right covenantal relationships, and of doing so with integrity (i.e., as a holy, just and loving God).[49]

Furthermore, covenant not only makes room for both retributive and restorative justice, it helps reveal how the two relate. It is the one and same God who gives the law of the covenant and who points toward the goal of the covenant: the Lord dwelling with his people in the new creation. Retributive justice has a restorative goal. Michael Bird is right to contend that "we do not have to choose between retributive and restorative schemes of divine justice.... There can be no reconciliation without recompense; otherwise the disorder, destruction, and decay of evil prevent peace from lasting."[50] The laws of the covenant are given by the Lord of the kingdom.

CONCLUSION

We have seen that covenant greatly informs the doctrine of atonement. If Christ's work is painted in many different colors, covenant is the canvas upon which they are painted. It is the relational backdrop of Christ's

---

46. Adonis Vidu, *Atonement, Law, and Justice: The Cross in Historical and Cultural Contexts* (Grand Rapids: Baker, 2014), xv.

47. Stephen Travis, for example, argues strongly against retributive justice. See Stephen H. Travis, *Christ and the Judgment of God: The Limits of Divine Retribution in New Testament Thought*, 2nd ed. (Milton Keynes, UK: Paternoster, 2008).

48. Kevin Vanhoozer, "The Atonement in Postmodernity: Guilt, Goats, and Gifts," in *The Glory of the Atonement: Biblical, Theological, and Practical Perspectives*, eds. Charles Hill and Frank James (Downers Grove, IL: InterVarsity, 2004), 375–81.

49. Ibid., 380–81, italics his.

50. Michael Bird, *Evangelical Theology: A Biblical and Systematic Introduction* (Grand Rapids: Zondervan, 2013), 306; cf. Leon Morris, who says, "Punishment must in fact be retributive if it is to be reformatory." Leon Morris, *The Cross in the New Testament* (Exeter, UK: Paternoster, 1965), 386); Henri Blocher, "God and the Cross," in *Engaging the Doctrine of God: Contemporary Protestant Perspectives*, ed. Bruce McCormack (Grand Rapids: Baker, 2008), 140.

multifaceted work. Christ fulfills the covenant obligations with his life, bears the covenant sanctions through his sacrificial death, and reconciles God and sinners into a covenant relationship. Prabo Mihindukulasuriya is correct to argue that when we understand atonement within the storyline of Scripture, we see "how the covenantal expectations of the Hebrew Scriptures are fulfilled in Christ, indicating the significance of his life and ministry, as well as his death and resurrection, and links seamlessly the themes of the kingdom of God and the cross."[51] Covenant is significant for both a biblically faithful understanding of Christ's work and a theologically rich account of atonement.

---

51. Prabo Mihindukulasuriya, "How Jesus Inaugurated the Kingdom on the Cross: A Kingdom Perspective of the Atonement," *Evangelical Review of Theology* 38 (2014): 213.

CHAPTER 6

ATONEMENT IN GETHSEMANE

The Necessity of Dyothelitism for the Atonement

R. LUCAS STAMPS

INTRODUCTION[1]

By the time the church convened what would become its sixth ecumenical council in Constantinople in the fall of 680, Maximus the Confessor had been dead for over eighteen years. But it was the work of Maximus, as much as anyone else in the preceding decades of the monothelite controversy, that laid the Christological groundwork for the decision that the bishops would render at the Third Council of Constantinople (680–81).[2] The question that the council addressed is well known: Does the incarnate Christ possess one will or two? In large measure, the parties of the debate were seeking to tease out the logic of the fourth ecumenical council, the Council of Chalcedon (451).

---

1. Some of this material originally appeared in R. Lucas Stamps, *"Thy Will Be Done": A Dogmatic Defense of Dyothelitism in Light of Recent Monothelite Proposals*, unpublished dissertation, The Southern Baptist Theological Seminary, 2014.

2. On the history of the monothelite controversy, see Jaroslav Pelikan, *The Christian Tradition: A History of the Development of Doctrine 2, The Spirit of Eastern Christendom (600–1700)* (Chicago: University of Chicago Press, 1974), 62–75; Leo Donald Davis, S.J., *The First Ecumenical Councils (325–787): Their History Theology* (Wilmington, DE: Michael Glazer, 1987), 258–89; Paul Verghese, "The Monothelite Controversy—A Historical Survey," *Greek Orthodox Theological Review* 13 (1968): 196–208; Justo L. Gonzalez, *A History of Christian Thought*, vol. 2, *From Augustine to the Eve of the Reformation*, rev. ed. (Nashville: Abingdon, 1987), 88–91, 98–100; Harold O. J. Brown, *Heresies: Heresy and Orthodoxy in the History of the Church* (Peabody, MA: Hendrickson, 1988), 186–92.

Both parties, the monothelites and the dyothelites, agreed with Chalcedon that Christ is a single person with two natures, but the pressing question was simply this: To which of these categories (person or nature) does the will—the faculty of choice and intention—properly belong?[3] Do wills inhere in persons or in natures? If the former is the case, then by Chalcedonian logic, Christ can have only one will. But if the latter is the case, then by that same logic, Christ must have two wills. Maximus's answers to these questions were clear and unambiguous. Wills belong to natures, not persons, and therefore the incarnate Christ possesses two wills: the one divine will that he shares eternally with the Father and the Spirit and the discrete human will that he assumed in the incarnation.

Part of what compelled Maximus to adopt this position was exactly what motivated Gregory of Nazianzus three centuries earlier in the Apollinarian controversy, namely, the soteriological task of Christ in his assumption of human nature. Indeed, Maximus echoed Gregory's famous maxim, "The unassumed is unhealed," and applied it not only to the soul of Christ generally but also to the distinctive, volitional faculty of the soul: the will.[4] Maximus also linked Christ's assumption of a human will to his redemptive work as the Last Adam; Christ reverses the curse of sin at the very place where it entered the human race: the human will.[5] In short, Maximus defended dyothelitism on explicitly soteriological grounds: only if Christ possesses a human will can he serve as an adequate redeemer and healer of fallen human wills.

In the history of Christian thought, Maximus is hardly alone in drawing a close connection between the Son's assumption of a human will and his atoning and reconciling work. John of Damascus closely follows Maximus's logic on this point, as does Thomas Aquinas.[6] Though the soteriological

---

3. Cyril Hovorun demonstrates that the monothelite controversy was largely an intra-Chalcedonian, even intra-Cyrillian, dispute. Cyril Hovorun, *Will, Action and Freedom: Christological Controversies in the Seventh Century* (Leiden: Brill, 2008).

4. "So, if according to them the Word when He became incarnate did not have this [faculty of will] along with the nature, then I shall never be set free from sin. And if I cannot be freed from sin, then I have not been saved, since what is not assumed is not healed." Joseph P. Farrell, trans., *The Disputation with Pyrrhus of Our Father among the Saints Maximus the Confessor* (Waymart, PA: St. Tikhon's Seminary Press, 1990), 46. See also Gregory of Nazianzus, "To Cledonius Against Apollinaris (Epistle 101)," in *Christology of the Later Fathers*, ed. Edward R. Hardy (Louisville: Westminster John Knox, 1954), 218–19.

5. Maximus argues that Christ's assumption of a complete human nature brought about the dissolution of "all the divisions introduced by the transgression of the old Adam, through which nature has been condemned to death." Maximus, *Opuscule 7*, in Andrew Louth, *Maximus the Confessor* (London: Routledge, 1996), 185.

6. John of Damascus, *The Orthodox Faith*, in John of Damascus, *Writings*, trans. Frederic H. Chase, Jr., Fathers of the Church, vol. 37 (New York: Fathers of the Church, 1958), 3.14; Thomas Aquinas, *Summa Theologica*, trans. Fathers of the English Dominican Province, ed. Daniel J. Sullivan (Chicago: Encyclopedia Britannica, 1952), 3.18.1.

models of the Reformation differed in many respects from those of the Eastern Fathers, Reformation theologians such as John Calvin and Peter Martyr Vermigli also defended dyothelitism for reasons closely associated with Christ's atoning work.[7] Within the Reformed tradition, the same trend continued through the post-Reformation period and into the nineteenth and twentieth centuries in the works of such Reformed luminaries as John Owen, Charles Hodge, William G. T. Shedd, and Thomas F. Torrance.[8]

The classic proof text for the dyothelite position is, of course, Jesus' prayer in Gethsemane: "Nevertheless not my will, but thine, be done" (Luke 22:42). Christian interpreters have often appealed to this passage, not only to defend the dyothelite position, but also to explain its particular soteriological utility: Christ assumes a human will precisely in order to overturn the consequences of sin and to "bend the will of man back into oneness with God," to cite Torrance's memorable phrase.[9]

This essay explores this important link between dyothelitism and the atonement. Its purpose is twofold. The primary aim is to suggest from both Scripture and the Christian tradition that dyothelitism undergirds the trinitarian, vicarious, and holistic nature of the "whole course" of Christ's obedience and every volitional act that comprises it.[10] A secondary purpose of this essay is to speak into contemporary debates over monothelitism. In recent decades, several theologians and philosophers have critiqued the church's dyothelite consensus and have sought to rehabilitate the monothelite position.[11] Operating from an "abstractist" understanding

---

7.   John Calvin, *A Commentary on A Harmony of the Evangelists: Matthew, Mark, and Luke*, trans. William Pringle, in *Calvin's Commentaries* (Grand Rapids: Baker, 2003), 3:233; idem., *Institutes of the Christian Religion*, ed. John T. McNeill, trans. Ford Lewis Battles (Louisville: Westminster John Knox, 1960), 2.16.12; Peter Martyr Vermigli, "Letter No. 267, To the Illustrous Polish Nobleman," cited in Torrance Kirby, Emidio Campi, and Frank A. James III, eds., *A Companion to Peter Martyr Vermigli* (Leiden: Brill, 2009), 331.

8.   John Owen, *Christologia*, vol. 1 in *The Works of John Owen*, ed. William H. Goold (Carlisle, PA: Banner of Truth, 1850–53), 15; William G. T. Shedd, *Dogmatic Theology*, 3rd ed., ed. Alan W. Gomes (Phillipsburg, NJ: P&R, 2003), 656–57; Thomas F. Torrance, *Incarnation: The Person and Life of Christ*, ed. Robert T. Walker (Downers Grove: InterVarsity, 2009), 212; idem., *Atonement: The Person and Work of Christ*, ed. Robert T. Walker (Downers Grove, IL: InterVarsity, 2009), 70.

9.   Torrance, *Incarnation*, 212.

10.   The language of the "whole course" of Christ's obedience comes from Calvin and figures prominently in Torrance's Christology as well. See Calvin, *Institutes*, 2.16.5; Torrance, *Incarnation*, 80–81.

11.   For example, see Alvin Plantinga, 'On Heresy, Mind, and Truth,' *Faith and Philosophy* 16, no. 2 (April 1999): 183–84; J. P. Moreland and William Lane Craig, *Philosophical Foundations for a Christian Worldview* (Downers Grove, IL: InterVarsity, 2003), 611–12; Garrett J. DeWeese, "One Person, Two Natures: Two Metaphysical Models of the Incarnation," in *Jesus in Trinitarian Perspective: An Introductory Christology*, eds. Fred Sanders and Klaus Issler (Nashville: B&H Academic, 2007), 114–53; Gordon R. Lewis and Bruce A. Demarest, *Integrative Theology*, 3 vols. (Grand Rapids: Zondervan, 1990–1996), 2:317.

of Christ's human nature and often from a kenotic model of the incarnation, these contemporary monothelites believe that the dyothelite position is demanded neither from Scripture nor from the Chalcedonian definition.[12] Indeed, according to these scholars, the dyothelite position risks Nestorianism by threatening the volitional unity of Christ's hypostasis.

This essay is not the place for a complete adjudication of these issues, but the retrieval of this particular rationale for dyothelitism (what we might call "the atonement rationale") may cast light on these contemporary debates over the volitional life of Christ. It may at least encourage proponents of monothelitism to consider how their own understanding of the incarnation can account for the full range of Christ's atoning work as the God-Man.

The essay will proceed in three steps: (1) a brief examination of the interpretive challenges posed by the Gethsemane Narrative, (2) some soundings in the history of interpretation, and (3) an attempt to draw some constructive conclusions from this scriptural and traditional material. These three steps correspond roughly to the triangulation of factors described by Marilyn McCord Adams in her discussion of medieval understandings of Christ's human nature: scriptural interpretation, systematic assumptions, and soteriological tasks.[13]

SCRIPTURAL INTERPRETATION: THE GETHSEMANE NARRATIVE

PRELIMINARY OBSERVATIONS

As mentioned above, the *locus classicus* for the monothelite/dyothelite debate is the Gethsemane Narrative, which is recorded in all three Synoptic Gospels (Matt 26:36–46; Mark 14:32–42; Luke 22:39–46). More specifically, the debate hinges on Jesus' prayer, "My Father, if it be possible,

---

12. In contemporary philosophical discussions of the incarnation, a distinction is sometimes made between transformational/abstractist models on the one hand and relational/concretist models on the other. In the former approach, the Son becomes incarnate by acquiring the abstract properties common to human nature, viewed as a universal. In the latter approach, the Son becomes incarnate by acquiring a certain relation to a specific human nature, viewed as a concrete particular. Alvin Plantinga seems to be the first to suggest this abstractist/concretist terminology, but the actual positions go back much further, perhaps even to the Council of Chalcedon itself. See Alvin Plantinga, "On Heresy, Mind, and Truth," *Faith and Philosophy* 16, no. 2 (April 1999): 182–93. See also Anna Marmodoro and Jonathan Hill, eds., *The Metaphysics of the Incarnation* (Oxford: Oxford University Press, 2011), 10–19. For a multi-disciplinary defense of kenoticism, see C. Stephen Evans, ed., *Exploring Kenotic Christology: The Self-Emptying God* (Oxford: Oxford University Press, 2006).

13. Marilyn McCord Adams, *What Sort of Human Nature? The Metaphysics and Systematics of Christology: The Aquinas Lecture, 1999* (Milwaukee: Marquette University Press, 1999). See also Adams, *Christ and Horrors: The Coherence of Christology* (Cambridge: Cambridge University Press, 2006), 55.

let this cup pass from me; nevertheless, not as I will, but as you will" (Matt 26:39 ESV). The discussion below will focus attention on Matthew's version of the Gethsemane Narrative, but before we get to this examination, a few preliminary observations are in order.

First, it is noteworthy that this single prayer brings together the two halves of this essay's subject matter: the will of Christ ("not as I will") and the atonement of Christ (the "cup" of Jesus' impending death). Christian interpreters have good reason, then, to argue that the volitional experience of Christ described in this passage has profound implications for the doctrine of the atonement.

Second, it is obvious that Jesus' will is contrasted here with the will of the Father, at least in some sense: "Not as I will, but as you will." As will be suggested below, how one understands the precise nature of this contrast is decided, at least in part, by factors that lie outside of this text—especially by theological convictions that interpreters bring to this text concerning the Trinity and the unity of the divine will. But at the outset, it must be admitted that some kind of contrast or tension between the will of the Father and the will of Christ is implied by the words of Jesus' prayer.

Third, and related, the Gethsemane Narrative cannot stand alone as a proof text for dyothelitism. The main theological/philosophical question under consideration in the monothelite debate is simply this: Do wills belong to persons or to natures? No single text can answer this complicated christological question. In Gethsemane, Jesus' will is clearly contrasted with his Father's. But the passage is still underdetermined when it comes to the number of Christ's wills. One could argue that wills belong to persons, and since there are two divine persons involved in the Gethsemane prayer (the Father and the Son), one would naturally expect to see a distinction of their personal wills. J. P. Moreland and William Lane Craig seem to suggest this kind of interpretation in their defense of monothelitism:

> Passages in the Gospels usually used as proof texts of this doctrine [i.e. dyothelitism]—such as Jesus' prayer in Gethsemane, "Yet, not my will but yours be done" (Lk. 22:42)—do not contemplate a struggle of Jesus' human will with his divine will (he is not, after all, talking to himself!), but have reference to the interaction between Jesus' will ("my will") and the Father's will ("yours"). Possessing a typical human consciousness, Jesus had to struggle against fear, weakness and temptation in order to align his will with that of his heavenly Father. The will of the Logos

had in virtue of the Incarnation become the will of the man Jesus of Nazareth.[14]

So, for Moreland and Craig, the Son possesses one will, which is distinct from the Father's, and this one will has, by virtue of the incarnation, been contracted to the limitations of Jesus' human consciousness. Moreland and Craig seem to be assuming that wills belong to persons, not natures. The Son is not talking to himself, after all. The will that is contrasted with Jesus' will is the Father's alone. The Son's will, like his person, is distinct from the Father's, and in his incarnate state it has taken on human properties, which make possible the kind of volitional tension we see in Gethsemane. On this account, one will in Christ would imply three wills in the Godhead and thus some version of social trinitarianism, an implication to which we will return in due course.[15]

A dyothelite reading, on the other hand, would argue that the "will" in view in the Gethsemane Narrative is the Son's *human* will, which is distinguished from the divine will of the Father. To be sure, on the dyothelite reading, the Son in his divinity also possesses this very same divine will, but this broader trinitarian point is not the issue under consideration in this text.[16] Instead, as Christian interpreters have always acknowledged, the Gethsemane Narrative is a deeply human account of Jesus' experience.

While we cannot divide or separate the natures of Christ, we can distinguish the attributes that belong properly to each. The traditional view has argued that Jesus' agonizing prayer in the garden reveals his human struggle at the prospect of his looming death.[17] The text shows how the Son's human will is perfectly conformed to the divine will. Though it is functionally one with the divine will, Christ's human will is ontologically

---

14. Moreland and Craig, *Philosophical Foundations*, 611. Jordan Wessling also explores how this "trithelitic" understanding of the divine nature could yield a "straightforwardly monothelitic" interpretation of Jesus' Gethsemane prayer. See Jordan Wessling, "Christology and Conciliar Authority: On the Viability of Monothelitism for Protestant Theology," in *Christology, Ancient and Modern: Explorations in Constructive Dogmatics*, ed. Oliver D. Crisp and Fred Sanders (Grand Rapids: Zondervan, 2013), 154.

15. So, it is no accident that monothelite Christologies often go hand-in-glove with social accounts of the Trinity. See, for example, Moreland and Craig, *Philosophical Foundations*, 575–88.

16. So, no, Christ is not talking to himself, as Moreland and Craig suggest the dyothelite interpretation implies. The person of the Son *in and through his human nature* is addressing the Father, who possesses the divine will. The fact that the Son also possesses the divine will is simply not addressed in this passage. It is an implication from other biblical and theological considerations regarding the unity of the divine nature.

17. Maximus the Confessor, *On the Cosmic Mystery of Christ*, trans. Paul M. Blowers and Robert Louis Wilken (Crestwood, NY: St. Vladimir's Seminary Press, 2003), 173–76; Aquinas, *Summa Theologica*, 3.18.1; John Calvin, *Commentary on a Harmony of the Evangelists, Matthew, Mark, and Luke*, trans. William Pringle, in *Calvin's Commentaries* (Grand Rapids: Baker, 2003), 17:233.

distinct and must undergo a trial of conformity to the divine will. In the words of Hebrews, "Although he was a Son, he learned obedience through what he suffered; and being made perfect he became the source of eternal salvation to all who obey him" (Heb 5:8–9).[18]

MATTHEW'S GETHSEMANE NARRATIVE

But the question remains: Are there any clues in the Gethsemane Narrative itself that point in the direction of the dyothelite interpretation? Once again, a final determination must take into account theological factors that lie outside of this single text, but we can at least discern in the Gethsemane Narrative a strong emphasis on the humanity of Christ and, especially relevant for the purposes of this essay, on the representative nature of Christ's suffering. If we adopt the rule of Gregory of Nazianzus—that some texts speak of the Son of God as such and others of the Son in his incarnate and mediatorial role—then we would no doubt place the Gethsemane Narrative in the latter category.[19]

Focusing on Matthew's version of the Gethsemane Narrative, two lines of evidence suggest that it is Jesus' uniquely human experience that is in view in this passage. First, the literary connections between Matthew's Gethsemane Narrative and Matthew's account of the Lord's Prayer (Matt 6:7–15) suggest that Jesus' representative (and thus fully human) role is in view in Gethsemane. As commentators have noted, there are several verbal parallels between the "Lord's Prayer" in Matthew 6 and the Lord's prayer in Matthew 26: "our/my Father" (Matt 6:9; 26:39, 42); "into temptation" (Matt 6:13; 26:41); and "your will be done" (Matt 6:10; 26:42).[20] Thus, the Lord takes upon his own lips the prayer that he taught his disciples. He is the Son of the Father *par excellence*. Through agonizing prayer, Jesus' human will was perfectly conformed to the Father's will.

This exemplary and representative role seems to require a human will for its accomplishment. To cite Hebrews, "He had to be made like his brothers in every respect, so that he might become a merciful and faith-

---

18. This Hebrews text seems to have the Gethsemane Narrative in view. On the parallels, see Raymond E. Brown, *The Death of the Messiah: From Gethsemane to the Grave; A Commentary on the Passion Narratives in the Four Gospels* (New York: Doubleday, 1994), 227–34, cited in R. T. France, *The Gospel of Matthew*, NICNT (Grand Rapids: Eerdmans, 2007), 1,002.

19. "What is lofty you are to apply to the Godhead, and to that nature in him which is superior to sufferings and incorporeal; but all that is lowly to the composite condition of him who for your sakes made himself of no reputation and was incarnate." Gregory of Nazianzus, "Third Theological Oration," in Hardy, *Christology of the Later Fathers*, 173.

20. W. D. Davies and Dale C. Allison, Jr., *Matthew 19–28*, ICC (London: T&T Clark, 1997), 497.

ful high priest in the service of God, to make propitiation for the sins of the people" (Heb 2:17 ESV). Here, we have our thesis in short order: the Son's reconciling work ("propitiation for the sins of the people") seems to require the Son's assumption of all that it means to be human, including a human will ("like his brothers in every respect").

Second, the high drama of the Gethsemane Narrative itself also points in the direction of Jesus' human representative role. Jesus is presented as more than an exemplary sufferer in this text. He is also presented as the representative, indeed the substitute, of God's people. In the garden, the disciples sleep while Jesus is praying the prayer he taught them to pray (Matt 26:40, 44). He alone watches and prays. He alone is wholly committed to the petition, "Thy will be done." He alone is the obedient Son of the Father. Jesus' prayer in Gethsemane is, in a sense, a dramatic enactment of his substitutionary work. Christ's passion begins in the garden: he suffers while his followers sleep. A few chapters earlier, James and John had promised that they could share in his "cup" of suffering (Matt 20:22), but in the final hour Jesus alone must drink the cup of God's wrath in their place (Matt 26:39, 42).[21]

Perhaps the garden setting further illustrates this representative work. Adam disobeyed in a garden of paradise; the Last Adam obeyed in a garden of agony.[22] All of this substitutionary evidence only makes sense if Christ can truly stand in the place of Adam, Israel, and the disciples.[23] We can state the matter as follows: Christ *wills* salvation through a human *will* in the place of human *wills*—in spite of the agony that this choice produces. Some kind of human volitional equipment seems necessary in order for him to serve as an adequate substitute in this manner. In short, volitional function implies volitional ontology. Christ can will and act as a human representative only because he has assumed human volitional equipage. What this means for Christ's ongoing relation to the divine will remains to be seen, but it seems clear that Matthew wishes to portray Jesus as the human representative and substitute for his faltering disciples.

---

21. The Old Testament background to the "cup" (ποτήριον) language in v. 39 strongly suggests a penal substitutionary interpretation of this text. See especially Isaiah 51:17, "Wake yourself, wake yourself, stand up, O Jerusalem, you who have drunk from the hand of the Lord the cup (LXX, ποτήριον) of his wrath, who have drunk to the dregs the bowl, the cup of staggering." For an argument along these lines, see Steve Jeffery, Michael Ovey, Andrew Sach, *Pierced for Our Transgressions: Rediscovering the Glory of Penal Substitution* (Wheaton: Crossway, 2007), 68–70.

22. Such a reading could find inspiration in St. Irenaeus, *The Demonstration of the Apostolic Preaching*, 34, trans. J. Armitage Robinson (London: SPCK, 1920), 100–102.

23. This emphasis on Jesus' representative role runs throughout Matthew's gospel. For a brief but excellent treatment of Matthew's Israel-Jesus typology, see R. T. France, *Matthew: Evangelist and Teacher* (Eugene, OR: Wipf & Stock, 1989), 207–10.

SYSTEMATIC ASSUMPTIONS: SOUNDINGS IN THE HISTORY OF INTERPRETATION

For theologians committed to showing deference to the Christian tradition, there is a sense in which the whole history of orthodoxy functions as a set of systematic assumptions for the task of contemporary theologizing. This is especially true with regard to the ecumenical councils of the church and the exegetical and theological consensus that they represent. When it comes to the Gethsemane Narrative, the history of interpretation bears out the vicarious reading sketched above, and when this interpretation is coupled with the traditional understanding of the unity of the divine will, it yields the conciliar two-wills position.

In other words, the dyothelite model of the incarnation is built in two steps, as it were. The first step involves interpreting the Gethsemane Narrative in the manner suggested above: in Gethsemane, it is the human nature, not the divine nature, that is underscored in Jesus' volitional struggle. The second step involves certain trinitarian assumptions that are brought to the interpretation of this text. Specifically, they are assumptions concerning the unity of the divine will: because the divine will inheres in the divine nature, the three trinitarian persons each share in a numerically singular will. Both halves of this dyothelite equation can be seen in the historical survey that follows. Three representative figures are explored: Maximus the Confessor, John Calvin, and Thomas F. Torrance.

MAXIMUS THE CONFESSOR

Though there were dyothelite precursors in the centuries prior to the monothelite controversy,[24] we begin with Maximus, since he stands at the fountainhead of the medieval dyothelite tradition.[25] Regarding the Gethsemane Narrative, Maximus writes,

> Therefore, in his natural capacity, the Saviour is distinguished as a human being, willing in a fleshly way the shrinking in the face of death together with the rest of the passions, showing the economy to be pure of fantasy,

---

24. Dyothelitic tendencies predated the monothelite controversy by several centuries. At the risk of anachronism, we might describe several Fathers of the first four centuries (including Irenaeus, Origen, Gregory of Nazianzus, and Augustine) as proto-dyothelites. As Cyril Hovorun has shown, there were monothelite precursors in the centuries preceding the seventh-century controversies, so it should be no surprise to discover that there were dyothelite precursors as well. Hovorun, *Will, Action, and Freedom,* 5–51.

25. On the life and theology of Maximus, see Demtrios Bathrellos, *The Byzantine Christ: Person, Nature, and Will in the Christology of Saint Maximus the Confessor* (Oxford: Oxford University Press, 2004); and Andrew Louth, *Maximus the Confessor* (London: Routledge, 1996).

and redeeming the nature from the passions to which it has been condemned as a result of sin.[26]

A couple of things are worthy of note here. First, Maximus believes that the Son's assumption of a human will is necessary for *the genuineness of his incarnation*. In order for God's redemptive economy to be "pure of fantasy," the Son had to assume the capacity to will in a "fleshly way," that is, the capacity to experience ordinary (and non-sinful, we should add) human passions.[27] Second, Maximus believes that the Son's assumption of a human will is necessary for *the effectiveness of his redeeming work*. Christ's experience in Gethsemane not only shows the genuineness of his human volition, but it also highlights his redemption of fallen human volition.

Maximus goes on to say that Christ "shows his eager desire, putting death to death in the flesh, in order that he might show as a human being that what is natural is saved in himself, and that he might demonstrate, as God, the Father's *great* and ineffable *purpose*, fulfilled in the body." So Christ's work of redemption must be understood in a twofold manner corresponding to his two natures and two wills. Through his human will, Christ saves fallen human volition from the inside out, as it were. And through his divine will, Christ demonstrates the united purpose of the Godhead to redeem humanity through the incarnation and passion of Christ.

For Maximus, there can be no distinction of wills between two divine persons. Wills belong to natures, not persons, after all; and since there is only one divine nature, there can be only one divine will. Indeed, in his disputation with Pyrrhus, Maximus makes precisely this trinitarian argument against monothelitism. If a "willer"—that is, a person or hypostasis—requires a distinct will, then one of two trinitarian heresies would follow. Either there is only one willer in the Godhead and we are left with Sabellian modalism, or else there are three wills in the Godhead and we risk Arianism (or tritheism).[28]

In another place, Maximus highlights the Adamic task of Christ that required his assumption of a human will. Maximus argues that since the will was the first human faculty to succumb to sinful passion, then the will must also be the locus of sin's undoing. He then cites Gregory's axiom and applies it to the human will: "So, if according to [the monothelites] the Word when He became incarnate did not have this [faculty of will] along

---

26. Maximus, *Opuscule 3*, in Louth, *Maximus*, 197.
27. For Maximus, while the Son possesses a discrete human will, he does not possess a "gnomic will," that is, a will inclined against the divine will by virtue of sin and ignorance. Farrell, *Disputation*, 29–32.
28. Farrell, *Disputation*, 5–6.

with the nature, then I shall never be set free from sin. And if I cannot be freed from sin, then I have not been saved, since what is not assumed is not healed."[29] Thus, Maximus lays the biblical and theological groundwork for the subsequent dyothelite tradition, arguing for the two-wills position on both soteriological and trinitarian grounds.

JOHN CALVIN

Maximus's dyothelite reading of the Gethsemane Narrative was echoed throughout the medieval period and into the Reformation era as well. John Calvin's interpretation is representative in this regard. In his commentary on the Gethsemane Narrative, Calvin explicitly addresses the monothelite heresy. Especially relevant is his exposition of Jesus' prayer, "Yet not my will, but thine be done" (Luke 22:42 par.):

> This passage shows plainly enough the gross folly of those ancient heretics, who were called *Monothelites*, because they imagined that the will of Christ was but one and simple; for Christ, as he was God, *willed* nothing different from the Father; and therefore, it follows, that his human soul had affections distinct from the secret purpose of God.[30]

Calvin's logic seems to be as follows:

Premise 1: Christ *qua* divine possesses the same will as the Father.

Premise 2: Christ's prayer in Gethsemane indicates that he possesses a will distinct from the Father.

Conclusion: Therefore, Christ must have assumed a human will, in addition to his divine will, when he assumed a human soul; that is, Christ *qua* human possesses a will distinct from the Father.

According to Calvin, Christ "as he was God" cannot will anything different from the Father. This assumption is absolutely critical for Calvin; the persons of the Godhead share an identical will.[31] The logic of the

---

29. Ibid., 46.

30. John Calvin, *A Commentary on A Harmony of the Evangelists: Matthew, Mark, and Luke*, trans. William Pringle, in *Calvin's Commentaries* (Grand Rapids: Baker, 2003), 3:233.

31. Perhaps one could interpret Calvin minimalistically here. That is, perhaps Calvin is merely saying that the divine persons share a common *functional* will—a common purpose or plan. In this interpretation, social trinitarianism would be still a Reformed possibility; Calvin has left open the possibility that the divine persons possess distinct *ontological* wills as a part of their distinct personhood. But this Social Trinitarian interpretation does not seem to fit the evidence. Calvin moves seamlessly between talking about "the will of Christ" and the act of Christ's willing. In other words, it seems that, for Calvin, a Triune volitional function demands a Triune volitional ontology. Christ's will is not "one and simple" because he shares the numerically same will as the Father and has taken to himself a distinct human will. Furthermore, in a social trinitarian interpretation of Calvin, there would have to be four wills, rather than merely two, in the field of play: the three divine wills and the distinct human will of Christ. Ockham's razor would seem to be helpful in this complicated scheme.

monothelites—that wills belong to persons, not natures—when pushed back into the Trinity would demand three distinct wills within the Godhead. This notion is unthinkable for Calvin.

But just as crucial for Calvin is the assumption that Christ possesses a will distinct from the Father. Otherwise, how could he pray this conflicted prayer in Gethsemane? If the Son's will is in some sense distinct from the will of the Father, as is implied in the Gethsemane narrative, then it must be the Son's *human* will that is in view. Hence, for Calvin, the Son possesses two distinct wills united in his one person.

Calvin also addresses Jesus' Gethsemane experience in the *Institutes of the Christian Religion*, where he writes of the Gethsemane Narrative,

> Now this refutes the error of Apollinaris, as well as that of the so-called Monothelites. Apollinaris claimed that Christ had an eternal spirit instead of a soul, so that he was only half a man. As if he could atone for our sins in any other way than by obeying the Father! But where is inclination or will to obey except in the soul? We know that it was for this reason that his soul was troubled: to drive away fear and bring peace and repose to our souls. Against the Monothelites, we see that he did not will as man what he willed according to his divine nature. I pass over the fact that, with a contrary emotion, he overcame the fear of which we have spoken. This plainly appears to be a great paradox: "Father, save me from this hour? No, for this purpose I have come to this hour. Father glorify thy name" [John 12:27–28]. Yet in his perplexity there was no extravagant behavior such as is seen in us when we strive mightily to control ourselves.[32]

Note that Calvin draws a parallel between Apollinarianism and monothelitism. Calvin explicitly places "inclination" and "will" at the level of the human soul. For Calvin, wills belong to natures, not persons. More specifically, human wills belong to human souls, and Christ must have assumed both in order to carry out his redemptive mission. Atonement and reconciliation demand the Son's assumption of a complete human nature: body and soul, inclination and will.

THOMAS F. TORRANCE
Finally, we turn our attention to the twentieth-century Scottish Reformed theologian Thomas F. Torrance. In many ways, Torrance is reliably Calvinistic in his Christology, but his defense of dyothelitism is refracted

---

32. Calvin, *Institutes*, 2.16.12.

through his own idiosyncrasies, as it were, especially his understanding of Christ's vicarious humanity and fallen flesh.

> But again, unless we take seriously at this point the fact that Christ assumed our will, the will of estranged man in estranged adamic human nature, in order to suffer all its temptations and to resist them and condemn sin in our human nature, and then to bend the will of man back into oneness with the divine will, it is difficult to give the temptations of Christ their due place. It is difficult therefore to give the human obedience of Christ, in struggle against the onslaught of evil and sin, its full and proper place in atoning reconciliation. If Christ assumed neutral or perfect human nature, and assumed it into oneness with his own divine person who could not choose to sin any more than he could choose not to be God, then the humanity of Christ is merely instrumental in the hands of God. But if so, then salvation is only an act of God done upon us and for us, and not also a real human act done in our place and issuing out of our humanity.[33]

Following Edward Irving and Karl Barth, Torrance argues that Christ assumed a fallen human nature.[34] To be sure, Christ is sinless, but he is not unfallen. He assumed the form of human nature possessed by those he came to save, namely, corrupted human nature. "If it were otherwise," Barth asks, "how could Christ really be like us?"[35]

For those committed to a more Western understanding of original sin, the idea that Christ could assume a fallen human nature and yet remain free from culpability is untenable.[36] But even theologians who would balk at Torrance's "fallen flesh" proposal can still appreciate what we might call his Gregorian logic: Christ must assume all that it means to be a human precisely in order to redeem and restore fallen humanity. The unassumed is unredeemed, and this applies equally to the human will of Christ as to his human soul.

SOTERIOLOGICAL TASKS: CONSTRUCTING A DYOTHELITE MODEL OF THE ATONEMENT

Having briefly considered the interpretive issues surrounding the Gethsemane Narrative and some representative readings from the his-

---

33. Torrance, *Incarnation*, 212.
34. Edward Irving, *The Collected Writings of Edward Irving*, 5 vols., ed. G. Carlyle (London: Alexander Strahan, 1865), 5:114–46; Karl Barth, *Church Dogmatics*, 4 vols. (Edinburgh: T&T Clark, 1956–1975) I/2: 153.
35. Barth, *Church Dogmatics*, I/2:153.
36. For a critique of the fallen flesh position, see Oliver Crisp, *Divinity and Humanity: The Incarnation Reconsidered* (Cambridge: Cambride University Press, 2007), 90–117.

tory of interpretation, we now seek to draw some conclusions at a more constructive level. Much remains to be said, especially in response to the challenges posed to the traditional view by contemporary monothelite proposals, but the following three propositions are offered in an attempt to sketch out the basic contours of a contemporary dyothelite model of the atonement.

TRINITARIAN INTENTION

Proposition 1: Dyothelitism is necessary for the atonement because it preserves the unity of trinitarian operations in the economy of redemption.

On a dyothelite model of the incarnation, there can be no tension between the will of the Father and the will of the Son when it comes to the divine plan of redemption. Indeed, there can be no *distinction* between the will of the Father and the will of the Son in this regard. The divine will, like the divine nature in which it inheres, is numerically singular. All three divine persons immutably will the same redemptive purpose. It is only by virtue of the incarnation, and the Son's assumption of a finite but unfallen human will, that the incarnate Christ can experience a genuine volitional trial and painful choice of the cross.

As argued above, the Gethsemane Narrative taken alone is underdetermined when it comes to the monothelite controversy. We must bring other biblical and theological considerations to bear on our interpretation of this text in order to make a determination about the number of wills in the incarnate Christ. The most important of these considerations is trinitarian in nature. Is the Trinity trithelitic or monothelitic? Are there three wills in the Godhead or one? If one assumes, with the majority Christian tradition, the unity of the divine will, the Gethsemane Narrative serves rather straightforwardly as evidence for the Son's assumption of a discrete human will.[37] If, on the other hand, one assumes a three-willed Godhead, then the passage would be taken, again rather straightforwardly, as evidence for a distinction of personal wills between the first and second persons. As Jordan Wessling has argued, perhaps both of these interpretive options are responsible ways of dealing with the passage.[38]

But consider for a moment what the latter interpretation would entail for the volitional life of the Godhead. Can it be the case that there exists a real, existential conflict between two divine wills? How could such a view

---

37. On the unity of the divine will in the pro-Nicene Fathers, see Khaled Anatolios, *Retrieving Nicaea: The Development and Meaning of Trinitarian Doctrine* (Grand Rapids: Baker, 2011), 41–78.
38. Wessling, "Christology and Conciliar Authority," 155–56.

be reconciled with the unity of the Godhead? Even the strongest versions of social trinitarianism identify the unity of the Godhead as a unity of purpose, with some kind of perichoretic activity preserving the union.[39] But on a monothelitic understanding of Gethsemane, one has to assume that for a moment in time (and perhaps others besides, during Christ's state of humiliation), this unity of purpose was threatened or suspended in the experience of the incarnate Christ. So, while the monothelitic-Christ/trithelitic-Trinity view can provide a defensible interpretation of the Gethsemane Narrative, it does so at a high trinitarian cost.

In any event it seems that dyothelitism provides us with a ready-made metaphysical mechanism by which we can affirm both the divine act of redemption in Christ and the human obedience of Christ without diminishing either or collapsing one into the other. Dyothelitism preserves both sides of the Christological coin, so to speak. It preserves what we might call the unity of trinitarian *intentions* as well as the appropriation of human suffering to the incarnate Son alone.[40] Dyothelitism enables us to affirm, on the one hand, the undivided intention of the Trinity to save a people through the death of the Son and, on the other, the reality of Christ's genuine human struggle and vicarious obedience in the face of trial and temptation. Monothelitism, by contrast, seems to demand some kind of kenotic understanding of Christ's Gethsemane experience, in which the Son's numerically singular will has undergone a transformation that makes possible his temptation in the face of death.

Whatever the merits of kenotic Christology as a coherent Christological model, the Gethsemane Narrative at least points up a potential weakness. If the Son has but one will, which has been contracted to the limitations of human experience, then it seems that he has given up more than a few nonessential divine attributes, and he may have surrendered volitional oneness with the Father as well. This is not to suggest that monothelites posit a final, functional dissonance between the wills of the

---

39. On the different versions of social trinitarianism, see Brian Leftow, "Anti-Social Trinitarianism," in *The Trinity: An Interdisciplinary Symposium on the Trinity*, ed. Stephen T. Davis, Daniel Kendall, and Gerald O'Collins (Oxford: Oxford University Press, 1999), 203–49. For a more recent discussion of classical versus social/relational models of the Trinity, see Jason Sexton, ed., *Two Views on the Doctrine of the Trinity* (Grand Rapids: Zondervan, 2014).

40. The traditional doctrine of inseparable operations would seem to imply inseparable intentions. St. Augustine provides the classic expression of the unity of trinitarian operations: "[A]ccording to the Catholic faith, the Trinity is proposed to our belief and believed—and even understood by a few saints and holy persons—as so inseparable that whatever action is performed by it must be thought to be performed at the same time by the Father and by the Son and by the Holy Spirit." See Augustine, Ep. 11.2, translation from Lewis Ayres, *Augustine and the Trinity* (Cambridge: Cambridge University Press, 2010), 59–60.

Father and the Son, but they do introduce a real distinction between the divine wills, which at least places strain upon the unity of the Godhead.[41] Dyothelitism avoids these trinitarian problems by locating the distinction of wills in Gethsemane in the two natures of the incarnate Son.

ADAMIC ROLES

Proposition 2: Dyothelitism is necessary for the atonement because it underscores Christ's Adamic work of recapitulation and representation.

Dyothelitism enables contemporary theologians to give a full-throated affirmation of the genuineness of Christ's volitional struggle at the prospects of his impending death and of the saving significance of his obedience as the Last Adam, without the trinitarian problems introduced by monothelitism. Because he possesses two wills, one divine and one human, Christ can function as both Lord and Servant in the covenant of grace, to use the traditional Reformed categories.[42] Christ is, at once, the Lord who commands and the human covenant partner who obeys. His assumption of a distinct human will underscores this Adamic work.

Irenaeus, of course, is the theologian most commonly identified with the theme of Adamic recapitulation, but this theme is also picked up by Gregory of Nazianzus and Maximus the Confessor, among others.[43] Maximus explicitly connects Christ's human volition to his Adamic work. If the human will of the first Adam was instrumental at sin's inception, then the human will of the Last Adam must be engaged in sin's defeat. Christ's assumption of a human will, with all of its weaknesses and passions, makes his work of redemption and recapitulation possible.

Calvin and Torrance also highlight the representational implications of the Son's assumption of a human will. Calvin was concerned to show that Christ assumed a complete human nature, including a human soul equipped with a human will, in order to atone for sin. Torrance's burden was to demonstrate that Christ assumed humanity as it actually stands, with all of the horrors of fallen existence, in order to bend the will of fallen humanity back into oneness with God. For these Reformed theologians, Christ's work as the federal representative of his people cannot

---

41. If the Son's will has taken on human properties by virtue of the incarnation, then it cannot be identical with the will of the Father, since the Father's will does not possess those human properties. But again, if wills belong to persons, then this distinction would have predated the incarnation anyway. Eternal personal distinctions would imply eternal volitional distinctions.

42. Michael Horton, *Lord and Servant: A Covenant Christology* (Louisville: WJK, 2005).

43. On the theme of recapitulation in Irenaeus, see Eric Osborn, *Irenaeus of Lyons* (Cambridge: Cambridge University Press, 2004), 97–140.

be fulfilled if he is lacking human volition. These recapitulative and representational themes demand the Son's assumption of a human will. In other words, these soteriological tasks require human volitional equipage for their execution.

But how might proponents of monothelitism answer these kinds of objections? Perhaps they could argue that since wills inhere in persons, not natures, nothing is lost if the Son does not assume a human will. After all, no one who affirms the doctrine of anhypostasis would argue that the Son's failure to assume a distinct human person constitutes a deficiency in his incarnation.[44] The Son brings his own person to the table, so to speak, when he assumes an anhypostatic human nature. According to the doctrine of enhypostasis, the human nature of Christ receives its personhood in the person of the Son. This fact in no way detracts from the Son's full humanity. Similarly, monothelitism could argue that the Son's failure to assume a distinct human will does not detract from his full humanity. In other words, they could argue for the *antheletic* nature of Christ's human nature; it is "without a will" (*thelēma*), just as it is "without a person." Likewise, they could argue for an *entheletic* human nature of Christ; his human nature receives its will in the will of the Son.

Aside from the trinitarian problems that this monothelitic redefinition of "nature" and "person" creates,[45] it is also unclear how this position can account for the ways in which the Scriptures speak of the will of Christ vis-à-vis his redemptive work. The Gethsemane Narrative seems to highlight the humanity, not the divinity, of the incarnate Christ in his volitional struggle. The same truth is implied in the book of Hebrews. It was precisely as a human that Christ learned obedience through what he suffered (Heb 5:8). It was through a human nature fashioned by God that he "came to do" the will of God (Heb 10:7). These passages cannot prove the dyothelite position beyond doubt, but they do seem to connect Jesus' volitional obedience to the humanity that he assumed rather than to his essential divinity.

Furthermore, if the incarnate Christ possesses only one will, then what kind of will is it? Is it a divine will? If so, how could he serve as an adequate representative for human wills? Wouldn't this leave us with a kind

---

44. The anhypostasis/enhypostasis distinction, rooted in the thought of Leontius of Byzantium (d. 543), is especially prominent in Torrance's Christology. See, for example, Torrance, *Incarnation*, 84, 105, 228–32. It was prominent in Barth's thought as well. For more on Barth's use of these terms, see Paul Dafydd Jones, *The Humanity of Christ: Christology in Karl Barth's Church Dogmatics* (Edinburgh: T&T Clark, 2008), 23–25.

45. To restate, defining the will out of the nature and into the person, so to speak, entails that there are three wills in the Godhead.

of volitional Apollinarianism, in which the will of the Son replaces the human will of Christ? Or perhaps in the incarnation the will of the Son is transformed into a human will. The will of the Son does not so much *replace* the human will as it *becomes* a human will, by taking on a certain set of human properties. This seems to be the kind of move that Alvin Plantinga makes in his defense of an "abstractist" understanding of Christ's human nature.[46] On this understanding of the incarnation, the person of the Son simply acquired a new set of abstract properties that enabled him to will and act as a human without necessarily surrendering his ability to will and act as God.

But wouldn't this position suggest a kind of hybrid divine-human will? In this case, wouldn't we be left with a kind of volitional Eutychianism, in which the will of the incarnate Christ is neither human nor divine but a kind of *tertium quid*? These Christological problems can be avoided on a dyothelite model. In the dyothelite scheme, the Son retains his divine will, which he shares eternally with the Father and the Spirit, and in the incarnation he assumes a discrete human will, on account of which he is adequately suited to serve as a representative and substitute for fallen humanity.

HOLISTIC REDEMPTION

Proposition 3: Dyothelitism is necessary for the atonement because it undergirds the entirety of Christ's obedience and not merely his atoning death, narrowly construed.

In their own distinctive ways, Maximus, Calvin, and Torrance all asserted the saving significance of what Calvin called the "whole course" of Christ's obedience. The Son's assumption of a distinct human will undergirds this holistic understanding of Christ's obedience because it infuses every volitional act of the incarnate Christ with redemptive meaning. As such, a dyothelite model of the atonement holds promise for bringing together several realities that are often dichotomized.

First, dyothelitism brings the incarnation and the atonement into closer relation. As Torrance argued, Christ's work of atonement began the moment he was conceived in the Virgin's womb. The incarnation itself has saving significance. Christ's assumption of human nature already begins the work of reconciliation. More to the point, Christ's assumption of a human will already begins the work of redeeming and healing fallen

---

46. Plantinga, "On Heresy, Mind, and Truth," 182–88. Oliver Crisp points out that one of the potential weaknesses of the abstractist view is that it entails monothelitism, against the findings of an ecumenical council. See Crisp, *Divinity and Humanity*, 34–71.

human volition. Even for those wary of the universalistic tendencies of Torrance's (and Barth's) understanding of Christ's vicarious humanity,[47] the idea that the incarnation itself has saving significance can help to overcome a dichotomy between incarnation and atonement, even between participatory and forensic notions of redemption.[48] The incarnation is not merely preparatory for Christ's work of atonement; it is itself a constitutive part of that atoning work.

Second, dyothelitism also draws a closer connection between Christ's active and passive obedience. These traditional Reformed categories seek to account for the biblical testimony that Christ's life as well as his death has redemptive meaning. Christ came to fulfill all righteousness (Matt 3:15). He was born under the law in order to redeem those under the law (Gal 4:4–5). His obedience as the Last Adam reverses the cursed effects of the first Adam (Rom 5:19). In another context, N. T. Wright has accused the ancient creeds of undervaluing the life and vocation of Jesus in that they move directly from his virgin birth to his suffering and death.[49] Whatever we might say in defense of the creeds on this point, it is clear that traditional Reformed Christology cannot be accused of eliding the life of Christ. Calvin himself sums up this Reformed emphasis well:

> Now someone asks, How has Christ abolished sin, banished the separation between us and God, and acquired righteousness to render God favorable and kindly toward us? To this we can in general reply that he has achieved this for us by the whole course of his obedience.... In short, from the time when he took on the form of a servant, he began to pay the price of liberation in order to redeem us.[50]

Christ's active and passive obedience, however, should never have been seen as separable parts in his work of redemption. Instead, they should be seen as aspects of an integrated whole. Dyothelitism can do some of the heavy lifting in this integration. Because Christ has assumed a human will, his every act of obedience is vicarious in nature, from his obedience to the will of the Father as a child to his Spirit-filled ministry all the way to his surrender in Gethsemane and his subsequent passion. Furthermore, dyo-

---

47. On the question of Barth's alleged universalism, see Oliver Crisp, "On Barth's Denial of Universalism," *Themelios* 29, no. 1 (2003): 18–29.

48. Michael Horton puts forward the Reformed doctrine of union with Christ as a means of integrating forensic and participatory soteriological themes. Michael S. Horton, *Covenant and Salvation: Union with Christ* (Louisville: WJK, 2007).

49. N. T. Wright, *How God Became King: The Forgotten Story of the Gospels* (New York: Harper One, 2012), 10–20.

50. Calvin, *Institutes*, 2.16.5.

thelitism also undergirds his redemptive work on the other side of death. The redemptive significance of Christ's human volition applies equally to his state of exaltation as to his state of humiliation. So even in his resurrection, ascension, session, intercession, and parousia, Christ remains fallen humanity's volitional representative.[51]

Finally, dyothelitism may also help to overcome dichotomies between various models of the atonement.[52] When emphasis is placed upon Christ's volitional representation on behalf of his people, there is no need to choose between the substitutionary and victorious aspects of his work of atonement. He dies in the place of his drowsy disciples, drinking the cup of God's wrath as their representative and substitute. But he also does battle with their enemies, watching and praying as he faces the Tempter's worst assaults. Thus, as both vicar and victor Christ rises from the garden ready to complete the task before him and to exercise his human volition in the furtherance of human redemption.

CONCLUSION

The unassumed is unhealed. Maximus the Confessor believed that Gregory's axiom applied as much to the will as it did to the soul or mind of human nature. Maximus and the broader dyothelite tradition maintained that the Son's assumption of a human will is necessary for his atoning work. Only if Christ is equipped with human volition can he overturn the disastrous effects of sin that were unleashed on the world through human volition. Because of the unity of the divine will, any volitional tension that the incarnate Son experienced in relation to the Father can only be explained in terms of his incarnation.

But even then, his human will is only ontologically distinct from, never finally or functionally in conflict with, the divine will. As humanity's representative and substitute, Christ renders obedience to the divine will through a human will in order to redeem and heal those with cursed and corrupted human wills. Dyothelitism helps to preserve the unity of trinitarian intention in the death of the Son, the Adamic tasks that Christ came to fulfill, and the holistic nature of his redeeming work.

---

51. For a helpful and comprehensive biblical treatment of each phase in Christ's work, see Robert A. Peterson, *Salvation Accomplished by the Son: The Work of Christ* (Wheaton: Crossway, 2011).

52. For a window into the contemporary debate over atonement models, see James Beilby, ed., *The Nature of the Atonement: Four Views* (Downers Grove, IL: InterVarsity, 2006); and David Tidball, David Hilborn, and Justin Thacker, eds., *The Atonement Debate: Papers from the London Symposium on the Theology of the Atonement* (Grand Rapids: Zondervan, 2008).

Perhaps monothelitism can explain these realities by recourse to an "abstractist" understanding of Christ's human nature. In other words, monothelitism may wish to explain that the will of the Son becomes the will of Jesus of Nazareth by assuming the properties of human volition and that through these properties he accomplishes human redemption. But for those who are committed to the unity of the divine will and who are wary of transformational and kenotic approaches to the incarnation, this abstractist understanding of Christ's Gethsemane experience comes at too high a trinitarian and Christological cost.

Dyothelitism seems better equipped to explain both the divine intention and the human obedience of the incarnate Son in his work of atonement.

CHAPTER 7

ATONEMENT AND THE CONCEPT OF PUNISHMENT

Daniel J. Hill and Joseph Jedwab

INTRODUCTION

In a broad sense, *atonement* refers to the state or condition of being at one or reconciled. In a narrower sense, it refers to the means by which such reconciliation is achieved. In Christian theology, this narrower sense of atonement refers to Christ's sacrificial act by which such reconciliation between God and humans is achieved. Our sin creates an obstacle to right relationship with God. Christ's sacrifice is (at least) part of the means whereby God removes this obstacle to such right relationship. There are, however, different theories as to how Christ's sacrifice does this.

The penal-substitutionary theory of the atonement (PSA[1]) says that we deserve punishment for our sin, but instead of punishing us, God[2] imposes a punishment on Christ for our sin. PSA finds its basis in a number of texts from the Bible. One is Isaiah 53:4–5:

> Surely he took up our pain and bore our suffering, yet we considered him punished by God, stricken by him, and afflicted. But he was pierced for our transgressions, he was crushed for our iniquities; the punishment that brought us peace was on him, and by his wounds we are healed (NIV).

---

1. We shall use "PSA" as an abbreviation for "the doctrine of penal-substitutionary atonement" rather than simply for "penal-substitutionary atonement"
2. When we write "God," we shall omit the qualification "(or God the Father)."

This text is picked up in the New Testament and explicitly applied to Christ in 1 Peter 2:24 (NIV):

> "He himself bore our sins" in his body on the cross, so that we might die to sins and live for righteousness; "by his wounds you have been healed."

Defenders of PSA have typically said that these texts teach that Christ's sufferings and death on the cross were laid or imposed on him by God. God may have imposed them on Christ for many different reasons, but, according to the defender of PSA, one reason is penal in nature.

There are many different possible versions of PSA. One line of difference concerns whether Christ substitutes for a group (the church) collectively or for that group distributively, i.e., for each and every member of that group. Another line of difference concerns whether he substitutes (collectively or distributively) for a definite number of individuals, the view known as "definite atonement," or whether he substitutes (again, collectively or distributively) for an indefinite number of individuals, the view known as "general atonement." A further line of difference concerns whether Christ takes *all* the punishment due to those for whom he substitutes or only *some* of the punishment due to them. Yet another line of difference concerns whether those for whom Christ substitutes are said to be punished "in" Christ (or "in" his punishment), or not.

We shall not comment further on these differences, but now turn our attention to one final line of difference, whether Christ is punished by God or not. Here we find three views: what we shall call "the strong version," that God did indeed punish Christ; "the weak version," that God judicially imposed suffering (but in lieu of punishment, rather than as punishment) on Christ;[3] and "the intermediate version," that God imposed punishment on Christ, even though God did not punish Christ. We shall list some of the historical sources for these views in an appendix at the end.

In this paper we propose to defend the strong version of PSA against the conceptual argument as deployed in Mark Murphy's article "Not Penal Substitution but Vicarious Punishment."[4] The conceptual argument concludes that PSA is conceptually confused, and it derives this conclusion from the concept of punishment itself. While the moral argument may tell equally against all versions of PSA, the conceptual argument does not tell

---

3. NB that it is necessary that the suffering be *judicially* inflicted in order for this theory to be a version of PSA.
4. Mark C. Murphy, "Not Penal Substitution but Vicarious Punishment," *Faith and Philosophy* 26, no. 3 (July 2009): 253–73.

at all against the weak version. And if our defence of the strong version is successful, it will also be a successful defence of the intermediate version.

MURPHY'S ARGUMENT FOR THE INCOHERENCE OF STRONG PSA

Murphy starts from the premise that an essential feature of punishing is the "condemning of the agent who failed to live up to the standard, the violation of which justifies the punishment."[5] He also states that "punishment expresses condemnation of the wrongdoer, of the wrongdoer as performer of the wrong."[6] He thinks that it follows from this that "punishment will be non-transferrable"[7] and that "penal substitution is unintelligible."[8] But note that there is a jump here: Murphy assumes that one cannot condemn the wrongdoer by punishing someone else.[9] And the defender of PSA can deny this assumption.

So the defender of PSA can either (1) deny that it is necessary for punishment that the offender, rather than the offence, be condemned, or (2) deny that it is necessary for punishment that the offender be condemned by way of being punished. It seems to us that (1) is less plausible than (2). It might be responded, however, that a consideration of the larger issue of the nature of punishment might resolve the matter in favour of Murphy. So we shall now turn to his treatment of the nature of punishment in his earlier monograph *Philosophy of Law*.[10]

MURPHY ON THE NATURE OF PUNISHMENT

Murphy's analysis runs as follows, to extract the necessary conditions from his continuous text:

> First, it is essential to punishment that, in itself, it is an evil of some sort.... Second, a punishment is imposed for the failure to measure up to some binding standard.... Third, a punishment is imposed by a personal agency who is authoritative.... [Fourth,] whenever punishment is found, it expresses judgments of disapproval and attitudes of indignation and

---

5. Ibid., 257.
6. Ibid., 256.
7. Ibid.
8. Ibid., 257.
9. Murphy also states that "[p]unishing presupposes that the object of punishment has failed in particular respects," but he provides no argument for the move from "agent who failed to live up to the standard" to "object of punishment." Ibid.
10. Mark C. Murphy, *Philosophy of Law* (Oxford: Blackwell, 2007).

resentment.... The object of condemnation must be *the person ... as performer of this act.*[11]

We shall comment on each of Murphy's conditions in turn.

(A) "An evil of some sort." Murphy explains that "[p]unishment involves the deprivation of goods or the imposition of bads,"[12] so it need not be a positive evil, so to speak, and the evil could be mental or physical. We add that it does not have to be felt as an evil by the victim: the imposition of pain could still be a punishment for someone (like a masochist) who would not think it such. It will follow from the fourth condition that for something to be a punishment, the imposer must think it an evil: it would not be a punishment if someone administered a whipping in the belief that a whipping were a jolly good thing with no bad consequences.

(B) "Punishment is imposed for the [supposed] failure to measure up to some binding standard." We have added the word *supposed* here to make clear what Murphy accepts,[13] that it is possible to impose punishment mistakenly or falsely—there does not need to be an actual failure on account of which the punishment is imposed. So it is possible to impose punishment on someone for stealing even if in fact no theft occurred, provided that, for example, the one imposing the punishment mistakenly believed the supposed offender was a thief or falsely asserted this.

Next we comment on the word *for.* This means that if A is imposing the punishment, then A is doing so on account of, or for the reason of, the supposed failure. It would not be a case of punishment if B's failure to measure up to some binding standard somehow caused the evil to be imposed without B's failure's constituting a reason in A's mind. Suppose that a schoolmaster, A, can punish a pupil at boarding school for going outside after hours by sentencing him or her to stay indoors for a week. Now suppose that a pupil, B, goes outside after hours and gets a chill, and A says that B must stay in the sanatorium for a week in order to recover. In the case described there is no punishment, because the staying inside is not for the breach of norms in going outside after hours, even though there is a causal relation between the two.

Third, Murphy is clear (rightly, we suggest) that "binding standard" applies more widely than just to breaches of morality or breaches of the

---

11. Ibid., 113–16.
12. Ibid., 113.
13. Ibid., 114.

law. For example, it also applies to a child's breaking house rules, or, as in our previous example, to a pupil's breaking school rules.

(C) "Imposed by a personal agency who is authoritative." Murphy offers an explanation for each of the two main parts of this condition. First, he explains "personal agency": "The imposition of a punishment is the work of beings who can think and judge; it is not, that is, simply a natural process."[14] We agree with this, and note that the word *simply* allows for the possibility of God's punishing people through natural processes. We also think that the condition does, rightly, allow for courts and states to impose punishment too.

Next, Murphy explains "who is authoritative": "Punishment is an activity by an authority, whether that authority is genuine or de facto only...: a private person can carry out vigilante justice, but he or she cannot punish."[15] The first thing to note here is that something can be a punishment even if it is imposed by a self-appointed authority like a Mafia boss, whose authority is not recognized beyond his or her immediate sphere of influence. That said, we also agree with Murphy that vigilante justice is not the same as punishment, and that an injured party merely executing revenge for the failure to measure up to some binding standard is not imposing punishment.

Moreover, this point holds even if the injured party executing revenge is in fact authoritative: a judge is authoritative, but that does not license him or her to impose evils outside the courtroom. So it is not sufficient that the person imposing the evil be authoritative; the person has to be *acting authoritatively* in imposing the evil.

(D) "Expresses judgments of disapproval and attitudes of indignation and resentment." Murphy gives three examples in which, he says, the first three conditions are met without there being punishment. The point is that this, if correct, shows that a fourth condition is needed. The clearest example is probably that of tort remedies, such as the award of damages. Damages are evils, and they are authoritatively imposed by personal agencies (e.g., judges) for the (supposed) failure to measure up to some binding standard. Nevertheless, awards of damages and other tort remedies are, intuitively, not punishments; punishments belong to criminal courts, not civil ones. And we agree with Murphy that the reason why they are not

---

14. Ibid.
15. Ibid.

punishments is that they do not in and of themselves express judgments of disapproval.[16]

We agree with Murphy that, in the light of this and other cases, the notion of punishment needs a fourth condition. We are, however, less happy with his precise formulation of the fourth condition. In particular, it does not seem to us that indignation and resentment are necessary features of punishment at all. Nevertheless, it does seem to us that disapproval or condemnation of the wrongdoer as performer of the wrong is indeed a necessary ingredient of punishment, as Murphy says.

MURPHY'S ANALYSIS APPLIED TO CHRIST'S SUFFERINGS AND DEATH

Could Christ's sufferings and death on the cross qualify, on Murphy's definition, as a punishment imposed by God? Yes. The defender of PSA can say that Christ's sufferings and death on the cross constituted an evil imposed by God for the failure to measure up to some binding standard, and that they expressed a judgment of disapproval and condemnation. But, it will be objected, Christ did not fail to measure up to any binding standard of God's, and, further, God did not condemn him. Indeed not, but it is not a feature of Murphy's definition that the one punished has to be the one who failed to measure up to the binding standard, nor does his definition specify that the one punished has to be the one condemned. Even Murphy's gloss, "The object of condemnation must be *the person . . . as performer of this act*,"[17] does not specify that the one punished is the object of condemnation. Of course, this could be added as a fifth condition, but in the absence of argument, this would simply beg the question.

At this point we may be asked whether the defender of PSA has any non-question-begging argument of his or her own for the contention that Christ could have undergone our punishment. It seems to us that there is a relatively common practice to which the defender of PSA could appeal: the practice of imposing suffering on every member of a group, or a representative of a group, for an offence committed by only some of the group. This is a form of punishment. (Whether or not it is just is not to the present point.) For example, sometimes schoolteachers impose suffering (e.g.,

---

16. We concede that sometimes disapproval of the action is expressed *along with* the award of damages or other tort remedy, but we maintain that this disapproval is not *part and parcel of* the award itself or the damages themselves.

17. Ibid., 116.

a detention) on every member of a class for an offence committed by only some of the class.

This practice is sometimes, but not always, motivated by ignorance as to the real culprits. Nor is it the case that the reason for the whole class's being detained is that their not preventing the culprits from committing the offence is considered itself an offence worthy of punishment. No, the idea is often that the solidarity of the class is such that it can be treated as a unit for purposes of punishment and reward, even if only some members performed the action punished or rewarded. The practice is perhaps more frequent with rewards—e.g., the granting of a half-day holiday to a school if one pupil distinguishes himself or herself—than it is with punishments, but, as Murphy remarks,[18] the principle is the same. For a similar example, a teacher might accept the offer from the class president (form captain) to accept responsibility for the class by taking the punishment due to the whole class.

A second kind of example can be found in the armed forces. Here again it is common for a sergeant to impose suffering on every soldier in the squad because of the actions of only some of its members, and—rather more rarely—to give out good treatment to every soldier in the squad because of the actions of only some of its members. For a similar example, a sergeant might accept the team leader's offer to take the punishment due to the whole fire team. It seems to us that there is good reason to count these as punishments or rewards (again, whether just or not is not to the present point).

These examples seem to us to show that it is not a necessary truth that if A imposes punishment on B, then the punishment thereby condemns B for a supposed failure on B's part to measure up to a binding standard. And if this is not a necessary truth, then it is hard to see on what grounds PSA could be ruled conceptually incoherent.[19]

WHAT IS IT TO PUNISH?

The foregoing analysis, however, has defended only the thesis that it is possible that Christ suffered a punishment for our sin, as asserted by the intermediate version of PSA. It might be objected that this does not show it is possible that God punishes Christ for our sin, as the strong version of

---

18. Murphy, "Not Penal Substitution," 256–57.
19. Of course, this does not address the objection that penal substitution is unjust.

PSA asserts. In what follows, we shall build on Murphy's analysis of punishment, as discussed above.

It seems to us that to punish it is necessary that one either impose punishment (as judges do when they sentence offenders) or implement punishment (as executioners do when they carry out a sentence). It might at first seem as though the broader notion underlying this disjunction was simply the notion of causation, such that the correct definition of *punish* would boil down to this:

(D0) A punishes B if and only if A causes B to suffer a punishment.

In fact, we do not accept (D0) since the concept of causation seems to cast the net too widely: By the transitivity of causation, anyone who caused the judge to punish the offender (say, by forcing the judge to adopt this course of action) would count as punishing the offender, and that seems to us wrong.

If it is not simply a matter of causation, then what is it to impose a punishment, and what is it to implement a punishment? It seems to us that for A to impose a punishment on B is for A authoritatively to mandate that B suffer a punishment, and for A to implement a punishment on B is for A authoritatively to implement the mandate that B suffer a punishment.[20] It is to be noted that we think these notions of imposition and implementation in and of themselves imply that A is a personal agent acting authoritatively; if this is right, then Murphy's third condition in his definition of *punishment* will in fact also be covered by this part of the definition of *punish*.

At first sight it might seem that the disjunction of imposition and implementation is not only necessary for punishing but also sufficient, so that the correct definition of *punish* is:

(D1) A punishes B if and only if A imposes a punishment on B or A implements a punishment on B.

It seems to us, however, that the first disjunct, "A imposes a punishment on B," does not suffice for punishing B. This is because, intuitively, one might impose a punishment on B without the mandate's ever being implemented. For example, B might die before the punishment is executed. Or another might undergo the punishment in B's stead. Or the court or law enforcement agency might suspend, or simply forget to

---

20. It is necessary that the mandate be logically prior to the implementation but not necessary that the mandate be temporally prior to the implementation. After all, it is possible simultaneously to impose and implement a punishment.

enforce, the punishment. In these cases it seems clear to us that if the punishment is not implemented on B, then B is not actually punished. (The corresponding point does not hold for "A implements a punishment on B," since it is in the nature of implementing a punishment that the punishment implemented has been imposed.)

A third attempt at the correct definition of *punish* might be this:

(D2) A punishes B if and only if A imposes on B a punishment whose mandate is authoritatively implemented or A implements on B a punishment.[21]

This, however, raises another concern. Suppose A imposes on B the punishment of being hanged in five days' time, and, because of a delay, B is hanged in six days' time. It is obvious that B is still punished by A in this situation. Indeed, if B is executed by lethal injection instead of being hanged as A directed, it still seems to us that B is punished by A. The potential problem here is that it might seem that B does not suffer the exact punishment that A imposes. To avoid this problem, we shall add a clause yielding:

(D3) A punishes B if and only if (1) A imposes on B a punishment, x, whose mandate is authoritatively implemented, or A implements on B a punishment, x; and (2) B suffers x or something close enough to x.

Whether a given evil suffered, y, will be close enough to x will depend on the context. It is certainly conceivable that in some contexts, if A sentences B to a horrible mode of death but the executioner actually executes B humanely, then A will not have punished B, since the evil suffered will not be deemed close enough to the evil imposed as sentence.

It might seem as though we need to add a clause specifying that for it to be the case that A punishes B, it must be the case that A intends to impose or implement a punishment on B. Punishing is not something that can be done by accident. We are of the opinion, however, that this is already implicit in the notions of imposition and implementation, such that stating it is unnecessary: one cannot impose or implement a punishment by accident either, since one cannot mandate something by accident or implement a mandate by accident.[22] Suppose, for example, that A is an executioner preparing to implement an imposed death penalty on B, but that A accidentally discharges the firearm while preparing it for B's

---

21. The phrase "on B" here rules out B's being punished if, say, B pays the fine imposed on another.

22. NB Implementing a mandate is different from merely acting in such a way that the mandate's conditions are fulfilled.

execution and accidentally kills B. We say that in this situation, A neither punishes B nor implements any punishment on B, since the accidental killing of B does not implement the death penalty.

Of course, it is still possible to impose or implement a punishment on B mistakenly, e.g.. in the wrong belief that one is imposing or implementing it on C (as when the defendant's identical twin takes his or her place in the dock for sentencing or on the gallows for hanging). But by the same token, it is possible to punish B in the wrong belief that one is punishing C.

The main question under our consideration here is whether it follows from our definition, (D3), together with the previously established definition of *punishment* drawn from Murphy's work, that it is necessary, in order for A to punish B, that the punishment condemn B as the one thought to have failed to have measured up to the binding standard. (We have seen already that it is not necessary that B or anyone have *actually* failed to measure up to a binding standard.) It does not follow. It is compatible with our definition, (D3), that A punish B intending thereby to condemn C (or C's offence).

Does there, then, have to be any connection at all in A's mind between the one that failed to measure up to the binding standard, C, and B in order for A to punish B? Suppose A thought that the "breach in the moral fabric of the universe could be shown up, condemned, and repaired" if he or she caused a random passerby to suffer an evil. Could that action count as (unjust) punishing? It seems to us that it could. To take a clearer example: suppose that A believed that anybody genetically related to the doer of the evil were fair game for punishing. We contend that this could indeed be a case of (unjust) punishing. Similarly, if the person causing B to suffer the evil believed that anybody spatially or temporally connected with the doer of the evil were fair game for punishing; then again we contend that this could indeed be a case of (unjust) punishing. And the examples we gave earlier in connection with the imposition of punishments also work for punishing, we think: it is possible for a school teacher to punish all the pupils in the class for a deed that he or she knows was performed by only some of them, and it is possible for a sergeant to punish all the soldiers in a squad for a deed that he or she knows was performed by only some of them. (Whether in these examples the punisher justly punishes is not to the present point.)

Now, is this definition met in the case of God and Christ? It seems to us that defenders of the strong version of PSA above will say yes: on the cross God punishes Christ on account of a failure (by the people collectively or distributively, for whom he substitutes) to measure up to moral standards. Presumably, God both imposes and implements a punishment on Christ. God authoritatively mandates that Christ suffer a punishment, and God authoritatively implements this mandate. And in God's punishing Christ, the punishment expresses condemnation of such people as wrongdoers. And whether or not there must be any connection in God's mind between such people and Christ in order for it to be conceptually possible that God punish Christ, God knows that Christ *is* connected in an appropriately intimate way (by union) with those whose sins are atoned for on the cross.

WHAT ARE THE NECESSARY CONDITIONS FOR PENAL SUBSTITUTION?

So for C to be B's substitute in being punished by A, it is necessary that A punish C, the conditions for which have been explained above. A particular implication of this is that a penal substitute must be capable of being punished. So if B is due to receive forty lashes and substitutes for himself or herself a waxwork that looks like B, then there is no penal substitution since the waxwork is not capable of being punished. Similarly, if B thinks that he or she will be sentenced to pay a huge fine and substitutes for him- or herself a bankrupt, C, in the dock before the judge, A, then while A may impose a penalty on C, C will not suffer it, and hence not be punished by A, since C is unable to bear it. So there is no penal substitution in this case either, even though it is attempted.[23] To apply this point to PSA, it seems to us that Christ is capable of being punished.

A further condition is that somebody has to intend that C substitute for B. Is it necessary, then, that C intend to be a substitute? We think not. If another party, D, subtly removes B from the dock and replaces B with C, then D has substituted C for B, and in consequence, C is B's substitute, whether C intends it or not. Moreover, it is not even necessary that C know that he or she is a substitute or that he or she is going to be, or is, being punished. Nor is it necessary that B know or intend that he or she is being substituted. Nor is it necessary that the one punishing, A, know or intend that a substitution occur. It is necessary, however, that for there to be a substitution, the person bringing about the swap intend that there

---

23. Somebody might define *penal substitution* more broadly than we have done, so that if C substitutes for B as the subject of A's imposition of a punishment, then C penally substitutes for B. As we are using the phrase, however, C penally substitutes for B only if C is punished in B's stead.

be a substitution. If there is a genuine mixup, and A punishes C under the wrong impression that C is B, without anybody intending this outcome, then there is no substitution—just a mistake. Finally, to apply this point to PSA, it seems to us that (at least) God substitutes Christ for us and intends such a substitution.

We have not addressed in this paper the question whether penal substitution is ever just, and, if so, under what circumstances. The defender of PSA will, of course, go further than we have been able to do in this paper, and insist that Christ's penal substitution for us on the cross shows that, no matter how serious the offence, it can be just for one person to be substituted for another. But the defender of PSA may also insist that the case of the cross is unique, since Christ was unique, and that features of this case cannot necessarily be generalized to merely human punishments. In consequence, the defender of PSA may think that arguments by analogy with the injustice of penal substitution in human judicial systems are not persuasive. There is no space here, however, to consider all the many arguments that have, in fact, been levelled against the justice of PSA.[24]

HISTORICAL APPENDIX

It has been alleged that PSA has *never* historically included the assertion that God punished Christ.[25] In response to this, we now set out a representative sample of Christian thinkers who have held this view, the strong version:[26]

(1) Gregory the Great:

But we must consider how He is righteous and ordereth all things righteously, if He condemns Him that deserveth not to be punished. For our Mediator deserved not to be punished for Himself, because He never was guilty of any defilement of sin. But if He had not Himself undertaken a death not due to Him, He would never have freed us from one that was

---

24. We'd like to thank Gert van den Brink, Stephen Clark, Tony Garrood, Simon Gathercole, Crawford Gribben, James Heather, Paul Helm, Sarah Hill, Howard Marshall, Richard Muller, Mark Murphy, Alexander Pruss, Stephen Rees, Sebastian Rehnman, John Ross, Eleonore Stump, Peter J. Williams, and Caleb Woodbridge. We'd also like to thank Oliver Crisp and Fred Sanders for hosting LATC 2015. Of course, none of them is to be held responsible for what we say.
25. "It is not a case of God punishing Christ but of God in Christ taking on himself the sin and its penalty. Indeed, at some point the challenge needs to be issued: where are these evangelicals who say that God punished Christ? Name them!" Howard Marshall, "The Theology of the Atonement," in *The Atonement Debate: Papers from the London Symposium on the Theology of Atonement*, eds Derek Tidball, David Hilborn, and Justin Thacker (Grand Rapids: Zondervan, 2008), 63.
26. Translations not listed in the footnotes as coming from a translation were done by Daniel J. Hill.

justly due to us. And so whereas "The Father is righteous" in punishing a righteous man, "He ordereth all things righteously," in that by these means He justifies all things, viz. that for the sake of sinners He condemns Him Who is without sin.[27]

(2) John Wycliffe: "Just as God justly and righteously punished Christ for the offence of his brothers."[28]

(3) Martin Luther: "God himself struck and punished Christ."[29]

(4) Johan Piscator: "But he punished us in Christ, or, what comes to the same thing, he punished Christ for us and in our place."[30]

(5) Samuel Rutherford: "The Lord punished Christ for us to declare the glory of his Justice in punishing sin in his own Son.... He punished Christ, who was not inherently, but only by imputation the sinner, with no hatred at all, but with anger and desire of shewing and exercising revenging justice, but still loving him dearly, as his only Son."[31]

(6) John Owen: "The person punishing is Jehovah, the person punished called 'him,'—that is, he who is spoken of throughout the whole prophecy, the Messiah, Jesus Christ."[32]

(7) Francis Turretin: "Christ is justly punished by God the judge both in body and soul in order to make expiation for sinners."[33]

(8) Solomon Stoddard: "God punished Christ with death for sin."[34]

27. "Qui Deus Christum innocentem poenis affecit.—Sed pensandum est quomodo justus sit, et omnia juste disponat, si eum, qui non debet puniri condemnat. Mediator etenim noster puniri pro semetipso non debuit, quia nullum culpae contagium perpetravit. Sed si ipse indebitam non susciperet, nunquam nos a debita morte liberaret. Pater ergo cum justus sit, justum puniens, omnia juste disponit; quia per hoc cuncta justificat, quod eum qui sine peccato est, pro peccatoribus damnat." Gregory the Great, Morals on The Book of Job, tr. Anonymous (Oxford: John Henry Parker, 1844 [original around 591]), bk. 3, ch. 14, §27, 148–49.
28. "Ideo cum Deus iuste et debite punivit Christum pro delicto suorum fratrum." John Wycliffe, Sermones, Volume 1: Super Evangelia Dominicalia, ed. Johann Loserth (London: Wyclif Society, 1887 [original 1383/4]), sermon 42, §284.
29. "Ipse Deus percussit et punivit Christum." Martin Luther, Werke: Kritische Gesamtausgabe: Volume 40, Part III (Weimar Ausgabe), ed. J. K. F. Knaake (Weimar: Böhlaus, 1930 [original 1543/44]), 715.
30. "At punivit nos in Christo, seu quod idem valet punivit Christum pro nobis, et loco nostri." Johan Piscator, Analysis logica epistolae Pauli ad Romanos (Herborn: Corvinus, 1608 [original 1595], 4th ed.), 106, comment on Romans 5:16. We do not ourselves agree that these come to the same thing, though. Particular thanks are due to Richard Muller for the reference.
31. Samuel Rutherford, The Covenant of Life Opened (Edinburgh: Robert Broun, 1655), pt. 1, chap. 7, §32; pt. 2, ch. 7, §251, accessed December 30, 2014, http://reformedlayman.com/CovenantOfLifeOpened/THE%20COVENANT%20OF%20LIFE%20OPENED.htm.
32. John Owen, Works: Volume 9, ed. Thomas Russell (London: Baynes, 1826 [first edition 1655]), 443, accessed December 30, 2014, http://www.ccel.org/ccel/owen/vindicevang.i.xxxi.html.
33. "At Christus a Deo Judice ex Justitia punitur et in corpore et in anima ad peccatorum expiationem." Francis Turretin, De Satisfactione Christi Disputationes (Geneva: De Tournes, 1666), Disputatio VI, Quae Quarta est de Veritate Satisfactionis, pt. 4, ch. 20, §163.
34. Solomon Stoddard, The Safety of Appearing at the Day of Judgment, In the Righteousness of Christ: Opened and Applied (Boston: Samuel Phillips, Stoddard, S. 1687), ch. 3, §51.

(9) Christopher Love: "It may well consist that God punished Christ for our sins."[35]

(10) John Downame: "It would not indeede haue stoode with Gods iustice, to haue punished Christ as he was innocent and righteous, nor to haue acquitted and absolued vs who were vnrighteous and wicked; but he punished Christ in respect that he had taken vpon him the sins of all the faithfull."[36]

(11) Edward Philips: "Christ and we are ioyned together, for otherwise it had not stood with Gods iustice to haue punished Christ in our flesh, nor to haue accepted our obedience in Christs person, if wee had not beene in him and he in vs."[37]

(12) Charles Wesley: "For what you have done, his blood must atone; The Father hath punished for you his dear Son."[38]

(13) A. A. Hodge: "Christ is the one satisfied as well as the one satisfying, the one punishing as well as the one punished; but he loves us enough to punish himself in our place."[39]

(14) Herman Bavinck: "God condemned sin in his flesh [Rom. 8:3] and punished him with the accursed death on the cross."[40]

The clearest historical example of the weak view, that God judicially implemented suffering on Christ but did not punish Christ, is that of Archbishop William Magee of Dublin:

> I will not contend, that this should be called suffering the *punishment* of those sins, because the idea of punishment cannot be abstracted from that of *guilt*. . . . But it is evident, that it is notwithstanding a judicial infliction; and it may perhaps figuratively be denominated *punishment*, if thereby be implied a reference to the actual transgressor, and be understood that suffering which was *due* to the offender himself; and which, *if* inflicted on him, would then take the name of punishment. In no other sense, can

35. Christopher Love, *The souls cordiall in two treatises: Volume 3* (London: Nathaniel Brooke, 1652), 165.

36. John Downame, *The Christian Warfare* (London: Kyngston, 1604 [first edition 1603]), ch. 16, §196.

37. Edward Philips, sermon on Romans 8:1 in *Certain godly and learned sermons* (London: Arn. Hatfield, 1607), 395.

38. Charles Wesley, "All Ye That Pass By" (Hymn 707), in *A Collection of Hymns*, ed. John Wesley (London: Wesleyan-Methodist Book-Room, 1889 [first edition 1779]), accessed January 1, 2015, http://www.hymntime.com/tch/htm/a/y/e/ayetpaby.htm. "Punished" was changed to "bruised" in George Booth, *The Primitive Methodist Hymnal* (London: Edward Dalton, 1889), 71.

39. Archibald Alexander Hodge, *The Atonement: Its Nature, Design, and Application* (Grand Rapids: Eerdmans, 1953 [first edition 1867]), 308.

40. Herman Bavinck, *Reformed Dogmatics: Volume 3*, ed. John Bolt and trans. John Vriend (Grand Rapids: Baker, 2006 [original: fourth edition, 1928]), 398.

the suffering inflicted on one, on account of the transgressions of another, be called a punishment; and, in this light, the bearing the punishment of another's sins, is to be understood as bearing that, which in relation to the sins, and to the sinner, admits the name of punishment, but with respect to the individual on whom it is actually inflicted, abstractedly considered, can be viewed but in the light of suffering.[41]

It is much harder to find a text explicitly and unambiguously declaring the intermediate view that Christ suffered a punishment imposed as a punishment by God, but was not punished by God. This reading would, however, be the face-value interpretation of a number of texts; for example:

> He bore the punishment of our transgressions, the punishment needed to bring us peace.... Yet we must be very careful in stating the truth of vicarious punishment not to go beyond what is written. Expressions like "God punished Christ" and still more "God was angry with Christ" should not be used.[42]

---

41. William Magee, *Discourses and Dissertations on the Scriptural Doctrines of Atonement and Sacrifice* (London: Henry Bohn, 1859 [first edition 1816]), 118, italics original.

42. H. E. Guillebaud, *Why the Cross,* (London: InterVarsity, 1946, 2nd ed.), 145.

CHAPTER 8

ATONEMENT AND THE WRATH OF GOD

ERIC T. YANG AND STEPHEN T. DAVIS

We must see, feel and appreciate His love to us even in His anger, condemnation and punishment. —Karl Barth (*Church Dogmatics* II/1)

I

The doctrine of atonement, as we understand it, is the affirmation that human beings are reconciled to God through the death of Christ.[1] Nowhere in Scripture is it precisely explained how or why the death of Christ atones for our sins. Accordingly, Christian theologians throughout history have felt free to propose various competing theories of atonement.

Interestingly, there is a related biblical theme that is pervasively affirmed throughout Scripture and yet is, so far as we can tell, almost completely ignored by many contemporary theologians and preachers. This is the notion of the wrath of God. This is unfortunate, since we believe that locating at least some of what occurs in the atonement in this divine attribute will aid us in making some headway toward a more complete and explanatorily adequate account of the atonement.[2] Although we would

---

1. We prefer to claim that our salvation is due to the life (including the incarnation, teachings, and deeds), death, and resurrection of Christ, though focusing on Christ's death will not affect our main argument.

2. When divine wrath is mentioned in the context of the atonement, it is often associated with the picture of Christ's death as placating a vindictive God. We seek to disassociate ourselves from such a picture while remaining faithful to the biblical data. Moreover, we do not take the notion of divine wrath to be central or fundamental to atonement; rather, we merely advance the more modest thesis of favoring the inclusion of the notion of divine wrath in an overall theory of atonement.

claim that highlighting the wrath of God as it relates to various issues in Christian theology can bear other interesting results, our focus will be on its relation to the doctrine of atonement.

We begin by addressing and responding to some of the objections or concerns that have been brought up as reasons for rejecting divine wrath altogether.[3] In particular, some have argued that wrath or anger is an emotion unfitting for God, either because God experiences no emotions at all or because that emotion is incompatible with an all-good and all-loving being. Others have claimed that wrath is inextricably linked to hatred, which goes against God's loving nature. We will show that these concerns fail to provide a reason to abandon anger or wrath as a divine attribute. We then present our own understanding of divine wrath and offer some reasons for why Christians should regard God as possessing such an attribute. Finally, we explain how such a notion can aid our theorizing about the doctrine of the atonement. To be clear, we are not offering a theory of atonement but instead making some suggestions on how future theological discussions concerning the atonement might be carried out.

II

We define God's wrath as his opposition to sin and evil.[4] Such opposition, we maintain, involves an emotive state of anger as well as God's actions on the basis of that emotion. As the psalmist says, "We are consumed by your anger; by your wrath we are overwhelmed. You have set our iniquities before you, our secret sins in the light of your countenance" (Ps 90:7–8 NRSV). Given the existence of sin and evil, the possession of such an emotion seems necessarily to follow from any being that has a morally perfect nature, for anger would be the appropriate response to the horrendous evils that exist due to human sin.[5] Furthermore, it is difficult to deny the pervasiveness of divine wrath found in the Bible. As Abraham Heschel notes,

> [It is] impossible to close one's eyes to the words of the wrath of God in Scripture. To interpret it on allegorical lines or as a metonymy, and to

---

3. We do not wish to deny that the wrath of God has been overemphasized at various points in the history of Christian teaching and preaching.

4. Cf. Tony Lane, "The Wrath of God as an Aspect of the Love of God," in *Nothing Greater, Nothing Better: Theological Essays on the Love of God*, ed. Kevin Vanhoozer (Cambridge: Eerdmans, 2001), 138–67; and Leon Morris, *The Apostolic Preaching of the Cross* (London: Tyndale, 1965), 180.

5. Though we maintain that divine wrath is not an essential attribute of God since it is possible for God to exist without evil (such as a world in which God never creates).

regard wrath as a synonym for punishment, is to misread the authentic meaning of the word and to misrepresent biblical thought.[6]

Arthur Baird also states that "wherever in the Old Testament one finds a reference to the love of God, his wrath is always in the background, either explicitly or implicitly, and we neglect this element to the impoverishment of the Hebrew concept of love."[7] When Scripture affirms God's love for us, we take that to be true; similarly, we take the affirmations of God's anger over evil and its perpetrators also to be true.[8]

Before focusing on the relationship between divine wrath and the atonement, we want to respond to some of the reasons the notion of divine wrath has been rejected by some theologians. Throughout the medieval period, it was common to regard God as being impassible—that he undergoes no suffering or no emotions. We will not here offer a critique of such a position, though we merely point out that such a view is no longer the dominant view of theologians or philosophers of religion. (Of course, there are still those who do espouse a strong version of divine impassibility.)

In a recent work, Anastasia Scrutton argues for a distinction between *passiones* and *affectiones*, where the former involves irrational and involuntary emotive attitudes, whereas the latter involves rational and voluntary ones.[9] She goes on to show that even within the Christian tradition, it is not obvious that those theologians who are associated with the idea of divine impassibility (such as Augustine and Aquinas) rule out *affectiones* and therefore rule out all emotions. Whatever the case, we are not convinced by the arguments for divine impassibility (in such a strong sense as to rule out even *affectiones* from God) and so will assume that it is coherent to construe God as having some emotions.

Another reason that some theologians deny that God possesses the attribute of divine wrath is that such a characteristic seems too anthropomorphic or anthropopathic—that by ascribing divine wrath to God we are somehow foisting our own limited human features onto God.[10] Rather

---

6.   Abraham Heschel, *The Prophets* (New York: Harper & Row, 1955), 359.
7.   J. Arthur Baird, *The Justice of God in the Teaching of Jesus* (London: S.C.M., 1963), 46.
8.   For additional treatment on this subject, see Anastasia Scrutton, *Thinking through Feeling: God, Emotion and Passibility* (New York: Continuum, 2011). Scrutton argues that God's expression of anger is rehabilitative as opposed to retributive (see ch. 5). A loving father may express anger for his child who has harmed a fellow playmate, and such anger does not have as its end the desire or motive to inflict harm for the sake of inflicting harm but rather to seek the good of the other child, the good for future communities, and especially the good for his own child.
9.   Ibid.
10.   For such a criticism, see Charles Harold Dodd, *The Epistle of Paul to the Romans* (London and Glasgow: Collins, 1959), 47–50.

than attributing the emotion of wrath or anger to God, some theologians have claimed that wrath is better construed as the experience of the consequence of sin—the cause-and-effect sequence from sinful action to the just deserts of harm or discipline.[11]

Certainly there are aspects of human anger that are not attributable to God, such as irrational or erratic behavior that stems from our emotion of anger.[12] However, God's wrath is only analogically related to the kind of anger that is experienced by humans. When humans experience anger or wrath, it often involves responsive actions where complete information of the entire situation is lacking. Thus, humans sometimes fly into a rage without knowing the motives of the putative offender or the circumstances involving the event. Accordingly, we are commanded by God to be "slow to anger," for our lack of omniscience may yield problematic behavior. However, God is never lacking in information and knows precisely how to respond appropriately against the offender.

We might even say that God's wrath is more akin to "righteous indignation" (stripped of its negative connotations), since that too is an attitude that involves opposition to evil. So when we attribute wrath to God, we are not including the human limitations and imperfections involved in our experience of wrath; we merely claim that God, in light of his full knowledge of the situation, undergoes an emotion of anger that is directed at sin and sinners. It does not fall into athropophaticism since the errors that are associated with human anger—such as irrationally flying into a rage and responding inappropriately—will never be committed by God.

Finally, the concept of divine wrath has been rejected given that it seems to be linked to hatred, and it cannot be the case that God exhibits such a negative emotion as hatred. God's love seems to be one of those theological axioms that no Christian, whether conservative or liberal, denies, and it is often relied upon as a central tenet for various theological claims (e.g., consider arguments for universalism that rely on the premise that God loves all human persons). Indeed, Scripture does speak much about the love of God, but it also includes various passages that indicate God's hatred for certain elements of creation—and quite strikingly, it is aimed at both sin and sinners alike. For example, consider the passages in Malachi 1:2–3, "I have loved Jacob but I have hated Esau," and in Hosea 9:15, "All their evil is at Gilgal; indeed, I came to hate them there! Because of the wickedness of their

---

11. Anthony Tyrrell Hanson, *The Wrath of the Lamb* (London: SPCK, 1957).
12. For a response to such charges, see Scrutton, *Thinking through Feeling*, ch. 5.

deeds I will drive them out of my house! I will love them no more" (NASB). Of course God also loved Esau and the residents of Gilgal. So we seem to require the claim that God can both love and hate certain individuals.

Following this line of thought, John Calvin approvingly cites Augustine, who made similar remarks about God's attitude of love and hatred toward us, which we quote here at length:

> Incomprehensible and immutable is the love of God. For it was not after we were reconciled to him by the blood of his Son that he began to love us, but he loved us before the foundation of the world, that with his only begotten Son we too might be sons of God before we were any thing at all. Our being reconciled by the death of Christ must not be understood as if the Son reconciled us, in order that the Father, then hating, might begin to love us, but that we were reconciled to him already, loving, though at enmity with us because of sin. To the truth of both propositions we have the attestation of the Apostle, "God commendeth his love toward us, in that while we were yet sinners, Christ died for us," (Romans 5:8). Therefore he had this love toward us even when, exercising enmity towards him, we were the workers of iniquity. Accordingly in a manner wondrous and divine, he loved even when he hated us. For he hated us when we were such as he had not made us, and yet because our iniquity had not destroyed his work in every respect, he knew in regard to each one of us, both to hate what we had made, and love what he had made.[13]

Calvin himself states that "[a]ll of us, therefore, have that within which deserves the hatred of God ... in respect, first, of our corrupt nature; and, secondly, of the depraved conduct following upon it."[14] Taking the popular slogan "love the sinner, hate the sin," it would be easy to suppose that God's hatred is directed only at sin and not at the sinner; however, such an emotion is regarded by Augustine and Calvin as being also directed at human sinners. Moreover, the tragedy of sin is that it has the effect of ruining and ultimately destroying one's "self," and hence it is difficult to divorce the sin from the sinner. William Temple points out this close connection: "My sin is the wrong direction of my will; and my will is just myself as far as I am active. If God hates the sin, what He hates is not an accretion attached to my real self; it is myself, as that self now exists."[15] Insofar as we have identified ourselves with our sin, God's wrath and therefore hatred is aimed at us.

---

13. Augustine, *Tractates on the Gospel of John* 110.6.
14. Calvin, *Institutes of the Christian Religion* 2.16.3.
15. William Temple, *Christus Veritas* (London: Macmillan, 1924), 258.

We maintain, therefore, that there is a sense in which God hates certain individuals, but such a statement obviously needs various qualifications. No such view of God should preclude his love for all creatures. There is a plausible sense in which, following Augustine and Calvin, we can assert that God both loves and hates certain individuals. Relying on a Thomistic account of love, Eleonore Stump distinguishes between two senses of hate, one that is opposed to love and one that is not. Under the Thomistic account, love involves willing the good of another and seeking (an appropriate kind of) union with that individual. Thus, hatred would be either to seek the bad for someone or to desire separation. Of course there can be instances of hate in which my desire for harm or aversion precludes my love for that person. However, Stump argues that there are some cases when such desires are compatible with love depending on the motive and circumstances. She goes on to state:

> Desiring the bad for someone and desiring not to be united with that person can be the desires of love if the person in question is bad enough that the bad of losing what he wants and having people alienated from him is the best thing for him in the circumstances. The difference between the two varieties of hatred consists primarily in the ultimate desire encompassing the desires for the bad and for alienation.[16]

Under this account, it becomes evident that God can both hate and love certain individuals. God may permit certain harms to befall someone or may permit that individual to feel distant from him in order to aid in his or her process of reconciliation and transformation. In fact, such an account of hate seems to provide the basis for a theodicy for both the problem of evil (since divine wrath permits evil or enacts discipline for the ultimate good of his creatures) and the problem of divine hiddenness (since divine wrath may permit the sense of separation that might lead us into recognizing our need for rescue and redemption).[17] The experience of such wrath and hatred, then, just is the experience of God's love by rebellious sinners.[18]

Though the notion of God possessing hatred for any individual may seem initially abhorrent, we have shown that such an idea is compatible with God's love. Indeed, the possession of such an emotion seems to elevate

---

16. Eleonore Stump, *Wandering in Darkness* (Oxford: OUP, 2010), ch. 5, endnote 74.
17. See Peter van Inwagen, *The Problem of Evil* (Oxford: OUP, 2006), who takes separation from God as a central feature of his response to the problem of evil.
18. Emil Brunner, *Man in Revolt* (London & Redhill: Lutterworth, 1939), 187.

our status and our relationship with Him. Scrutton offers several reasons for this. For one, God's hatred demonstrates his regard for us as autonomous agents—God does not have the same attitude for rocks, trees, or puppies.[19]

God, then, is a respecter of our dignity by regarding us in the way that autonomous agents should be regarded. Moreover, it also shows that God is seeking a loving union with us, for He is not merely a judge who pronounces his verdict in a detached manner but rather is personally invested in the outcome.[20] As Scrutton states, "God's anger, as an aspect of his passionate character as a whole, is indicative of the fact that God is not merely an abstract principle, but a fully relational person; and so God's anger is linked to the possibility of human communion and fellowship with God."[21] It is apparent that the degree to which one experiences anger is proportional to the relationship and level of personal intimacy between the offender and the offended.[22] We conclude, then, that no decisive objection has been offered against ascribing wrath or anger to God.

III

Having dealt with some of the objections, we now turn to our understanding of God's wrath and our reasons for ascribing wrath to God. As we take it, the wrath of God is an expression of God's just and righteous nature, where divine justice provides some measure of moral equilibrium in a broken and morally imperfect world. God's justice is not only eschatological, for we believe that without divine justice, the world would fall into greater moral chaos. The manifestation of divine wrath reminds us of moral standards and the consequences of both right and wrong actions. In a morally relativistic climate, the notion of God's wrath undermines such relativistic thinking and elevates the value of moral actions.[23]

To be clear, we are not here endorsing any particular meta-ethical or normative theory, but we do claim that divine wrath precludes any relativistic account that results in no objectively wrong actions. Whether morality

---

19. Scrutton, *Thinking through Feeling*, 107.
20. Ibid., 109, 120.
21. Ibid., 106.
22. Lane also states that "God's love itself implies his wrath [such that] without his wrath God is simply not loving in the sense that the Bible portrays his love," in Lane, "Wrath of God," 139. See also Aaron Ben-Ze'ev, *The Subtlety of Emotions* (Cambridge: MIT Press, 2000), 398, who claims that "the closer the person is to us, the more we care about the person, and the angrier we are when this person hurts us."
23. For more development on this idea, see Stephen T. Davis, "Universalism, Hell, and Fate of Ignorant," *Modern Theology* 6 (1990), 184–85.

is independent of God or is commanded by God or is a part of his divine nature (or whatever other account one may prefer concerning the relationship between God and morality), God's wrath indicates that there are some actions that are truly wrong to perform and that "the wrath of God comes on those who are disobedient" (Eph 5:6 NIV). As Paul says elsewhere, "Put to death, therefore, whatever in you is earthly: fornication, impurity, passion, and greed (which is idolatry). On account of these the wrath of God is coming on those who are disobedient" (Col 3:5–6 NRSV). Whether one personally experiences the force of the moral law or not, the experience and recognition of divine wrath serves as a reminder that there nevertheless is a moral law.

The absence of such wrath at the pervasive wickedness in our world would be considered a moral defect.[24] But given that God is morally perfect, it follows that he must be angry at evil and its perpetrators, for God loves both the victim and the offender and so must act for the good of both. Consider the following example from Lane:

> Suppose a child willfully and maliciously hurts another child. In what way is the disciplining of that child an expression of love? It expresses the parent's love for righteousness and detestation of cruelty. It expresses love for the victim in the form of concern for what has been done. It expresses love for the perpetrator in that it is intended as discipline. Finally, it expresses love for society in the disciplining of the child. Those who let undisciplined children loose on society show not love but lack of concern for their children and even greater lack of concern for their future victims in the rest of society.[25]

In Stump's treatment of the events in Job concerning the problem of evil, she argues that God truly demonstrates love for everyone, not only to Job but even to his friends as well as Satan.[26] What God does or permits, then, is for the benefit of all the parties involved. So out of love for the victims of wrongdoing, God must restrain, discipline, and sometimes severely punish wrongdoers to protect not only the victims but also potential future victims. However, God's actions also seek to benefit the offender, with the hope that seeking the bad or separation from the wrongdoer may eventually lead that individual to restoration and reconciliation with other human beings and ultimately with God.

---

24. C.E.B. Cranfield, *A Critical and Exegetical Commentary on the Epistle to the Romans*, vol. 1 (Edinburgh: T&T Clark, 1975), 1:109.

25. Lane, "Wrath of God," 166.

26. Stump, *Wandering in Darkness*, ch. 9.

IV

What, then, is the relation of divine wrath and the atonement? It is not uncommon for the notion of God's wrath to be raised in connection with the penal substitutionary theory of atonement, but we want to argue that any theory of the atonement would do well to consider divine wrath as an integral part of an adequate account. We take there to be at least three desiderata that any adequate account of the atonement must satisfy. The first is that any adequate theory must explain how Christ's death deals with our guilt for the sins that we have committed. Regarding guilt, it is not merely felt guilt that is at issue but the objective guilt that we have taken on by our offense. The second desideratum is that any adequate theory must deal with our disposition or propensity to fall into sin.

The rationale for these two desiderata follows from what can be taken as the main problem that the atonement is supposed to solve—viz., our separation from God. This separation is due to the sin we have committed (and perhaps even due to original sin), and such separation becomes wider because of our guilt—for we may try to avoid God's discipline or avoid communion with him because of the guilt and shame that we experience. Moreover, such separation expands given our continuation of sin, which follows from our proneness to do what is wrong.[27]

We also add a third desideratum: any adequate theory of atonement must explain why Christ's suffering and death was "fitting" (as some medieval theologians put it), or at least, effective.[28] God is also loving and merciful and so is willing to forgive sinners. So why doesn't God just forgive them without the ordeal of sending his Son to die on a cross? In fact, some theories of atonement seem not to require Christ to have died at all. It seems that if there was some other means to accomplish the reconciliation between God and human beings besides the suffering and death of Jesus, then such a means is not only preferable but perhaps even obligatory for God to bring about—for God should not bring about gratuitous or meaningless suffering, especially on a completely innocent individual. Thus, if we take seriously the plan that God had carried out in the death

---

27. These desiderata line up with what Stump calls the "backward-looking desideratum" and the "forward-looking desideratum" in Stump, "The Nature of the Atonement," in *Reason, Metaphysics, and Mind,* eds. Kelly Clark and Michael Rea (Oxford: Oxford University Press, 2012), 130–34.

28. We leave open the question of whether Christ's suffering and death was necessary for the atonement to be achieved, though we are inclined to think that it is possible for God to have accomplished atonement and reconciliation by other means—but perhaps the means he actually carried out in Christ's death conformed best to the natural order, including human nature.

of his own Son, then we need to explain why that gruesome feature had to be a part of the plan at all.

Incorporating the notion of the wrath of God provides a way of partially satisfying these desiderata. We are not claiming that the notion of divine wrath sufficiently answers all the questions surrounding the atonement or even completely satisfies these desiderata; we only claim that significant headway can be made when we take seriously the wrath of God (though we only provide a sketch here). Considering the first desideratum, divine wrath is directed at the very elements that cause guilt in human beings. If that element (human sin in 1 Peter 2:24 or "the curse" in Galatians 3:13) was taken up in Christ, then divine wrath is aimed at destroying that element. Insofar as that element resides in us, divine wrath attempts to destroy that in us while preserving us—which fits with the theme of God loving us and hating us.

It may seem that initially such anger and hatred will aggravate our guilt and shame because we will fear discipline and punishment (and so believe God is seeking what we take to be bad for us) as well as rejection and separation. However, understanding that hatred is not opposed to love, we can experience God's anger as a means of removing the source of our guilt and shame, whether that is by means of destroying it in the body of Christ or destroying it in us.[29]

We can also learn to regard God's anger as an experience of the love that he has for us. That is, we learn to regard such anger not as the fits of rage from a tyrant or the impersonal declaration and enactment of punishment from an impersonal judge but as the personal and parental care and concern that involves both emotional anger and severe discipline. There is a significant difference between the acts of anger from an abusive parent and the acts of anger from a loving parent, and we can, through growing in our knowledge of God, understand and construe his wrath as his love. If so, then we need not fear that God will reject us or desire separation, for his very anger and acts of discipline are signs that he is seeking out a restoration in the relationship. Again, we are leaving open the various ways of pursuing this approach, since we are not here offering a full-blown account of atonement. But part of the problem can be overcome by reference to God's wrath.

Divine wrath can also help make sense of how the atonement deals with our disposition toward sinful behavior. As stated earlier, there is a

---

29. We recognize that much is left unstated, and perhaps it is ultimately a mystery exactly how our guilt and shame are destroyed in Christ's body at his death.

legitimate sense in which we can say that God both loves and hates us as sinners. But his hatred, which involves both the experience of suffering or discipline and (for those saved) the temporary separation from God, is ultimately aimed at reconciliation between God and human beings. As Lane notes,

> God loves sinners, not in the sense that he does not hate them along with their sin, but in the sense that he seeks their salvation in Christ. While his attitude to sinners as sinners is antagonism and wrath, his good will toward them actively seeks their conversion and forgiveness.[30]

Such experiences of suffering or discipline, being manifestations of divine wrath, seek to transform our minds and wills so that we no longer are prone to sin. We leave it open whether such a transformation can take place here on earth (at least in principle, as some interpreters of Wesley seem to believe) or only after death. But the wrath that involves our experiences of what we take to be bad for us (including the sense of rejection) may in fact be for our benefit. Again, this is quite incomplete; we would also have to add the activity of the Holy Spirit among other things involved in the process of our transformation. Yet by incorporating the notion of divine wrath, it becomes clear that God is engaged in processes that are directed at our salvation, which involves not only the forgiveness of our sins but also the removal of the disposition to sin.

The third desideratum of an adequate theory of atonement requires that the theory provide an explanation as to why Christ had to die. As an example of what we take to be an inadequate theory, consider exemplarist accounts of atonement that place great emphasis on the life and teachings of Christ and on the need for Christians to work for peace and justice. They appear to have no strong notion of human sinfulness and thus no need for any strong notion of atonement. Their view appears to be that God is loving and merciful and will forgive anyone who sincerely confesses and repents. There is no need for anyone to die on the cross.

Divine wrath shows us just how bad it is to engage in immoral or sinful behavior. The gruesomeness of sin corresponds to the gruesomeness of the sacrificial system in the Old Testament. One cannot merely offer junk ("spotted animals"), for God rejects such offerings (Mal 1). Rather, something of great value must be surrendered. Thus, the author of Hebrews can write, "Without the shedding of blood, there is no forgiveness of sin"

---

30. Lane, "Wrath of God," 155.

(Heb 9:22). As such, we uphold the principle that it is always difficult and costly to rectify a terribly wrong situation.[31]

In ancient Greek and Roman tragedies, the expression *deus ex machina* (i.e., "God out of a machine") referred to any easy solution to the problem or conflict that a play had created. For example, suppose that in the last act Zeus was lowered to the stage by a machine and declared something like, "I do not allow things like this to happen. I now command that *x*, *y*, and *z* occur" (which is an edict that in effect resolves the play's central problem). It was recognized early in Western literature that novels or plays with a *deus ex machina* ending were unrealistic and deficient. The reason they are considered inferior is, we think, the almost universal human recognition that it takes a great cost to rectify a terribly wrong situation.

That great cost was the death of the Son of God. Such a cost must be paid on account of the moral instability brought about by human (and perhaps demonic) sin. Since divine justice is the moral equilibrium of the world, it is appropriate that expressions of divine anger be wrought against all that has been infected by sin. Again, God's wrath does not preclude his love, but it does evince that things are not right and that they must be made right through costly (and sacrificial) means. Once again, we think incorporating divine wrath takes us some steps closer to understanding why such a great cost as Christ's death had to be paid.

V

Again, we are not recommending here any particular theory of atonement. We merely claim that taking seriously the notion of God's wrath goes some way toward developing an adequate and more complete account. In this section we provide a sketch of how this can be accomplished by using as an example two current accounts: the penal substitutionary theory and Swinburne's version of the satisfaction theory.

Considering penal substitution theory, one striking objection involves the worry that to exact reparation from someone for the offense he or she has committed precludes any genuine forgiveness offered by the offended. In response, we note that it is part of scriptural teaching that Christ had taken the sin of the world ("he became a curse"), and hence it is fitting that God's wrath be placed on his own Son. We do not pretend to be able to

---

31. See Stephen T. Davis, "The Wrath of God and the Blood of Christ" in *Christian Philosophical Theology* (Oxford: Oxford University Press, 2006) for additional defense of this claim.

explain the mechanism by which such a transfer of sin or guilt takes place; we only regard *that* it had happened, not *how* it happened.

As noted earlier, great wrongs demand a great cost. In some cases, forgiveness might involve merely pardoning someone or no longer holding someone to their debt. But God's wrath for us is not the wrath of a banker or an impartial judge; rather, it is the wrath of a loving parent. As such, genuine forgiveness and reconciliation cannot take place without a great cost. Of course this does not explain exactly why or how it is that Christ's taking the penalty of our sins achieves our reconciliation. But including a proper understanding of divine anger in the context of a loving parent evinces the cost that the Son had freely decided to pay, thereby demonstrating the depth and magnitude of God's grace and love for us.[32]

Next, consider Swinburne's satisfaction theory. Without assaying the details of his account, Swinburne argues that apology, repentance, reparation, and penance are required for atonement. Though human beings can offer an apology and can repent, we lack the resources to offer the appropriate reparation as well as to undertake the appropriate penance when it comes to our offense against God. However, Christ's sacrifice allows a way for the appropriate reparation and penance to take place. Now Richard Cross has argued that the only reparation that is required for humans to make to God is merely an apology.[33] He distinguishes between two types of deprivation of service, one of which involves an additional deprivation and another which does not. Here is his example to clarify this distinction:

> Suppose I have a son, and that I ask him to do the washing up. He fails to do this, and in so doing fails not only in a duty of service, but also brings it about (in a loose sense) that I have to do the washing up. But suppose instead I ask him to tidy his bedroom. He fails to do this, but in so doing fails me in no more than a duty of service. The only other harm he does is to himself, not to me.[34]

Cross claims that our duty to God is of the latter sort, for nothing that we fail to do can cause God any harm.

That God cannot be harmed in any way whatsoever is a view fitting for those who endorse divine impassibility. But as noted earlier, we reject divine impassibility and believe that there are good reasons to ascribe emo-

---

32. We are not suggesting that all problems of the penal substitutionary theory are resolved by the notion of wrath; we are only trying to show how these theories can overcome *some problems* and provide deeper and more comprehensive explanations of the process of reconciliation.
33. Richard Cross, "Atonement without Satisfaction," *Religious Studies* 37 (2001), 397–416.
34. Ibid.

tions to God, and especially the emotion of divine anger. Given what we have said so far about God's wrath, it should be clear that there is a sense in which God can be harmed—whatever is the analogue to the harm done to a parent who perceives his or her children harming themselves. Though the children may be engaged in some activity that is directly harming themselves—say, they are using harmful narcotics on a frequent basis—there is a sense in which the parent is also being harmed. Certainly the parent is not undergoing neurological damage or experiencing other problematic side effects, but any loving parent will experience not only grief but anger.

So taking seriously the notion of divine wrath permits the proponent of Swinburne's satisfaction theory to deny the claim that God cannot be harmed in any way.[35] Furthermore, by including God's wrath in our understanding of atonement, it becomes clear that mere apology is insufficient for full reparation—as we argued that a great wrong requires a great cost. Mere verbal utterances won't be enough. As we stated earlier when discussing penal substitution theory, the requirement for reparation does not preclude forgiveness, for we see that the desire for genuine reconciliation, which is motivated by God's love for us, involves a great reparation that we humans cannot make.

To reiterate, we have only provided a mere sketch of how such theories can utilize the notion of God's wrath as a way of mitigating some of the objections and problems. And though we lack space to say more here, we believe that taking divine wrath seriously can also aid other accounts of atonement. Thus, we believe it has been detrimental to theology to ignore or eschew the idea of divine wrath, and we hope for further exploration into this attribute of God and the ways in which it broadens and deepens our understanding of other theological issues.[36]

---

35. A distinction can be made between being *harmed* and being *damaged*. A subject S is *harmed* whenever an occurrence takes place that S would desire not to obtain, whereas a subject S is *damaged* whenever the value, capacities, or essential activities of S are reduced, undermined, or eliminated. Thus, God is not damaged by our sin since nothing we can do would diminish his essence, though we maintain that God can be harmed in our sense above.

36. We would like to thank Eleonore Stump, Oliver Crisp, Joseph Jedwab, and those who attended our presentation at the 2015 Los Angeles Theology Conference for their helpful and insightful comments.

CHAPTER 9

FROM "I HAVE DONE WRONG" TO "I AM WRONG"

(Re)Constructing Atonement as a Response to Shame

T. MARK MCCONNELL

IN DECEMBER 2010, Brené Brown, a social work researcher from the University of Houston, gave a TED talk entitled "The Power of Vulnerability," which turned out to be one of the most watched, downloaded, and shared TED talks over the past five years.[1] In the talk, Brown speaks about the importance of embracing vulnerability. In her research she found that vulnerability is the birthplace of joy, creativity, belonging, and love. But vulnerability also lies at the heart of fear, disappointment, grief, the struggle for a sense of worthiness, and shame.[2]

In a follow-up TED talk, Brown unpacked the meaning and significance of shame. One of the many reasons people do not embrace vulnerability, and so fail to live in a wholehearted way, is because they are afraid to embrace their own shame. For Brown, shame is universal. It is part of the human condition.

---

1. TED (Technology, Education, Design) is a nonprofit organization that aims to spread ideas usually in the form of eighteen-minute talks given at conferences at various international locations. More than 1,500 talks can be found on the main TED website and YouTube.

2. See Brené Brown, "Transcript of 'The Power of Vulnerability,'" accessed February 2, 2015, https://www.ted.com/talks/brene_brown_on_vulnerability/transcript.

To understand shame, one has to understand that it is different from guilt. As Brown states, shame is a focus on self; guilt is a focus on behavior. Shame is "I am bad." Guilt is "I did something bad." And for Brown, shame is never good.[3]

In Western Christianity, discussions about the human condition have largely been focused on guilt rather than shame. This has led to the atonement, at both a popular and theological level, particularly among conservative evangelicals, being viewed as the solution to the problem of human guilt. The following will consider how the atonement might be understood if the problem of the human condition is the reality and experience of shame. In other words, it will consider how the atonement might be understood if the location of that atonement is the problem of shame rather than the problem of guilt.

Recent research in the social sciences will be examined in order to more fully understand the nature of shame, particularly in contrast to guilt. The beginnings of an account of the atonement will be offered. Since shame is focused on one's experience of "being" rather than merely on action, although having significant consequences for action, this account will build upon a basic recapitulation framework as found in Irenaeus and Athanasius. It will also propose that Thomas F. Torrance's understanding of the vicarious humanity of Christ provides a significant resource for understanding the atonement as a response to the human problem of shame.

Shame Defined

One of the problems in understanding the essence and nature of shame is the limitation and potential confusion caused by language. There is the noun *shame* itself, but there is also the verb *to shame* and cognates such as *ashamed*, *shameful*, and *unashamed*, many of which can be found in most English language translations of both the Old and New Testament texts. From a cursory review of how such words are used, in both common speech and academic writing, it is clear that there is a wide variety of usage that will lead to confusion unless definitions are clear.

One of the basic divisions in meaning is between cultural anthropology approaches and modern Western psychological understandings of shame. The former can be traced to the 1946 book by Ruth Benedict, *The*

---

3. See Brené Brown, "Transcript of 'Listening to Shame,'" accessed February 2, 2015, https://www.ted.com/talks/brene_brown_listening_to_shame/transcript.

Chrysanthemum and the Sword: Patterns of Japanese Culture, in which Benedict differentiated between guilt cultures and shame cultures, arguing that Japan was shame-based in contrast to Western guilt-based.[4]

In shame cultures the focus is on social conformity. Such conformity is generated by external sanctions. The main forms of "punishment" for offending against the social rules are public shaming and ostracization. The focus is therefore on conformity and appearance. Significantly, and surprisingly to most Westerners, in shame cultures "shame is not perceived or felt to be an internal psychological condition."[5] The motivation for "moral" behavior is therefore approval, esteem, and honor in the eyes of the community.

In guilt cultures the focus is on the individual's internalized sense of wrongdoing, which produces a feeling of guilt and ideally motivates the person to better behavior. At a societal level, serious acts of misbehavior are dealt with by specific legal process of punishment and redress in which the person "pays for" their misbehavior.[6] Typically, so this paradigm suggests, shame cultures are non-Western and more communal, and guilt cultures are Western and more individualistic. Shame is thought of as an external public phenomenon. Guilt is thought of as an internal private phenomenon.

Various missiologists, particularly those holding an evangelical perspective, have taken up this apparent basic distinction in reflecting on how the gospel ought to be communicated in non-Western societies.[7] Such

---

4. Ruth Benedict, *The Chrysanthemum and the Sword: Patterns of Japanese Culture*, 1946.
5. Stephen Pattison, *Shame: Theory, Therapy, Theology* (Cambridge, UK; New York: Cambridge University Press, 2000), 54.
6. Ibid.
7. See for example Barbara Ellen Bowe, "Reading the Bible through Filipino Eyes," *Missiology* 26, no. 3 (July 1, 1998): 345–60; David J. Hesselgrave, "Missionary Elenctics and Guilt and Shame," *Missiology* 11, no. 4 (October 1, 1983): 461–83; David J. Hesselgrave, *Communicating Christ Cross-Culturally: An Introduction to Missionary Communication*, 2nd ed. (Grand Rapids: Zondervan, 1996); C. Norman Kraus, *Jesus Christ Our Lord: Christology from a Disciple's Perspective* (Scottdale, PA: Herald Press, 1987); C. Norman Kraus, "The Cross of Christ—Dealing With Shame and Guilt," *Japan Christian Quarterly* 53, no. 4 (September 1, 1987): 221–27; Ruth Lienhard, "A 'Good Conscience': Differences Between Honor and Justice Orientation," *Missiology* 29, no. 2 (April 1, 2001): 131–41; Andrew M. Mbuvi, "African Theology from the Perspective of Honor and Shame," in *The Urban Face of Mission: Ministering the Gospel in a Diverse and Changing World*, eds. Harvie M. Conn, Manuel Ortiz, and Susan S. Baker (Phillipsburg, NJ: P & R Pub., 2002), 279–95; Bill A. Musk, *Touching the Soul of Islam: Sharing the Gospel in Muslim Cultures* (Crowborough: Marc, 1995); Bruce J. Nicholls, "The Role of Shame and Guilt in a Theology of Cross-Cultural Mission," *Evangelical Review of Theology* 25, no. 3 (July 1, 2001): 231–41; Robert J. Priest, "Cultural Anthropology, Sin, and the Missionary," in *God and Culture*, eds. D. A. Carson and John D. Woodbridge (Grand Rapids: Eerdmans, 1993), 85–105; Timothy C. Tennent, *Theology in the Context of World Christianity* (Grand Rapids: Zondervan, 2007); Bruce Thomas, "The Gospel for Shame Cultures: Have We Failed to Reach Muslims at Their Point of Deepest Insecurity?" *Evangelical Missions Quarterly* 30, no. 3 (July 1, 1994): 284–90.

missiological reflection on the role of shame in non-Western cultures has been accompanied and reinforced by the work of biblical scholars who have made efforts to take into consideration the shame-honor cultural context of much of the Old and New Testaments. Non-Western shame-based cultures, so it is argued, are significantly culturally closer to both Ancient Near Eastern cultures and first-century Mediterranean cultures than Western guilt-based cultures.[8]

Benedict's typology has come under significant criticism. Working within a Freudian framework, Benedict, who perhaps tellingly did no actual fieldwork in Japan, thought of guilt cultures, which focus on individual autonomy, as being developmentally superior to shame cultures that were more group-focused. Such a position has become increasingly unacceptable. A number of non-Western writers have also criticized Benedict as misreading so-called shame-based cultures (e.g., Japanese culture) by failing to recognize the presence of a guilt dynamic. For example, Takeo Doi states that "what is characteristic about the Japanese sense of guilt ... is that it shows itself most sharply when the individual suspects that his action will result in betraying the group to which he belongs."[9] In addition, Benedict's binary typology, which defines shame as a public matter and guilt as a private one, has been criticized as being overly simplistic. In the same culture one person may internalize the consequences of wronging where another person, in relation to the same instance of wrongdoing, may not.[10] Shame and guilt may be present in the same culture.[11]

This is not to say that a shame-honor dynamic is not present in Japanese and other non-Western cultures, or that the shame-honor dynamic in Ancient Near Eastern culture and first-century Mediterranean culture should be downplayed. What it does mean is that the understanding of shame in the traditional cultural anthropological model is rather limited. Shame in the shame-honor model would appear to have a particular meaning associated with ensuring acceptable behavior.

---

8.   The literature in this area is substantial. For an extensive bibliography, see "Complete Bibliography of Honor-Shame Resources," accessed February 2, 2015, http://honorshame.com/wp-content/uploads/2014/01/Complete-Bibliography-of-HS-Resources.pdf.

9.   Takeo Doi, *The Anatomy of Dependence* (Tokyo: Kodansha International, 1973), 49. Quoted in Young Gweon You, "Shame and Guilt Mechanisms in East Asian Culture," *Journal of Pastoral Care* 51, no. 1 (March 1, 1997): 57.

10.   Young Gweon You, "Shame and Guilt," *Journal of Pastoral Care*, 58.

11.   It should be noted that despite the criticism of Benedict's differentiation, David Hesselgrave, a leading figure in evangelical missiology in the late twentieth century, states that "the guilt-shame distinction made by Benedict and others would seem to have validity [although] the distinction is not one that is generally recognized and utilized in the literature of psychiatry, psychology and counseling." See Hesselgrave, "Missionary Elenctics and Guilt and Shame," 479.

In contrast contemporary Western psychology provides a different account of shame in relation to guilt, one that is represented in the message of Brené Brown's TED talks. Erik Erikson, a developmental psychologist, was one of the first to make the distinction in the psychological literature between shame and guilt in his groundbreaking study on child development.[12] According to Erikson, in Western culture "shame is an emotion insufficiently studied, because in our civilization it is so easily absorbed into guilt." For Erikson, shame preceded guilt developmentally. If there is too much shame and doubt in the child's development, said Erikson, this resulted in failure to develop a healthy sense of autonomy, thus leading to "compulsive activity as the ego over compensated in its attempts to master and manage the expressions of will."[13] It is only after this stage that guilt, associated with initiative and sense of purpose, developed. Too much guilt would leave the child lacking a purpose in life.

Since Erikson, there has been significant work on the distinction between shame and guilt from a psychological perspective. According to James Fowler, well-known author of *Stages of Faith* and former director of the Center for Research on Faith and Moral Development at Emory University, the work of Helen Block Lewis in the early 1970s has been "fundamental in the revolution in psychology and psychoanalysis fostered by attention to shame."[14] In her work Lewis essentially refuted Benedict's cultural distinction between shame and guilt.[15] The distinction was not a matter of shame being a public emotion and guilt being a private one; rather, the distinction revolved around the role of the self in judging. With guilt, the self judges one's action or activity; with shame, the self judges "the inadequacy of the *self* itself."

As Lewis states:

> The experience of shame is directly about the self, which is the focus of evaluation. In guilt, the self is not the central object of negative evaluation, but rather the thing done or undone is the focus. In guilt, the self is negatively evaluated in connection with something but is not itself the focus of the experience.[16]

---

12. Stephen Parker and Rebecca Thomas, "Psychological Differences in Shame vs. Guilt: Implications for Mental Health Counselors," *Journal of Mental Health Counseling* 31, no. 3 (July 2009): 214–15.

13. Erik H. Erikson, *Childhood and Society* (New York: Norton and Company, 1950), 252.

14. James W. Fowler, "Shame: Toward a Practical Theological Understanding," *Christian Century* 110, no. 24 (August 25, 1993): 817.

15. Helen Block Lewis, *Shame and Guilt in Neurosis* (New York: International Universities Press, 1971).

16. Lewis, *Shame and Guilt in Neurosis*, 30.

Lewis's basic distinction, as opposed to the older anthropological distinction, has been confirmed by numerous qualitative and quantitative studies.[17] According to June Price Tangney, another leading researcher on issues of shame and guilt, "Empirical research has consistently failed to support the public/private distinction."[18]

Since shame has to do with one's sense of self, it is more pervasive and all-encompassing compared to guilt. Lewis illustrates the sense of the scope of shame when she compares the thinking of someone struggling with guilt as compared with someone struggling with shame.

[Guilt-laden thinking run as follows:] "How could I have *done that*; what an injurious *thing* to have done; how I *hurt so-and-so*, what a moral lapse that *act* was; what will become of *that* or of *him*, now that I have neglected to do it, or injured him. How should I be *punished* or *make amends*? Mea culpa!" Simultaneously, ashamed ideation says: "how could *I* have done that; what an *idiot I am* — how humiliating; what a *fool*, what an *uncontrolled person* — how mortifying; how unlike so-and-so, who does not do such things; how *awful and worthless* I am. Shame!"[19]

The origins of shame are highly debated. Following a similar path to Erikson, some theorists such as Gershen Kaufman argue that the origins of shame occur early in life in the parental bonding process.[20] In a healthy process an "interpersonal bridge" is formed between the parent and child.[21] If the parent shows rejecting disapproval to the child, the interpersonal bridge is ruptured and shame is the result. Others such as Silvan Tomkins and Donald Nathanson see shame as originating in neurobiological processes developed at birth.[22] Others such as Vicki Underland-Rosow and Carl Greinger

---

17. Parker and Thomas, "Psychological Differences in Shame vs. Guilt," 215.

18. June Price Tangney, "The Self-Conscious Emotions: Shame, Guilt, Embarrassment, and Pride," in *Handbook of Cognition and Emotion*, eds. Tim Dalgleish and Michael J. Power (Chichester: Wiley, 2000), 545. See also Ying-Yi Chiu, Chi-Yue Hong, "A Study of the Comparative Structure of Guilt and Shame in a Chinese Society," *Journal of Psychology* 126, no. 2 (March 1992): 171–74.

19. Lewis, *Shame and Guilt in Neurosis*, 36.

20. Gershen Kaufman, *Shame: The Power of Caring* (Cambridge, MA: Schenkman Pub. Co., 1985), 12–17.

21. Similar conclusions about the impact of early parent-child interaction can be found, *inter alia*, in Helen Block Lewis, "Shame and the Narcissistic Personality," in *The Many Faces of Shame*, ed. Donald L. Nathanson (New York: The Guilford Press, 1987), 93–133; Allan N. Schore, *Affect Regulation and the Origin of the Self: The Neurobiology of Emotional Development* (Hillsdale, NJ: Lawrence Erlbaum Associates, 1994); P. Gilbert, J. Pehl, and S. Allan, "The Phenomenology of Shame and Guilt: An Empirical Investigation," *British Journal of Medical Psychology* 67, no. 1 (March 1994): 23–36.

22. See Stephen Tomkins, "Shame," in *The Many Faces of Shame*, ed. Donald L Nathanson (New York: Guilford Press, 1987), 133–61; Donald L. Nathanson, *Shame and Pride: Affect, Sex, and the Birth of the Self* (New York: Norton, 1992).

see shame as a learned behavior taught by parents as a way of distracting or denying the infants feelings that are deemed undesirable by the parents.[23]

Whatever the source of shame, it is an affect and an experience that brings a person close to their sense of self. As Kaufman powerfully puts it:

> Shame itself is an entrance to the self. It is the affect of indignity, of defeat, or transgression, of inferiority, and of alienation. No other affect is closer to the experienced self. None is more central to the sense of identity. Shame is felt as an inner torment, a sickness of the soul. It is the most poignant experience of the self by the self, whether felt in the humiliation of cowardice, or in the sense of failure to cope successfully with a challenge. Shame is a wound felt from the inside, dividing us both from ourselves and from one another.[24]

Those researching shame argue that the effects of shame are extensive and varied. Tangney along with her fellow researchers has provided some of the clearest research.[25] A person suffering from shame is prone to blame others for the issues associated with the negative evaluation of their sense of self. The externalization of blame is in fact one of the chief markers of shame. Another key marker is a lack of empathy, because shame produces such a painful and overwhelming experience that it becomes difficult to respond to the needs of others. There are also strong links between shame and aggression/anger due to the difficulty in managing feelings. For Merle A. Fossum and Marilyn Mason, shame is the cause of a wide variety of addictive behaviors including substance abuse, workaholism, eating disorders, and family violence.[26]

One of the key defining experiences of shame described by a number of writers is the sense of exposure. Kaufman states:

> To feel shame is to feel seen in a painfully diminished sense. The self feels exposed both to itself and to anyone present. It is this sudden, unexpected feeling of exposure and accompanying self-consciousness that characterize the essential nature of the *affect* of shame. Contained in the experience of shame is the piercing awareness of ourselves as fundamentally deficient in some vital way as a human being.[27]

23. Vicki Underland-Rosow, *Shame: Spiritual Suicide* (Shorewood, MN: Waterford Publications, 1995); Carl Greinger, "Shame: A Psychiatric Perspective for Chaplains," *The Caregiver Journal* 10, no. 1 (1993): 2–17.
24. Kaufman, *Shame: The Power of Caring*, ix–x.
25. See the helpful summary of Tangney's work by Parker and Thomas, "Psychological Differences in Shame vs. Guilt," 215–18.
26. Merle A. Fossum and Marilyn Mason, *Facing Shame: Families in Recovery* (New York: W.W. Norton & Co., 1986), 123–47.
27. Kaufman, *Shame: The Power of Caring*, ix–x.

This sense of exposure leads to a withdrawal from others and a need to hide or escape.[28] Schneider defines shame as "a painful feeling of being exposed uncovered, unprotected, vulnerable."[29] In addition, shame is also often accompanied by "a sense of shrinking and being small, and by a sense of worthlessness and powerlessness" which produces a debilitating sense of impotence.[30] As Gregersen puts it, shame "defeats us, rendering us incapable of free agency."[31]

Despite the very personal nature of shame, focused on one's sense of self, it does not exist "on its own." For Laurel Arthur Burton, "Shame is always interpersonal and systemic. For there to be an experience of shame, there must be interrelatedness."[32] This is clear if one accepts that the roots of shame lie in the development of a child's sense of identity in relation to their parents and primary caregivers. As Mark E. Biddle states:

> In essence, shame constitutes an objectification of self. It is a focus on the self that involves the awareness that at least one other person is watching and evaluating one's behavior, an awareness that provokes a shift of view such that one regards oneself from the outside.[33]

One of the debates in the shame research literature is whether a sense of shame can be healthy. The belief that shame can be healthy is reflected in the general usage of the word "shameless." Carl D. Schneider, in his book *Shame, Exposure and Privacy,* is perhaps the most influential proponent of a "healthy sense of shame."[34] Noting that French has two words for shame whereas English only has one, Schneider makes the distinction between "discretionary shame" (in French, *pudeur*) and "disgrace shame"

---

28. In contrast to shame, Parker and Thomas state that, "Guilt ... moves one toward others in attempts to repair damage done, often through confession and restitution." See Parker and Thomas, "Psychological Differences in Shame vs. Guilt," 217.

29. Interestingly, as Biddle notes, "the Indo-European root *(skam* or *skem)* for the modern English word, 'shame,' could either denote the 'hide' (skin) of an animal or function as the verb 'to hide.'" See Mark E. Biddle, "Genesis 3: Sin, Shame and Self-Esteem," *Review & Expositor* 103, no. 2 (March 1, 2006): n.22, 369.

30. June Price Tangney, "Moral Affect: The Good, the Bad, and the Ugly," *Journal of Personality & Social Psychology* 61, no. 4 (October 1991): 599.

31. Niels Henrik Gregersen, "Guilt, Shame, and Rehabilitation: The Pedagogy of Divine Judgment," *Dialog: A Journal of Theology* 39, no. 2 (Summer 2000): 111.

32. Laurel Arthur Burton, "Original Sin or Original Shame," *Quarterly Review* 8, no. 4 (December 1, 1988): 37.

33. Biddle, "Genesis 3," 363.

34. Carl D. Schneider, *Shame, Exposure and Privacy* (New York: W. W. Norton, 1992). Others who take a similar position on healthy shame include John Bradshaw, *Healing the Shame That Binds You* (Deerfield Beach, FL: Health Communications, 1988); David W. Augsburger, *Pastoral Counseling across Cultures* (Philadelphia: Westminster Press, 1986); Lewis B. Smedes, *Shame and Grace: Healing the Shame We Don't Deserve* (San Francisco: Harper, 1993).

(*honte*). Discretionary shame relates to the private aspects of relationship and sexuality.[35] It has a role in safeguarding modesty, privacy, and propriety. It guards the boundaries of the self.

Robert Albers, a leading Christian writer on the nature of shame, argues that this healthy form of shame manifests itself as awe before God. "It is an acknowledgement of the gap and the gulf between the human and the divine."[36] The prophet Isaiah in the reception of his call in Isaiah 6:1–8 and Peter in his confession of sinfulness in Luke 5:5 both experienced this healthy sense of shame. In contrast, Brené Brown states that shame is always bad. It may simply be a matter of language. What Brené Brown and others such as Lewis, Kaufman, and Tangney are talking about is "disgrace shame." Thus, rather than set out the arguments against the "healthy shame" position, it will be assumed that the subject of this paper is "disgrace shame" rather than "discretionary shame."

SHAME AS THE LOCATION FOR ATONEMENT

The need to consider, particularly in the West, how the atonement might be understood if its "location" is the reality and experience of shame, rather than guilt, can be justified for at least two reasons. First of all, in Western society people generally no longer carry a sense of sin as personal guilt for moral wrongdoing. Wolfhart Pannenberg states the contemporary situation as follows:

> In modern times a Christianity which takes its bearings from the problem of guilt has increasingly come up against lack of understanding and mistrust among people who do not feel themselves to be sinners and who consequently believe that they do not need the message of forgiveness either.[37]

However, as Capps argues in *The Depleted Self: Sin in a Narcissistic Age*, people still "feel bad about themselves"; they still feel "that something is seriously wrong."[38] The reason for this is shame, which has become the dominant emotion which people in Western culture struggle with. It is through the experience of shame, Capps argues, that people today will experience their sinful nature.

---

35. Fowler, "Shame," 217.
36. Robert H. Albers, *Shame: A Faith Perspective* (New York: Haworth Press, 1995), 11.
37. Wolfhart Pannenberg, *The Apostles' Creed in the Light of Today's Questions* (Philadelphia: Westminster Press, 1972), 163.
38. Donald Capps, *The Depleted Self: Sin in a Narcissistic Age* (Minneapolis: Fortress Press, 1993), 39.

Alan Mann in his book *Atonement for a 'Sinless' Society* argues a similar position. He uses the term "sinless," since most contemporary Westerners would equate sin with guilt. Mann argues that due to the intensity of emphasis placed upon the self in post-industrialized society, most people experience "a chronic, internalised, dis-ease," which is in fact shame.[39] Indeed, the modern, individualized self, which is acutely aware of the opinions of others and increasingly obsessed with self-esteem, is arguably more shame-prone than ever before.[40]

Secondly, in comparison to guilt, shame is in fact the deeper, more pervasive human experience and reality since its focus is on one's sense of self and worthiness rather than on one's behavior. It is one's sense of self that lies at the root of one's behavior—sinful or otherwise. Shame, as Erikson suggests, has always been the more significant experience, since it precedes guilt. And as we have seen, shame can be thought of as the root cause of much dysfunction/sinful behavior: anger, aggression, violence, addiction, self-centeredness, the inability to empathize and love, etc.

Despite what may be claimed by those in the Western theological tradition, it is arguable that shame has always been the more significant dynamic. For example, psychologist Paul Pruyser, in his study of Augustine's *Confessions*, found little that would indicate a guilt dynamic but much that indicated a struggle with shame.[41] The same has been argued by Donald Capps, former professor of pastoral theology at Princeton Theological Seminary.[42]

A relational anthropology rooted in trinitarian relationality, as articulated by various contemporary theologians, would also point to the consideration of shame for locating atonement, since shame is a relational concept.[43] The relational origins of shame, particularly in the context of the infant-parent relationship, have been noted. Shame disrupts relationship with self, with

---

39. Alan Mann, *Atonement for a 'Sinless' Society: Engaging with an Emerging Culture* (Milton Keynes: Paternoster, 2005), 31.

40. Pattison, *Shame: Theory, Therapy, Theology*, 144.

41. Paul Pruyser, "Psychological Examination: Augustine," *Journal for the Scientific Study of Religion*, 5 (1965–66).

42. See Donald Capps, "Augustine's Confessions: The Scourge of Shame and the Silencing of Adeodatus," in *The Hunger of the Heart: Reflections on the Confessions of Augustine*, eds. Donald Capps and James E. Dittes (West Lafayette, IN: Society for the Scientific Study of Religion, 1990), 69–92; Donald Capps, "Augustine as Narcissist: Of Grandiosity and Shame," in *The Hunger of the Heart: Reflections on the Confessions of Augustine*, eds. Donald Capps and James E. Dittes (West Lafayette, IN: Society for the Scientific Study of Religion, 1990), 169–84. See also Tianyue Wu, "Shame in the Context of Sin: Augustine on the Feeling of Shame in De Civitate Dei," *Recherches de Théologie et Philosophie Médiévales* 74, no. 1 (January 1, 2007): 1–31.

43. For example, see Stanley J. Grenz, *The Social God and the Relational Self: A Trinitarian Theology of the Imago Dei* (Louisville: Westminster John Knox Press, 2001).

others, and, as will be argued, with God. Shame causes a withdrawal from relationships. The "self" ironically becomes lost in its own sense of self. If sin fundamentally affects our humanity and our humanity is essentially relational, then shame must be seen as a more significant problem than guilt. Guilt is experienced at a behavioral level. Shame, if a relational anthropology is assumed, is experienced at an ontological level.

All of this coheres when the narrative of Genesis 3 is considered. Despite the fact that it is commonly employed to give a basis for seeing sin in terms of a guilt problem, the focus is shame. Guilt is not named, referred to, or implied. In eating the fruit and disobeying what God had said, Adam and Eve tellingly did not feel guilt or remorse. Rather, they felt shame with regard to their nakedness. Mirroring one of the key effects of shame, they experienced exposure and so felt the need to hide, first of all covering themselves with fig leaves (Gen 3:7) and then hiding in the bushes when they heard the Lord God walking in the garden in the cool of the day (Gen 3:8). It is too excruciating for them to be "in the open" and to continue to be in intimate relationship with God. Their sense of vulnerability is too painful. They are no longer willing to be seen in the eyes of a perceived "critical Other."

There are also a number of other key indicators of shame, based in the shame research described above. Adam and Eve each exhibit blaming, fear, a failure to take responsibility for their actions, passivity and powerlessness, and a preoccupation with appearance. There is alienation from self, from each other, and, perhaps most notably, from God. As Kaufman would say, the interpersonal bridges have been disrupted. The indicators of anger and aggression are not present, but significantly, these do arise in the narrative of Cain and Abel in Genesis 5, which can also be interpreted as a story that revolves around the issue of shame, this time between siblings.[44]

God's response would also indicate that the key issue is shame rather than guilt or even disobedience. God's immediate response, in asking the question "Where are you?" can be interpreted as God calling Adam and Eve out of their shame and back into intimate, open, and vulnerable relationship. God then compassionately provides Adam and Eve with a more permanent and durable covering for their sense of shame. In this picture God is not "a critical Other," but it appears this is now what Adam and Eve think and, more importantly, *feel* as they hide in the bushes. The

---

44. Robin Stockitt, *Restoring the Shamed: Towards a Theology of Shame*, Kindle Edition (Eugene, OR: Cascade Books, 2012), loc. 383ff.

interpretation of the world as a critical, unsafe place, and of God as an unsafe relational partner, again points to shame.

Dietrich Bonhoeffer stands out as one of the few Western theologians who have reflected on shame in relation to sin and the narrative of Genesis 3. For Bonhoeffer, shame was a result of humanity's grief over its estrangement from God. In *Ethics* he writes,

> Shame is man's ineffaceable recollection of his estrangement from the origin; it is grief for this estrangement, and the powerless longing to return to unity with the origin.... Shame is more original than remorse.[45]

Shame is the experience of "disunion" with God. In reflecting on Genesis 3 Bonhoeffer states, "In the unity of unbroken obedience man is naked in the presence of man, uncovered, revealing both body and soul, and yet he is not ashamed. Shame only comes into existence in the world of division."[46] In this place of division, or disunion, a person can really only see themselves and their nakedness, not God.[47] For Bonhoeffer, shame, therefore, can only be overcome when the original unity is restored.[48]

In the Genesis narrative it is possible to see the shame dynamic begin even before Adam and Eve's "act of disobedience," in their conversation with the serpent. The serpent's question (Gen 3:1), and then response (Gen 3:4–5), can be interpreted as a way of questioning and diminishing the inherent and God-given worth of Adam and Eve. Perhaps Adam and Eve were missing out on something? Perhaps their humanity is lacking in something? Perhaps their condition, naked and vulnerable, is not "fully acceptable"? Here are the seeds of shame: a basic questioning of Adam and Eve's goodness and worthiness and the creation of a sense of discomfort with their creatureliness. This is the lie of the serpent: Adam and Eve are not good enough, and God cannot be trusted.

Thus Biddle makes the following assertion:

> They consume the fruit, in part, because they disdain mere humanity. Rather than express the nobility and autonomy inherent in their status as bearers of God's image by asserting their confidence in God's trustworthiness, they allow themselves to be duped by their inferior, the serpent,

---

45. Dietrich Bonhoeffer, *Ethics* (New York: Macmillan, 1955), 20.
46. Ibid., 63.
47. See ibid., 145.
48. See ibid., 146–47. In an assessment of Bonhoeffer's reflections Pattison states, "Bonhoeffer's comments upon shame are tantalisingly brief. While suggestive and intriguing, they are unclear and unsystematic. Without the benefit of much modern psychological thinking about shame, Bonhoeffer's concept of this phenomenon seems to be based on a couple of verses in Genesis 3 in which humans recognise themselves to be naked and then cover themselves." See Pattison, *Shame: Theory, Therapy, Theology*, 192.

who is merely "cunning" (Gen 3:1) and not wise.... It is only fitting, then, that immediately upon consuming the fruit, they become acutely aware of their creatureliness.[49]

If Adam's problem is shame, then all humanity, bound up with Adam as the apostle Paul argues in Romans 5, also has a problem with shame. The universal human experience of shame, even across cultures, has been evidenced by the research on shame. It can even be thought of as the primary problem with regard to the human condition.[50]

CONSTRUCTING ATONEMENT AS A REMEDY FOR SHAME

Despite these considerations, as Stephen Pattison notes, "For most theologians, shame has not been a significant phenomenon as part of human experience or as a feature of the relationship between humans and God."[51] The result is that shame has received a negligible amount of sustained theological consideration. For example, in Barth's *Church Dogmatics* only three direct references to shame are indexed.[52]

If this is the case with regard to theological reflection in general, then it is particularly the case with regard to a theology of the atonement. Few, if any, recent scholarly works on the atonement consider the topic of shame as being of importance.[53] It should be noted that there are significant numbers of books written from a pastoral theology perspective, but few of them consider that a theology of the atonement might have a role to play in a response to those suffering from chronic shame.[54]

---

49. Biddle, "Genesis 3," 362.
50. For an argument that "original sin" ought to be thought of in terms of "original shame," see Burton, "Original Sin or Original Shame."
51. Pattison, *Shame: Theory, Therapy, Theology*, 190.
52. See ibid., 191. According to Pattison, "It appears that Barth almost incidentally identifies a number of different kinds of theologically significant shame in the pursuit of the more central theme of sin."
53. In his major work on shame, published in 2000, Pattison states, "A number of important recent British theological books that have heralded a revival of interest in atonement, Gunton (1988), Fiddes (1989) and Bradley (1995), find no space for shame as a category for thought and analysis. The word is not even mentioned in the indexes of these books." See ibid., 190.
54. For example, see Biddle, "Genesis 3"; Neil Pembroke, "Pastoral Care for Shame-Based Perfectionism," *Pastoral Psychology* 61, no. 2 (April 2012): 245–58; Robert H. Albers, "The Shame Factor: Theological and Pastoral Reflections Relating to Forgiveness," *Word & World* 16, no. 3 (June 1, 1996): 347–53; Rebecca Thomas and Stephen Parker, "Toward a Theological Understanding of Shame," *Journal of Psychology & Christianity* 23, no. 2 (Summer 2004): 176–82; Nancy Stiehler Thurston, "When 'Perfect Fear Casts Out All Love': Christian Perspectives on the Assessment and Treatment of Shame," *Journal of Psychology and Christianity Spring 1994*, April 1, 1994; J. Earl Thompson Jr., "Shame in Pastoral Psychotherapy," *Pastoral Psychology* 44, no. 5 (May 1, 1996): 311–20; John M. Berecz and Herb Helm, "Shame: The Underside of Christianity," *Journal of Psychology and Christianity Spring 1998*, April 1, 1998; Burton, "Original Sin or Original Shame."

There have, however, been some recent exceptions.[55] One of these is an article by Brad A. Binau entitled "When Shame Is the Question, How Does the Atonement Answer?" published in 2002.[56] Binau notes there that "I know of no approach to the atonement ... that seeks to frame the doctrine as a response to human shame."[57] In responding to this lack, Binau argues for a view of the atonement that is anchored in the concept of "recapitulation." The remainder of his paper agrees that recapitulation is a potentially helpful way of understanding the atonement if the human problem that atonement deals with is shame. It also argues that atonement as recapitulation becomes even more helpful if augmented by Torrance's understanding of the concept of the vicarious humanity of Christ.

The idea of recapitulation, which finds its origin in Irenaeus and then Athanasius, is well known.[58] Guided by the apostle Paul's thinking in 1 Corinthians 5 and Romans 5, Irenaeus saw Jesus as the "Second Adam," summing up all humanity and, through his life, death, and resurrection, recreating humanity. All that went wrong in Adam which was passed on to the entire human race has been undone in all the actions of Christ. As Binau helpfully puts it, "Irenaeus understood Christ to have entered the human situation as the new Adam, going over the same ground as the old Adam, but in a way that through perfect obedience leads to a different outcome."[59] This new outcome in Christ is trust, obedience, and faithfulness instead of mistrust, disobedience, and faithlessness. It is perfectly possible to also see the outcome as including openness and the embrace of vulnerability instead of hiding and shame. The "New Adam" way of being and living is played out during the whole of Christ's life. With a recapitulation framework, shame can be included in the work of Christ since it is part of the human situation.

---

55. Exceptions include Paul W. Pruyser, "Anxiety, Guilt, and Shame in the Atonement," *Theology Today* 21, no. 1 (April 1, 1964): 15–33; C. Norman Kraus, *Jesus Christ Our Lord: Christology from a Disciple's Perspective* (Scottdale, PA: Herald Press, 1987); Mark D. Baker and Joel B. Green, *Recovering the Scandal of the Cross: Atonement in New Testament and Contemporary Contexts* (Downers Grove, IL: InterVarsity, 2011); Mann, *Atonement for a 'Sinless' Society*; Stockitt, *Restoring the Shamed*.

56. See Brad A. Binau, "When Shame Is the Question, How Does the Atonement Answer?," *Journal of Pastoral Theology* 12, no. 1 (January 1, 2002): 89–113.

57. Ibid., 89–90.

58. The word *recapitulation* is based on the Greek word *anakephalaiōsasthai*, found in Eph 1:8–10, meaning "summing up."

59. Binau, "When Shame Is the Question," 99.

The reality of recapitulation on the part of Jesus means the recreation of humanity—a new humanity in Christ.[60] This is not simply the forgiveness of sins or guilt being dealt with. If forgiveness of sins was all that atonement did, then humanity would still be lost in its shame. Shame affects humanity ontologically and existentially; it affects humanity down to its core. A work of global recreation is needed—the scope of atonement needs to be as wide as the scope of shame. Those struggling with shame would be helped to know that in Christ God has recreated every aspect of their life in the renewed image of God. If true humanity is lost in shame as the research shows, it is recreated in Christ through recapitulation.

For Irenaeus, Christ's identification with humanity is of supreme importance. Kelly, in describing Irenaeus's view of the atonement, states, "Because he identified [with] the human race at every phase of its existence, He restores fellowship with God to all, perfecting man according to God's image and likeness."[61] The theme of identification is unmistakably present throughout Irenaeus's atonement theology. For example:

> But how could we be joined to incorruptibility and immortality, unless, first, incorruptibility and immortality *had become that which we also are*, so that the corruptible might be swallowed up by incorruptibility, and the mortal by immortality, that we might receive the adoption of sons?[62]

> The Word of God, our Lord Jesus Christ [did] through His transcendent love, *become what we are*, that He might bring us to be even what He is Himself.[63]

> The Word of the Father and the Spirit of God, having *become united with the ancient substance of Adam's formation*, rendered man living and perfect, receptive of the perfect Father, in order that as in the natural [Adam] we all were dead, so in the spiritual we may all be made alive.[64]

---

60. It is well known that Athanasius explains this recreation in terms of the image of God in man being renewed. He states, "You know what happens when a portrait that has been painted on a panel becomes obliterated through external stains. The artist does not throw away the panel, but the subject of the portrait has to sit for it again, and then the likeness is re-drawn on the same material. Even so was it with the All-holy Son of God. He, the Image of the Father, came and dwelt in our midst, in order that He might renew mankind made after Himself." See Athanasius, *On the Incarnation: The Treatise De Incarnatione Verbi Dei*, trans. Penelope Lawson (Crestwood, NY: St. Vladimir's Seminary Press, 1998), 41–42.

61. J. N. D. Kelly, *Early Christian Doctrines* (New York: Harper, 1959), 173.

62. Irenaeus, "Against Heresies," in *The Ante-Nicene Fathers*, ed. A. Cleveland Coxe, reprinted, vol. 1 (Peabody, MA: Hendrickson, 1994), 448–449. Italics added.

63. Ibid., 526. Italics added.

64. Irenaeus, "Against Heresies," 527. Italics added.

This identification is potentially an incredibly helpful reality for a humanity lost in shame. In this location, those experiencing shame wonder whether they are worthy, lovable, special, noticeable, etc. By identifying with humanity God has fully and wholeheartedly embraced our humanity and creatureliness. There is no fundamental shame in being a human, even with all its vulnerability, imperfection, and limitations. This identification with the shamed is a theme throughout the life of Christ, from his shame-filled birth, to his years of ministry where he has no fear in associating himself with the outwardly shamed of society, to his shame-filled death. Christ's identification as outlined by Irenaeus and Athanasius, and the testimony of the gospel narratives, are a denial of the counter-reality created by shame. In Christ's identification with humanity, God fully moves toward humanity even though humanity is lost in sin. Our humanity does not repel God. Our humanity leads God to embrace us in our shame. If the location of the first Adam was paradisiacal Eden, the location of the second Adam is shame-filled humanity.

From Irenaeus's statements, and from many others throughout the writing of the church fathers, the question arises as to whether the humanity that Christ takes on is pre- or postlapsarian. In other words, does Christ himself take on fallen human nature? What exactly was the human situation that Christ entered into as the new Adam?

There is *prima facie* biblical support for the view that Christ took upon himself fallen humanity. The writer to the Hebrews is clear that Christ was in all respects like other human beings but was without personal sin (Heb 2:14; 4:15). The apostle Paul states, Christ was sent "in the likeness of sinful flesh" (Rom 8:3). It should be noted, however, that in the contemporary theological context the issue is a controversial one.[65] One of the problems is how Christ's fallen humanity can/could be held together with his personal sinlessness. Nevertheless, for Barth, the assumption of our fallen humanity must be maintained:

> There must be no weakening or obscuring of the saving truth that the nature which God assumed in Christ is identical with our nature as we see it in the light of the Fall. If it were otherwise, how could Christ really be like us? What concern could we have with him? We stand before God

---

65. For example, see Oliver D. Crisp, "Did Christ Have a Fallen Human Nature?," *International Journal of Systematic Theology* 6, no. 3 (July 1, 2004): 270–88; Kelly M. Kapic, "The Son's Assumption of a Human Nature: A Call for Clarity," *International Journal of Systematic Theology* 3, no. 2 (July 1, 2001): 154–66.

characterised by the Fall. God's Son not only assumed our nature but He entered the concrete form of our nature, under which we stand before God as men damned and lost.[66]

This quote by Barth continues to raise questions when the problem of shame is at the forefront. Does the "concrete form" of our humanity that Barth speaks about actually include the experience of shame? If our shame is the location of the atonement, does Christ himself experientially remain outside of this location? Or, to put it in terms borrowed from Gregory of Nazianzus, if Jesus is going to heal human shame, does he need to assume it? Recapitulation pushes a positive answer to all these questions to the forefront. However, in seeking further help we turn to Torrance's understanding of the vicarious humanity of Christ and his understanding of incarnational atonement.

For Torrance, the mediation of Christ in atonement is of crucial importance. The hypostatic union means that all that Christ accomplishes as mediator is accomplished from within the being and life of Christ, not external to the person of Christ.[67] It is in Christ himself that the reconciliation between God and humanity occurs. For this to happen, the Son of God must assume our sinful and corrupt humanity. Torrance states:

> In his incarnation the Son of God penetrated into the dark recesses of our human existence and condition where we are enslaved in original sin, in order to bring the redeeming love and holiness of God to bear upon us in the distorted ontological depths of our human being.[68]

Unless there is an assumption of fallen humanity, there can be no reconciliation and no healing of corrupt human nature.[69] Here Torrance uses the same reasoning as Irenaeus, Athanasius, and Gregory of Nazianzus. Torrance expresses the relationship of Christ's assumption of fallen humanity and his healing of fallen humanity as follows:

> If the incarnate Son ... actually assumed our flesh of sin, the fallen, corrupt and enslaved human nature which we have inherited from Adam, then the redeeming activity of Christ took place within the ontological

66. Karl Barth, *Church Dogmatics*, trans. Geoffrey W. Bromiley, vol. I/2 (Edinburgh: T&T Clark, 1956), 153.
67. See Thomas F. Torrance, *The Trinitarian Faith: The Evangelical Theology of the Ancient Catholic Church* (Edinburgh: T&T Clark, 1988), 155.
68. Thomas F. Torrance, *Karl Barth: Biblical and Evangelical Theologian* (Edinburgh: T&T Clark, 1990), 203.
69. See Thomas F. Torrance, *The Mediation of Christ* (Grand Rapids: Eerdmans, 1984), 66.

depths of his humanity in such a way that far from sinning himself, he condemned sin in the flesh and sanctified what he assumed.[70]

Even though Torrance does not talk of the fallen human condition in terms of shame, it is relatively easy to extend his description of fallen humanity to include shame. Thus, if shame is the problem, then for Torrance, Christ's response must be made from within the reality of that shame "as one with us and one of us."[71] This would then mean that Christ assumed shame-filled humanity and all the fears, tensions, doubts, suspicions, and ways of seeing that accompany shame, yet he did this in such a way that he himself did not live out the behavior that comes from shame attested to by the shame research. In other words, Christ withstood the onslaught of shame. Shame, as argued above, affects humanity ontologically. If shame is the problem of the human condition, then atonement must take place at the same ontological level. This, according to Torrance, is what we find in Christ's atoning work in his assumption of fallen humanity.

To know that Christ assumed our shame at the ontological depths of his humanity is a powerful truth. Shame is different from guilt. It cannot be dealt with by external action. In other words, it cannot be dealt with simply by a word of forgiveness or an act of contrition or the bearing of some kind of punishment.[72] Torrance refers to versions of the gospel built around such actions as gospels of external relation. If shame is the problem, then such versions will not be sufficient. Shame requires something to take place within the reality of shame.

The vicarious humanity of Christ is a linchpin in Torrance's theological scheme. For Torrance, the whole of the Christ's earthly activity is done on behalf of humanity and in the place of humanity:

> Jesus steps into the place where we are summoned to have faith in
> God, to believe and trust in him, and acts in our place and in our stead
> from within the depths of our unfaithfulness and provides us with a faith-
> fulness which we may share.... That is to say, if we think of belief, trust
> or faith as forms of human activity before God, then we must think of

---

70. Thomas F. Torrance, "Incarnation and Atonement: Theosis and Henosis in the Light of Modern Scientific Rejection of Dualism," *Society of Ordained Scientists* Bulletin No.7 (Spring 1992): 12, quoted in Myk Habets, *Theosis in the Theology of Thomas Torrance* (Farnham: Ashgate, 2009), 72.

71. Thomas F. Torrance, *The Christian Doctrine of God: One Being Three Persons* (Edinburgh: T&T Clark, 1996), 101.

72. Albers, with regard to priestly words that declare forgiveness, states that "where disgrace shame is the operating dynamic, these gracious words cannot be heard, and the declaration of forgiveness may even exacerbate the sense of shame because the person now is shamed for not believing the word of God!" See Albers, "The Shame Factor," 350.

Jesus Christ as believing, trusting and having faith in God the Father on our behalf and in our place.[73]

It is the entire course of Christ's life that is lived for us and on our behalf, but it is perhaps most intense in Christ's passion and death. In Gethsemane and at Calvary, Christ "penetrates the utmost extremity of our self-alienating flight from God where we are trapped in death, and turned everything around so that out of the fearful depths of our darkness and dereliction we may cry with him, 'Our Father.'"[74] Thus, the prayer in Gethsemane is a vicarious one. For Torrance, Christ assumes our selfish human will and turns it back to God in willing obedience on our behalf and in our place.

If the problem, which the atonement answers, is shame, then we must say that Christ's vicarious humanity is lived out in the location of shame. This seems to clearly be the case when reflecting on the cross and, in particular, Christ's cry of dereliction.

The shame-fullness of the cross has been well documented in recent years, particularly by New Testament scholars who have wrestled with the shame-honor culture of first-century Mediterranean culture.[75] Albers refers to the cross as "God's shame-bearing symbol for the world."[76] The cross was reserved for those least worthy of respect. It was a vulgar word for civilized Romans and so not used in polite company. It was not uncommon for the condemned to be killed before crucifixion since the point was shame and humiliation rather than a mere painful death. Shame is used to destroy the person through destroying one's name and reputation.

For Christ, all of this is compounded by how he is treated prior to his crucifixion: rejected by the crowds who had previously acclaimed him, bound and silenced, teased and badgered, dressed up like a pretend, grotesque king, spat upon, used for humiliating sport, and beaten. All of this comes to a head on the cross itself. Christ is abandoned with a mocking

73. Torrance, *The Mediation of Christ*, 82–83.
74. Ibid., 79.
75. For some of the main examples, see Jerome H. Neyrey, *The Social World of Luke-Acts: Models for Interpretation* (Peabody, MA: Hendrickson Publishers, 1991); Jerome H. Neyrey, *Honor and Shame in the Gospel of Matthew* (Louisville: Westminster John Knox Press, 1998); Jerome H. Neyrey, "Despising the Shame of the Cross: Honor and Shame in the Johannine Passion Narrative," *Semeia* 68 (1994): 113–37; Bruce J. Malina, *The New Testament World: Insights From Cultural Anthropology* (Atlanta: John Knox Press, 1981); Martin Hengel, *Crucifixion in the Ancient World and the Folly of the Message of the Cross* (Philadelphia: Fortress Press, 1977); J. J. Pilch, "Death with Honor: The Mediterranean Style Death of Jesus in Mark," *Biblical Theology Bulletin* 25, no. 2 (1995): 65–70; Richard Bauckham, *Jesus and the God of Israel: God Crucified and Other Studies on the New Testament's Christology of Divine Identity* (Grand Rapids: Eerdmans, 2009).
76. Albers, "The Shame Factor," 352.

sign above his head, hearing the derision of passersby. Perhaps most significantly, in terms of shame, he died naked, exposed before the world. Here the two Adams are linked by shame and nakedness. It is in the midst of this shame and nakedness that the most ignominious shame is experienced: the feeling of abandonment by God. "My God, My God," Jesus cries, "why have you forsaken me?" (Matt 27:46 NIV).

> It is there that we are carried to the extreme edges of our existence, to the very brink of the abysmal chasm that separates us from God. It is there that we see the end of all of our theologizing, in sheer God-forsakenness, in the desolate waste where God is hidden from us by our sin and self-will and self-inflicted blindness and where, as it were, God has 'died out on us', and is no where to be found by any man.[77]

As with the prayer in Gesthemane, this cry of God-forsakenness is vicarious. C. Baxter Kruger powerfully and poetically describes this reality while also referring to the experience of shame contained in it:

> Who has cried this cry? Is this not the cry of Adam, blind and trembling in the bushes? Is this not the unspeakable fear of every human heart trapped in the great darkness, with no true vision of the Father? ... Under the shame of our angst-ridden imaginations, mocked by the endless misperceptions of the self-righteous and the all-seeing religious eye, Jesus ... identified with us. He heard the haunting harassing whisper, 'I am not acceptable, not good enough, not important,' and he felt the bitter curse of its judgment. With the leaves of the garden rustling with the rumor of our failure, he stared into the terrifying shadows of rejection and abandonment.[78]

It is here that it is possible to see in Christ that God himself has penetrated the depths of the shame that haunts and infects humanity. However, it is in this very location that Christ nevertheless is faithful to the Father and trusts his life over to his care and love. He turns our shame-filled humanity back to God in faith. "Father, into your hands I commit my Spirit" (Luke 23:46). He reconstructs and alters the existence of humanity "by yielding himself in perfect love and trust to the Father."[79] In the depths of shame, instead of moving away from "the Other," Christ moves toward "the Other."

---

77. Thomas F. Torrance, *Theology in Reconstruction* (Grand Rapids: Eerdmans, 1966), 124.

78. C. Baxter Kruger, "The Hermeneutical Nightmare and the Reconciling Work of Jesus Christ," in *An Introduction to Torrance Theology: Discovering the Incarnate Saviour*, ed. Gerrit Scott Dawson (New York; London: T&T Clark, 2007), 165.

79. Torrance, *Theology in Reconstruction*, 125.

By following Torrance here, it is possible to construct an understanding of the atonement in which the depths of humanity's shame are the location for the great atoning exchange. He becomes what we are so that we might become what he is.[80] For Torrance the exchange embraced the whole relation between Christ and humanity. And so Christ's obedience is exchanged for humanity's disobedience; Christ's life is exchanged for humanity's death; Christ's strength is exchanged for humanity's weakness.[81] To this list we can add: Christ's embrace of his own vulnerability is exchanged for humanity's shame.

ATONEMENT AS THE RENEWAL OF THE RUPTURED INTERPERSONAL BRIDGE

As noted above, according to Kaufman, the origins of shame can be traced to the rupture, or breakdown, of interpersonal relational bridges necessary for the healthy development of one's sense of self.[82] The most important of these bridges is that between a parent and a child. Because humans are relational beings, such a rupture can have a devastating effect on our humanity, on our ability to both receive and give love. The rupture can continue through adolescence and into adulthood, affecting all our relationships.

The Genesis 3 narrative can be interpreted as telling the story of the rupture of the interpersonal bridge between humanity and God and the resulting consequences. Such a rupture occurs not on God's part, but by humanity believing the lie of the serpent and by eating from the fruit. For Kaufman, the solution to shame lies in restoring the interpersonal bridge, which for Kaufman can take place in the relationship between a counselor and client. However, over and above any pastoral response, the solution to the problem of shame can be found in the atonement.

In Christ's atoning work of recapitulation and vicarious humanity, which takes place in the ontological depths of human shame, the ruptured interpersonal bridge is renewed between God and humanity in Christ himself. In Christ, humanity is able to once again love and receive love — not only in relation to God, but also in relation to other human beings. This then becomes the recovery of our humanity.

80. See Torrance, *The Trinitarian Faith*, 78.
81. Ibid., 181.
82. Kaufman, *Shame: The Power of Caring*, 12–17.

CHAPTER 10

ATONEMENT AND HUMAN SUFFERING

BRUCE L. MCCORMACK

INTRODUCTION

Most Christians do not know why Jesus died. Not really. There was a time when evangelicals thought they knew, but they do so no longer. Embarrassment over the penal substitution theory which most of us grew up with haunts us now; the faith of our parents and grandparents is not our own. The truth is that most of us would do almost anything to avoid having to answer the question in any great detail. That He died "for us"—most still would like to be able to say that much; that His death was somehow vicarious, an act of substitution—*maybe*.

Whether this is best understood in a judicial, an ontological, or an ethical frame of reference (to put the matter in the broadest terms possible) is a question we prefer not to have to answer, or that we answer in a highly disintegrative way (e.g., playing the "ontological" off against the judicial and the ethical to the obvious detriment of the latter two frames of reference).

The one thing many do seem to be sure of is this: The God we serve could not possibly have *willed* what took place on that final weekend in Jerusalem. Whatever else we say, we cannot and must not suggest that God willed the death of His Son, that in His death Christ served a divine purpose. God willed the incarnation, yes. God willed the healing of human nature in Christ and His triumph over death in the resurrection. But the death itself? No. Our God is a nonviolent God. But that is not the way the New Testament tells the story.

Hear the words of Karl Barth, a man not yet subject to our anxieties or prone to our rationalizations:

> In His passion, the name of God active and revealed in Him is *conclusively* sanctified; *His will is done* on earth as it is done in heaven; His kingdom comes, in a form and with a power to which as a man He can only give a terrified but determined assent. And in the passion He exists *conclusively* as the One He is—the Son of God who is also the Son of Man. In the deepest darkness of Golgotha, He enters supremely into the glory of the unity of the Son with the Father. In that abandonment by God He is the One who is directly loved by God. This is the secret that we have to see and understand.[1]

Notice carefully what Barth has said. In Christ's passion, God's will *was* done—*on earth as it is in heaven*. The answer to the prayer we pray in churches across the land, Sunday by Sunday, the prayer which Jesus taught His disciples, was answered decisively and definitively here in the passion and death of Christ.

But now see what Barth says next!

> What we have to say along these lines is ... in direct contradiction to the conception of the passion story which has found its classical exposition in the St. Matthew's Passion of Bach.... In an almost unbroken minor it is a wonderful cloud-pattern of sighs and lamentations and complaints, of cries of horror and sorrow and sympathy. It is a tragic ode culminating in a conventional funeral dirge ('Rest Softly'). *It is neither determined nor delimited by the Easter message,* and Jesus never once speaks in it as the Victor. When is the Church going to realize, and to make it clear to the thousands and thousands who have direct knowledge of the evangelical passion-story only in this form, that what we have here is only an abstraction and not the real passion of Jesus Christ?[2]

Jesus is Victor in His death because it is in His death that death itself dies. This understanding—expressed with great intuitive insight by Gregory Nazianzen when he said, "He dies, but He gives life, and by His death destroys death"[3]—was made central in Reformed soteriology in the seventeenth century. For John Owen, the death of death was understood to occur in the death of Christ, not in the resurrection.[4] The resurrection

---

1. Karl Barth, *CD* IV/2, 252 (emphases added).
2. Ibid., 252–53 (emphasis added).
3. Gregory of Nazianzus, "The Theological Orations" in Edward R. Hardy, ed., *Christology of the Later Fathers* (Philadelphia: Westminster Press, 1954), 175.
4. John Owen, *The Death of Death in the Death of Jesus Christ*, with an introduction by J. I. Packer (Edinburgh: Banner of Truth, 1995).

is the public and universal declaration of the death of death in the death of Jesus Christ, a declaration which is itself a creative and effective Word which brings new life, new creation. But it is not the cause of death's demise.

The negative significance of this insight is that Jesus was not, in His death, a victim. Or better perhaps: He was not only that. And to the extent that we focus our attention there, we miss the overarching story being told in the Gospels and concern ourselves instead with a spin-off, a sequel which cannot stand comparison with the original. The positive significance lies in the fact that Christ's death was willed by Him—and willed at the cost of enduring an excruciating spiritual struggle to unite His will with that of His Father. And make no mistake: this was the will of the Father. Jesus was not laboring under a misunderstanding. As Peter put it in his great prayer of thanksgiving in Acts 4:27–28:

> For in this city [Sovereign Lord] ... both Herod and Pontius Pilate, with the Gentiles and the peoples of Israel, gathered together against your holy servant Jesus, whom you anointed, to do whatever your hand and plan had predestined to occur (NRSV).

Let's be honest: The narrative structure of the Gospels is torn to shreds where it is not recognized that Jesus Christ came into this world to suffer and die. Historians of the New Testament may wish to deny it, with their attempts to devalue Jesus' predictions of His suffering and death. But even those who protest most loudly against historical-critical reconstructions of the life of Jesus often fail to take as seriously as they ought the fact that, as Hans Urs von Balthasar put it, "It is impossible to suppose that God could use this death to reconcile the world to himself if the one who died it was unaware of its significance."[5]

Of course, the minute one says such things today, the immediate response is going to be: It is not possible to make God responsible for the passion and death of Jesus without establishing some sort of "inner peace" on God's part with violence, with the torture and judicial murder of an innocent human being. If God willed the death of His only Son, then God Himself is capable of violence—which authorizes violence on the plane of human-to-human relations. Mind you, this objection is the most serious one that could be raised. It is a deeply moral objection, and it is to the

5.   Hans Urs von Balthasar, *Theo-drama: Theological Dramatic Theory*, vol. III, "Dramatis Personae: Persons in Christ" (San Francisco: Ignatius Press, 1992), 164.

credit of feminist theologians over the last decades to have raised it in a persuasive and compelling way that forces a good bit of rethinking where it is taken seriously.[6]

So how are we to think about God's will in the death of Jesus? Can we do so in a way that does not establish an "inner peace" between God and violence? Yes, I think we can—though the way forward is anything but obvious. It requires that we think systematically across a range of doctrines which are affected quite dramatically by the decisions that will be made here, *locating* the doctrine of the atonement in relation to the doctrine of sin, to Christology, the doctrine of the Trinity, and the being and attributes of God, to name but a few.

My task in this essay is to locate the atonement in relation to human suffering. To carry out that task, I must begin with a delimitation. Human suffering is, at best, an analogy to the sufferings of Christ. Not because of a quantitative calculus, mind you. Others have certainly suffered as much or more. No, the difference between Christ's death and those of others is qualitative, not quantitative. And it is qualitative because the death He died was *not merely* physical.

We confuse ourselves a second time when we focus our attention on Christ's physical agonies and on death as a "separation of soul and body." Death in the latter sense is continuous with the death toward which all living things move "by nature" in this world. To be sure, the traditional talk of a "separation of soul and body" was an attempt to distinguish the kind of death humans die from the death experienced by other life forms. But even if that attempt had been successful, it would have told us nothing with regard to what makes the death of Jesus redemptive—for a merely biological death cannot possibly be redemptive.

The truth is that biological death was in this world long before human beings came into existence and, therefore, long before the fall of the latter into sin.[7] But the death which Adam and Eve died when they ate from the forbidden tree was not this death anyway. In the day they sinned, they did indeed die—but not biologically. They were instead driven from the garden, driven from the presence of God into the death of alienation from God. The death that they died was a handing over to sin and its conse-

---

6. For a respectful engagement with this critique, see Bruce L. McCormack, "The Only Mediator: The Person and Work of Christ in Evangelical Perspective" in Richard L. Lints, ed., *Renewing the Evangelical Mission* (Grand Rapids: Eerdmans, 2013), 266–69.

7. See on this point Christopher Southgate, *The Groaning of Creation: God, Evolution, and the Problem of Evil* (Louisville/London: Westminster/John Knox, 2008).

quences (Rom 1:24, 26, 28)—which prefigured and provisionally realized in a less complete form the final and definitive handing over of Christ to the *full* consequences of sin as death in God-abandonment (Rom 8:32). If we do not understand Christ to have died *this* death, then we will not understand it at all.

In what follows, I will begin by giving some attention to the gospel accounts of Jesus' death. I will turn in a second section to a critical engagement with that treatment of the death of Christ that has been most influential where my thinking about these matters is concerned, that of Hans Urs von Balthasar. In doing so, I will touch upon the Christology which I think best supports an adequate theology of the cross. After that, a third brief section will be devoted to the problem of human suffering.

I. THE DEATH OF CHRIST IN GOSPEL NARRATIVE

The four Gospels do not say the same things of the death of Christ. But they supplement one another in interesting ways. Their differences, when taken together, can produce a synthesis of enormous power and, indeed, considerable unity. Christ is, in His death, *the sinner*; not merely the bearer of the guilt of others (though He is that too) but the sinner.

This is the great insight of Karl Barth, an insight which takes us beyond classical penal substitution theories into the realm not of metaphysical speculation but of apocalyptic: The in-breaking of God's reign through the death of death and a new creation which lifts the finite above the conditions of life proper to it in this world.[8] In the description that follows, I am not interested in every detail of the four renditions of the story but in those elements which contribute most directly to a theological construal of the meaning of Christ's death.

Mark's rendering is the briefest and the most raw, the most tragically beautiful. Here darkness enshrouds the land, from noon until three in the afternoon (Mark 15:33). It ends with the cry of dereliction, the surrender of

---

8. See, for example, Karl Barth, *CD* IV/1, 247: "We are dealing with the painful confrontation of God and this man not with any evil, not merely with death, but with eternal death, with the power of that which is not. Therefore, we are not dealing merely with any sin, or with many sins.... We are dealing with sin itself and as such ... the corruption which God has made His own, for which He willed to take responsibility in this one man." And again, ibid., 253: "In the suffering and death of Jesus Christ, it has come to pass that in His own person He has made an end to us as sinners and therefore of sin itself by going to death as the One who took our place as sinners. In His person He has delivered us up as sinners and sin itself to destruction."

bodily life, and the tearing of the temple curtain. That darkness should have descended upon the earth at high noon is, in all likelihood, an evocation of Amos 8:9—"And on that day, says the Lord God, the sun will set at midday, and the light will grow dark upon the land at daytime"—a passage which speaks of the "day of the Lord," a day of divine judgment and, indeed, of punishment (cf. Mark.13:24).[9] The darkness is, I would say, a sign, a portent, of the passing away of the old world so that the new might be born.

More than that, though, Adela Yarbro Collins says that it is at least possible that this passage is connected in the mind of the Evangelist with the image of the cup of wrath which Jesus accepts in 14:36 as in accordance with the will of God.[10] This seems to me all the more probable given that the darkness comes to an end with the cry of dereliction and expiration. This is certainly not the death of a tragic hero.[11] The darkness does not begin at the point at which Jesus dies and last until Easter morning (as our Good Friday liturgies might lead us to expect). In Mark, the darkness comes to an end at that point, suggesting that the passion has a significance that far transcends the merely physical. The passion, in its physical dimensions, is but a symbol of the outpouring of the eschatological wrath of God—an outpouring which culminates in the anguish of a deeply personal separation, rejection, dereliction.

Or does it? Many there have been who have wanted to soften the significance of the cry of dereliction—to find in it a demonstration of Jesus' sympathy for sinners who, in His place, would have felt abandonment (though He, in reality, did not). But of such sympathy, the text says nothing. This interpretation, found in thinkers as diverse as Cyril and Friedrich Schleiermacher,[12] is the result of the imposition of a conclusion drawn from an ontological construct which has been devised without regard for the lived existence of the Subject depicted in this narrative and brought to the text from without.

One might be tempted to say (on the basis of a certain reading of the Chalcedonian Definition) that the experience was real enough, yet one would

---

9. See on this point, Joel Marcus, *Mark 8– 10: A New Translation with Introduction and Commentary* (New Haven: Yale University Press, 2009), 1054, 1062. Marcus says of this darkness, precisely in its character as judgment, that it recalls the darkness of Exodus 10:21: "a darkness that can be felt." And he adds, "Jesus feels it," which is why he immediately gives voice to the cry of dereliction, for darkness is also a sign of divine absence. Ibid., 1062, 1063.

10. Adela Yarbro Collins, *Mark: A Commentary* (Minneapolis: Fortress Press, 2007), 751.

11. Cf. Ibid., 754: "What is clear is that Mark did not portray Jesus' last words on the model of the noble death."

12. St. Cyril of Alexandria, *On the Unity of Christ* (Yonkers: St. Vladimir's Seminary Press, 1995), 105–6; Friedrich Schleiermacher, *The Christian Faith* (Philadelphia: Fortress Press, 1976), 436.

like to see it confined to the so-called human "nature" alone—the divine Logos, on this view, being preserved inviolate from all threat of dissolution of that bliss which is His "by nature." But on this point, too, our text is silent. Indeed, the centurion's confession, "Truly, *this man* was God's Son!" (Mark 15:39 NRSV), would lead us to raise serious doubts about this particular application of the Chalcedonian Definition. No, it is from a unified Subject (the God-human in His divine-human unity) that this word of lament and, I would say, complaint, is forcibly wrenched.[13] And the abandonment itself— because we are speaking here of divine judgment—is all too real. More than that cannot be said exegetically. But that much can be said.

The truth is that death in God-abandonment is not "saving" simply because a human has experienced it. This death is the death which ought to have come to all if God were merely "just." Any and every human could and should experience it; therefore, insofar as it is merely a human experience, it has no value "for all." The fact that it *is* "for all" strongly suggests that it is not merely a human experience but a human experience *in God*; it is something taken up very directly into the life of God, which is what the unified Subject of Chalcedon might have led us to expect, were it not accompanied by an implicit commitment to the notion of divine impassibility.

I should say, before continuing, that the question often raised as to whether the cry is intended to call to mind in the reader the whole of Psalm 22 or merely the first verse (which is all that is actually ascribed to Jesus) rests on an effort to bring comfort to ourselves. That Psalm ends in praise to the God who does not leave the psalmist in abandonment. So if the whole of the psalm is alluded to here, then the often-drawn conclusion is that the abandonment, even if real, does not threaten Christ's trust and confidence in God in the least. But the cry is followed immediately by death. And just as immediately, the lights come back on—which strongly suggests that the victory takes place *in and through* abandonment, not as a response to Jesus' perception of it—an abandonment which clearly extends into death.[14]

"Then Jesus gave a loud cry and breathed his last" (Mark 15:37 NRSV)—at which point the temple curtain is torn in two. It has been suggested that the two events are joined; that the "loud cry" is evidence of

---

13. See on this point, Marcus, *Mark 8–16*, 1063, where Jesus is said to "complain searingly."
14. See on this point, W. D. Davies and D. C. Allison, *A Critical and Exegetical Commentary on the Gospel According to Saint Matthew*, vol. III (London: T&T Clark, 1997), 625. Davies and Allison rightly protest against the attempt to construe the cry of dereliction in terms of unrecited verses from Psalm 22. They also note that divine abandonment, while real, finds a limit in the resurrection. Death in God-abandonment is not the final act.

the Spirit's departure from Jesus (since a crucified person dies of asphyxiation and would have no breath left with which to cry aloud)—a departure which results quite directly in the tearing of the curtain.[15] Joel Marcus says that the foregoing narrative renders this suggestion implausible, since it "points in the opposite direction. Jesus dies forsaken."[16] But surely, the departure of the Spirit from Jesus could just as well be seen as sealing that forsakenness and making it complete.[17] In any event, the curtain is torn.

The tearing has both a negative and a positive significance, both of which point once again to the in-breaking of God's reign, the passing away of the old world and the birth of the new. Divine judgment is here shown to serve the interests of divine mercy. "The glory of God" which had been hidden behind the veil "begins to radiate out into the world"[18]—and it is significant that the first to acknowledge it is a Gentile, the Roman centurion. God alone could remove the temple veil. He it was who ordered it to be put in place; He alone possessed the authority to effectively erase the boundary between God and human beings which it symbolized.[19]

To the foregoing account, Matthew's version adds that an earthquake took place as the curtain was being torn. Coincident with the earthquake, tombs were opened and the bodies of deceased saints were raised. These resurrected ones appeared to many in Jerusalem after the resurrection of Jesus. Davies and Allison interpret this as an eschatological sign whose meaning is: "Jesus' death is a resurrecting death; the dead are revived by his dying."[20] Here again, redeeming power is ascribed to the death of Jesus as such. It does not await His own resurrection to be made effective. The "primary purpose" is, however, witness in Jerusalem.[21] This is not yet the general resurrection of the dead but a proleptic event which testifies to a future whose power is present even now.[22]

---

15. Howard M. Jackson, "The Death of Jesus in Mark and the Miracle from the Cross," *New Testament Studies* 33 (1987): 27.

16. Marcus, *Mark 8–16*, 1,066.

17. This answer to Marcus is also sufficient to address the criticism offered by Collins. She writes, "The idea that a strong wind came forth from Jesus directed specifically and only at the veil of the temple is bizarre." Collins, *Mark*, 763. The valid point in this complaint has to do, of course, with the equation of the Spirit's work with a naturally conceived wind. But the work of the Spirit does not have to be explained in this way.

18. Ibid., 1,067.

19. Ibid., 1,066–67.

20. Davies and Allison, *The Gospel According to Saint Matthew*, vol. III, 633.

21. Ibid.

22. Davies and Allison are right to say that there is no hint of the "traditional equation of our passage with the descent into hell." Ibid. Of course, the fact that the traditional rendering of that theme is not to be found here offers no reason in itself that a nontraditional construal might not render the whole more meaningful.

Taken together, Mark and Matthew place the death of Jesus in the framework of apocalyptic expectation even as they revise those expectations christologically: "The Day of the Lord dawns on Golgotha: the divine judgment descends, and the first-fruits of the resurrection are gathered. The end of Jesus is the end of the world in miniature."[23] But the disclosure of the depths of human depravity in this scene does not take place through the actions of those who tortured and put to death an innocent; such expressions of depravity are, sadly, all too commonplace. Disclosure takes place rather through the silence of God which declares that this man was in His death the *sinner*—One who had taken personal responsibility for the sins of all and who had identified Himself to the uttermost with their cause. The Christological modulation of apocalyptic expectation is revealed precisely here, in that the destruction of sinners takes place in and through the destruction of *the* sinner.

The death of Jesus in Luke's gospel retains some apocalyptic elements (the darkness and the tearing of the temple curtain). But the cry of dereliction is no longer to be found between these two events. The effect of that decision is to make the darkness to be more nearly a sign of divine displeasure with the human beings who crucified Jesus, rather than a sign of judgment upon Jesus as *the* sinner. In the place of the cry of dereliction we find the "more edifying and exemplary saying: 'Father, into your hands I entrust my spirit,'"[24] a saying which could easily be turned in the direction of interpreting the death of Jesus as the death of a tragic hero if Luke should be treated in isolation from Mark and Matthew (a non-canonical hermeneutic, to be sure) or valued more highly for one reason or another.

More generally, though, the dying Jesus appears in Luke's gospel as more "in control," one might say. As in Mark and Matthew, Simon of Cyrene is made to carry the cross (Luke 23:26), thereby suggesting that Jesus has been physically weakened by His ordeal. And yet, He is still able (in Luke's telling of the story) to have a conversation with the "daughters of Jerusalem" (vv. 27–31 NRSV) and to tell them, "Do not weep for me, but weep for yourselves and for your children" (v. 28). Luke's Jesus prays from the cross for those who crucified Him: "Father, forgive them; for they do not know what they are doing" (v. 34). He has a conversation with the penitent thief which ends with a promise: "Truly I tell you, today you will be with me in Paradise" (v. 43). More in control, then; more spiritually powerful—even as He endures the agony of crucifixion.

---

23. Ibid., 639.
24. Collins, *Mark*, 754.

But then, Luke also has Jesus being strengthened by an angel (Luke 22:43), an element in the story that is missing in Mark and Matthew. Interestingly enough, in spite of the heroic nature of much that is said in Luke—again, when read in isolation—the introduction of an angel testifies to the very human nature of the enterprise. There is no evidence here of a divine Person (the Logos) acting through the man Jesus instrumentally. That does not mean, of course, that a dyothelite Christology has been rendered impossible; far from it. It only means that the version of it which would make the human "nature" of Christ to be the instrument of the divine Person faces a challenge—even in Luke's treatment of the death of Jesus.

The saying to the penitent thief deserves further comment. That the thief should be with Jesus in paradise "today" might well seem to collide with the fact that God would not raise Jesus from the dead for three days. Francois Bovon solves the problem by suggesting that the statement is not to be taken in terms of a "chronological objectivity" but as an evocative expression of Luke's confidence that the righteous would be "with God" beyond death, as they await the final resurrection.[25] In any event, the "today" of this saying does not render impossible a "*being* in death" during the three days; indeed, it does not rule out a "descent into hell" (depending on how that theme is elaborated).

John's gospel is even more sparing in its description of the death of Jesus. He speaks from the cross only to arrange care for His mother now that He is dying (John 19:26) and to say that He is thirsty—a statement made in order, John says, that Scripture might be fulfilled. Having drunk some sour wine (which Mark's Jesus refused to do), Jesus says, "It is finished"—then lowers His head and gives up His "spirit" (John 19:30).

Taking a step back, it seems to me that a canonical reading of the four Gospels must inevitably be faced with the task of producing a synthetic picture which embraces as many of the details as possible. But we must prepare ourselves for a bit of awkwardness. No synthetic picture can be complete; the details cannot all be made to agree. Moreover, imagination will be needed: a theologically informed imagination, based not only on the evidence we find here but also on Paul's teaching especially, and on the contribution that can be made by the history of theology as well as by systematic/constructive reflection. I would add, as a matter of deeply

25. Francois Bovon, *Luke 3: A Commentary on Luke 9:28–24:53* (Minneapolis: Fortress Press, 2012), 313.

held personal conviction, that a canonical reading should *not* be played off against all historical-critical reconstructions without further ado. The two must inform each other, pose questions to each other.

A canonical reading, then, must never be confused with reading under the constraint of an ecclesial decision whose authority is placed beyond question. Protestants have no holy tradition in the Catholic sense; for them, every ecclesial pronouncement is inherently reformable; indeed, repairable.

So what do we get when we place the four gospel accounts of the death of Jesus alongside one another? It seems to me that Mark and Matthew ought to be granted a certain historical priority, if for no other reason than that the more offensive a text is to regnant philosophical opinions at work in its environment, the more likely it is to rest on traditions which find their origins in real history. But beyond that, Luke at least is clearly editing and altering the Markan and Matthean accounts—which also argues for the priority of the latter. And Luke can even introduce a new apocalyptic element with his talk of the paradise to which the penitent thief will go.

So the overarching horizon in the Synoptics (taken together) is, broadly speaking, apocalyptic in nature. And we would do well to try to understand the words from the cross in Luke and John in the light of the harder sayings found in Mark and Matthew,[26] and go from there. When we do that, it seems to me that the resulting synthetic picture is bound to look a great deal like that drawn by Hans Urs von Balthasar.

II. THE DEATH OF CHRIST: AN HOMAGE TO VON BALTHASAR—WITH A BIT OF CRITIQUE

To understand what made the death of Christ a "saving" event, we must first of all know who it is who dies here—and how He dies, the conditions under which He dies. That is to say, we must attend to Christology in the strict sense and to the full meaning of divine judgment. Hans Urs von Balthasar does both.

Basic to von Balthasar's Christology is the conviction that Christ's person simply *is* His mission. His mission is not something

> imposed on him from outside, like a "law." ... [H]e is the one who, from before all time, has had the task—indeed, he *is* the task—of fulfilling this universal design; everything in him, mind, intelligence and free will is oriented to it. We cannot say that they are "instrumental"; that would

---

26. Ibid., 312 (where Bovon finds a possible antecedent for "paradise" in *I Enoch* 60:8).

suggest that the mission takes precedence over his "I," whereas we must hold fast to the[ir] identity.[27]

Von Balthasar tries to offer a somewhat psychologized explanation for his identification of being and mission in Christ which is not entirely convincing, even though it is highly suggestive.

> Where a person is entrusted with a substantial mission that summons him to put his very existence at its disposal, the person thus sent [*der Gesendete*] can, as a result, become (to a degree) identified with the mission [*Sendung*].[28]

In such cases, identity is given with mission. And so it is, he thinks, with Jesus Christ, but with this qualitative difference: Jesus' "consciousness" of His mission is "absolute" in the sense that His mission is to reconcile the world with His God and Father—a "more than human mission."[29] The identity of being and mission in Him is therefore complete, total, and has always been so. Christ's mission is one that a mere human could not accomplish; it is a divine mission. Hence, what is said here of the unity of person and mission is rightly applied not to a "mere human" in the first instance but to the "person of the union" and, therefore, ultimately, to the second person of the Trinity. "Since the Subject in whom person and mission are identical can only be divine, it follows that 'God's being' really 'undergoes development' (E. Jüngel)." And so

> if Jesus, this man who is also God ... also has a *reciprocal* relation with God, that is, a relationship expressed in terms of genuine life, developing in decisive events, it is also clear that both elements—both *being* and *becoming* in the Incarnate One—express a single *being*, which, while we may not call it *becoming*, is the streaming forth of eternal life.... The dramatic dimension that is part of the definition of the person of Jesus does not belong exclusively to the worldly side of his being: its ultimate presuppositions lie in the divine life itself.[30]

What fails to convince here is the talk of a becoming that entails development and change. To seek to find the root of the identity of person and mission, of being and becoming, in the second person of the Trinity, as von Balthasar does, is good in my view; it is, in fact, a necessity if we are not to separate the being of God and the being of the man Jesus in quasi-Nestorian fashion.

---

27. Von Balthasar, *Theo-drama* III, 167–68.
28. Ibid., 154.
29. Ibid., 166.
30. Ibid., 158–59.

But we carry that task out wrongly, it seems to me, where we introduce any element of mutability into God. The "becoming" which the second person of the Trinity undergoes as incarnate must be *proper* to Him: not an *almost*-eternal obedience of the Son to the Father (which is actually made to belong to our time insofar as it is treated as resting upon a "contingent" decision) but one which is truly eternal and, therefore, proper to Him. God does not cease to be God, He does not become anything other than what He is eternally in that He gives Himself over in Jesus Christ to the human experience of that death which reconciles us to Him. He gives Himself wholly and completely to this experience, but, as Karl Barth rightly says, He does not give Himself away.[31]

Von Balthasar would certainly agree with this much. But his solution, unlike Barth's, is to *posit* (as a speculative act) a Being in God that is beyond the identity of being and becoming in Jesus Christ—or, to put it another way, an immanent Trinity which is somehow more than the economy.[32] He fails to honor the "rule" which Barth advanced in laying the foundations of his actualistic account of the divine life, viz., that "statements about the divine modes of being antecedently in themselves *cannot be different in content* from those that are about their reality in revelation."[33] And so von Balthasar assigns the identity of being and becoming to an "economy" which stands in no clear relation to the identity of the eternal Son in the immanent Trinity.

It did not have to turn out this way. In fact, consistently applied, the method which von Balthasar himself advocates could not have had this outcome. Von Balthasar tells us that he is pursuing a Christology "from below"[34]—from a starting point in a "Christology of consciousness" (i.e., a historically constructed understanding of the self-consciousness of Jesus with regard to the mission that He is) to a "Christology of being."[35] Such a "method" is quasi-transcendental in nature. He asks, "Who *must* he be, to behave and to act in this way"[36]—that is, in the way of One conscious of having a divine mission which can only be carried out humanly? We might say: What must God be "in Himself" if Jesus Christ, the God-human" is truly *God* "for us"? What are the ontological conditions in God for this outcome in time?

---

31. Barth, *Church Dogmatics* IV/1, 185.
32. Von Balthasar, *Theo-drama* III, 157.
33. Barth, *Church Dogmatics* I/1, 479 (emphasis added).
34. Von Balthasar, *Theo-drama* III, 150.
35. Ibid., 163.
36. Ibid., 149.

This is, as I say, a promising method, and the decision to start with Jesus' consciousness of having been sent into this world to achieve a divine purpose has a strong exegetical foundation. If only von Balthasar had been able to resist the temptation to engage in speculation, thereby lapsing back into a metaphysical conception of the immanent Trinity! For it was that fateful move which made it impossible to make consistent use of his preferred method in Christology.

Much more could be said about von Balthasar's Christology in a lengthier treatment. He does not yet have the Christology he needs to make his treatment of the atonement fully coherent and render it immune to moral objection. And that is a pity. Von Balthasar was heir to the version of dyothelite teaching set forth by Aloys Grillmeier, a version which is often hard to distinguish from a "two-subjects" Christology.[37] Every dyothelite faces the challenge, of course, of explaining how it is that *two* minds, wills, and energies of operation (one divine and one human) can yield one person—a single, unified subject. Cyril solved the problem by making the divine to be active, the human passive, thereby narrowing the distance between what might otherwise seem to be two (independent?) subjects whose unity could not rise above the level of a simple agreement of wills. In other words, Cyril instrumentalized the human nature of Christ.

But von Balthasar is negatively disposed toward this strategy; he understands Cyril to have revived the Apollinarian heresy, at least in part.[38] And he has his worries about the *enhypostatic* doctrine of Leontius. For, he asks, "How can an essentially self-subsistent being, equipped with reason and freedom, be the 'property' of another? Surely the latter, by definition, must rob it of its self-possession (*substantia*)?"[39] Von Balthasar is clearly concerned, as he puts it, to uphold "the christological distinction between the human conscious subject and the divine Person."[40]

In order to achieve this goal, von Balthasar makes the novel suggestion that a "nature"—even when understood as equipped with self-conscious agency—is not yet a "person" until he or she has a mission, an identity. In the case of Jesus, this happens in that God addresses Him and speaks to Him the truth as it has been known to God from all eternity: "You are my beloved Son."[41] At this point, the man Jesus becomes a "person"—and,

37. Ibid., 214.
38. Ibid.
39. Ibid.
40. Ibid.
41. Ibid., 207.

indeed, a divine person, since it is in this event that the Son identifies Himself with the man who has received God's identity-giving words. But now notice: the term *person* is being employed here to speak of the man Jesus, a man who *as such* is divine but who, in His divinity, remains other than the Son who identifies Himself with Him. The distance between them—indeed, the essential abyss that distinguishes God from all created things—has been preserved in this christological construct. That this is so is made all the more clear when von Balthasar goes on to say that "the *analogia entis* that prevails between God and the creature ... goes right through the incarnate Son of God."[42]

So von Balthasar cannot attain what he most wants, viz., to be in a position to show how it is possible to say that "a perfect man, endowed with reason and even possessing a free will ... can be God."[43] He cannot say this coherently because, at the end of the day, his Jesus is but an analogy of God. He is not fully God. Sadly, von Balthasar has not been able to free himself from a two-subjects Christology—a problem which, if left unresolved, would undermine his most brilliant achievement, viz., his treatment of the atonement.

My primary source for establishing von Balthasar's understanding of the atonement will be his 1969 work, *Mysterium Paschale.* What he says touching on atonement in the third volume of the *Theo-drama* (which has been our concern up to this point) is entirely commensurate with this earlier theology of the cross. But this earlier version is not entirely compatible with the later treatment found in volume IV of the *Theo-drama* (first published in 1980). *Mysterium Paschale* is a more useful resource for the model I would like to elaborate on here, and, it has to be said, it is more in line with the apocalyptic understanding which informs the Gospels.

The earlier von Balthasar knew full well that a real substitution in the event of the cross would be impossible if it were thought that "it is simply *some man or other* who suffers on others' behalf: it is only possible if "*unus ex Trinitate passus est*" [i.e., "One of the Trinity is suffered"] both in his human nature *and in his divine person.*"[44] He is right about this, which is why the shortcomings in his Christology are so hard to understand. But I will stay focused now on his theology of the cross.

---

42. Ibid., 203, 220–29.
43. Ibid., 215.
44. Ibid., 239–40.

Von Balthasar's theology of the cross is, from start to finish, a Christian modulation of what Martinus de Boer has called the "forensic" form of Jewish apocalyptic, according to which punishment with eternal death awaits those who have rejected their Creator, while eternal life is the reward of those who have believed.[45] For von Balthasar, what takes place in the cross of Christ is "a turning-point between the old aeon and the new"[46]—a turning which occurs with the outpouring of divine wrath on the Son of God made flesh.

Von Balthasar describes the way of the Son to the cross in kenotic terms of humiliation, self-emptying, surrender for the sake of the others. This way reaches its initial climax in the eschatological "trial" of Jesus in the garden of Gethsemane, at the point when Jesus pleads with His Father, "Abba, Father, for you all things are possible; remove this cup from me; yet, not what I want but what you want" (Mark 14:36 NRSV; cf. Matt 26:39b; Luke 22:42). Von Balthasar interprets the "cup" as the chalice of "eschatological wrath"[47] referred to in the Old Testament and apocalyptic literature (see, for example, Isa 51:17, 22; Jer 25:15; Eze 23:31–34; and Ps 75:8).[48] Jesus prays according to Mark's version (which von Balthasar regards as primary), as One who has been "dashed to the ground" and filled with horror as God distances Himself from Him.[49] His fear is the "fear of hell" (the *timor gehennalis*).[50] His obedience is not cheerfully offered; it is something to which He is reduced.[51] Moreover, the "not my will but yours" is the drinking of the chalice, signaling the entrance of sin. The "sin of the world"—its very being as sin—is made to be Christ's in body and soul.[52] And so in the event of the cross, God "condemned sin in the flesh" (Rom 8:3).[53] That means that the suffering endured by Christ was not just any suffering: it was suffering the eschatological wrath of God.[54]

45. Martinus de Boer, "Paul and Apocalyptic Eschatology," in John J. Collins, ed., *The Encyclopedia of Apocalypticism*, vol. 1 (New York/London: Continuum, 2003), 359.

46. Hans Urs von Balthasar, *Mysterium Paschale: The Mystery of Easter* (Edinburgh: T & T Clark, 1990), 56. It should be noted that the subtitle given to this work in its English dress is *not* original. The original referred to the "mystery of salvation"—a mystery centered not in Easter but in von Balthasar's treatment of the passion and death of Christ and his quite original treatment of Holy Saturday.

47. Ibid., 101.

48. Ibid., 123. The examples offered here are von Balthasar's.

49. Ibid., 100.

50. Ibid., 102. Cf. 104: "Christ's anguish was a co-suffering with sinners, of such a kind that the real loss of God which threatened them (the *poena damni*) was assumed by the incarnate Love of God in the form of a *timor gehennalis*."

51. Ibid., 105.

52. Ibid., 101.

53. Ibid., 119.

54. Ibid., 123.

It should be noted that von Balthasar argues that primacy, where the words from the cross are concerned, "must go to the cry of abandonment."[55] All other words are interpreted by him in its light. The Lucan words make clear theologically that the judgment of God which realizes itself in abandonment has a gracious goal in view. The Johannine *"consummatum est"* refers to the completion of Christ's commission, insofar as it is viewed as a consciously willed act.[56] But that is not the end of the experience of eschatological wrath. What happens next has nothing to do with consciously willed activity.

Of considerable importance, too, is von Balthasar's belief that the Holy Spirit is "freed" when Jesus breathes His last.[57] That the Spirit should depart from Him is the completion of His isolation and abandonment. Whatever happens next, Jesus will be alone: alone in death, alone in the experience of "hell."

Von Balthasar's notoriety — for those who disdain his theology — has everything to do with his theology of Holy Saturday, his meditation on the theme of Christ's "descent into hell." Hell for von Balthasar is not a place; it is a spiritual condition, a condition of the soul.[58] Indeed, it is (following Isaac of Ninevah) a timeless experience, one in which there can be no hope of change.[59] Von Balthasar describes this condition as one in which all spontaneous activity has ceased. It is complete and total passivity. That Jesus was "really dead" means that during the time between physical death and resurrection, He did not engage in "all manner of 'activities' in the world beyond." [60]

The traditional Catholic teaching with regard to the "harrowing of hell" would require that Jesus be doing things that only a living person can do, not a dead one.[61] So even the word *descent* has to be understood metaphorically as a "being with the dead." [62] But, of course, there is more to "hell" than simply being with the dead. The spiritual condition into which Christ enters as a consequence of the outpouring of the eschatological wrath of God is not adequately described in terms of a going to *Sheol* (though that may well be included) but of *Gehenna*.

---

55. Ibid., 125.
56. Ibid., 126.
57. Ibid., 127.
58. Ibid., 77, 162–63.
59. Ibid.
60. Ibid., 148.
61. Ibid., 149. In any case, 1 Peter 3:19, to which appeal is often made in an effort to find a basis for the harrowing of hell, speaks of a "preaching to the spirits in prison" but does not speak of a combat. Cf. Ibid., 152. Moreover, in relation to a passage like Colossians 2:14f., which speaks of a disarming of the powers and principalities, it is God who is the Subject, not Christ. Ibid., 154–55.
62. Ibid., 150.

What then is this spiritual condition called "hell"? Negatively expressed, it is that deprivation of the vision of God which is the *poena damni*.[63] More positively (and all the more horrifically), it is (following Nicholas of Cusa) the *visio mortis*—the contemplation (remember that the dead can engage in no spontaneous activity) of "the pure substantiality of 'Hell' which is 'sin in itself.'"[64] To contemplate this "object" is, for Christ, to contemplate His own victory (the grain of truth in the "harrowing of hell" idea) as the unintuitable (if I may put it that way) means to the vanquishing of the "second death."[65] But He is not in a condition to know all of that. In a "timeless" condition, He cannot experience its end in resurrection prematurely, so to speak.

"Hell in the New Testament sense," von Balthasar says in conclusion, "is a function of the Christ event."[66] Indeed, it is "a *product* of the Redemption,"[67] for Christ alone has measured "the depths of that abyss" and, in doing so, set its limits.[68]

Who is the Subject who dies *this* death? Who takes upon Himself the eschatological "No" of God to the sinner? It is "the Son, the Word of the Father."[69] Here again, to say this in the sense of understanding the divine Word to be the Subject of this human experience would require that identification with the man in whom this thoroughly human experience takes place be construed not merely in psychological terms but in ontological terms, i.e., in terms of what I would call an ontological *receptivity*. And if such receptivity is not to set aside divine immutability, then identification with the human Jesus must be *proper* to the second person of the Trinity, so that what happens to Him in the cross and the descent into hell constitute the realization in time of who and what He is in Himself eternally.

Thus far, von Balthasar on the death of God—and my christological correction.

III. THE PROBLEM OF HUMAN SUFFERING

Human suffering has many sources, many if not most unrelated to sin. Growth, degeneration, decay, and death are natural to the finite creature

---

63. Ibid., 164–65.
64. Ibid., 173.
65. Ibid.
66. Ibid., 172.
67. Ibid., 174.
68. Ibid., 168.
69. Ibid., 49.

in this world that is passing away—and suffering is part of that experience, an ever-present feature of life. It is quite true, of course, that human beings can increase the measure of suffering in this world artificially. But suffering in and of itself is natural.

What can we say then of the relation of atonement and human suffering? First, that it is not the atoning work of Christ as such which brings an end to physical and emotional suffering. It is only the general resurrection of the dead at the end of time which will do that. Resurrection is new creation; it is a lifting of the finite above its natural state, thereby making the finite to be more than finite. A creature who cannot die is not natural; she has been lifted above her finitude by a transfiguring of the finite through the power of the Holy Spirit. Christ's resurrection is a proleptic realization in time of this final end of all things. Still, the "sublation" of the finite (if I may put it that way) that occurs in the resurrection and results in unending and unbreakable fellowship with God can only follow the destruction of the sinfulness of human creatures who failed morally and spiritually to live in the world and under its conditions as those who are righteous—so that atonement must precede resurrection.

The last step is to see that there is a certain necessity in the movement from God to the creation of the finite and its eschatological transfiguration. It is a necessity grounded, I would say, in God's very being. God is, by nature, love—self-giving, self-emptying love (according to Philippians 2); a love which contains the object of that love in itself. And what can be truly "other" than God, and therefore other than the *telos* of the self-emptying activity that God is, but the finite, rational creature capable of responding to that love?

Does such a view make God dependent on the world in order to be God? In no way. The love that God is cannot be contained or privatized; it overflows its boundaries. Its going forth is not to remedy a defect or lack or any deficiency in being. And it cannot be the expression of need or it would not be the kind of love it is, viz., Self-giving love.

On this view, the fall into sin is not a catastrophe that God either did not foresee or was unable to do anything to prevent. It did not overtake Him unexpectedly. Does this mean that God wills natural evils and sin? Not as ends in themselves certainly.[70] What God wills is the redemption of the human race in Jesus Christ for the sake of unending and unbreakable fellowship. A finite world with all that this entails is the unavoidable result.

---

70. See on this point Matthew Levering, *Predestination: Biblical and Theological Paths* (Oxford: Oxford University Press, 2011), 78–79.

But this also means that the misery of this world is not the consequence of a contingent decision made by God—call it the "covenant of grace"—for which no sufficient reason can be given. To put it that way would be to elevate the divine will over the divine Self-knowledge and divine Self-love (God's love of the Self-giving love that He is), to the point where no reasons for what God does can be given beyond the stark statement that God willed it so. God's willing is, on this showing, its own justification—and in this bare assertion is grounded the glory of God. Classical Reformed theology treaded this path, but it should not have done so. To think of God in this way is to make Him ultimately indifferent—which is the final end of all voluntaristic conceptions of divine freedom. And as Jürgen Moltmann rightly observed, "To speak ... of an indifferent God would condemn men [and women] to indifference."[71]

CONCLUSION

Does God's redemptive activity as here described suggest that God has made an "inner peace" with the violence of this world? Not at all. We must remember that the physical dimensions of Christ's death are not, as such, redemptive. What is redemptive is death in God-abandonment. God wills this form of death as a way of bringing this world (and the moral evil that human beings do in it) to an end through making Himself the object of His own judgment.

Seen in this way, divine judgment is a wholly gracious activity whose goal is the destruction of the old world to make way for the new. And, it should be added, in the new creation, violence will be no more. It will have been made an ontological impossibility because the finitude itself will have been transfigured. And so, God's "No" is the instrument for realizing God's "Yes."

"For the Son of God, Jesus Christ ... was not 'Yes and No'; but in him it is always 'Yes.' For in him every one of God's promises is a 'Yes.' For this reason it is through him that we say 'Amen,' to the glory of God" (2 Cor 1:19–20 NRSV).

---

71. Jürgen Moltmann, *The Crucified God: the Cross of Christ as the Foundation and Criticism of Christian Theology* (New York: Harper & Row, 1973), 274.

CHAPTER 11

ATONEMENT AND EUCHARIST

ELEONORE STUMP

INTRODUCTION

In this paper, I want to explore the nature of the connection between the atonement of Christ and the Eucharist. (I recognize, of course, that the names for this rite vary among Christians, but it is necessary to have some name by which to refer to it, and so for purposes of this paper I will call the rite "the Eucharist." Nothing hangs on this name, and those who are uncomfortable with it should feel free to use the name they prefer.)

It is reasonable to suppose that, in order to explore the nature of the connection between the atonement and the Eucharist, one would first need a full account of each; only then could one begin to explore what the connection between the two of them is. But those are preconditions that are virtually impossible to fulfill, not least because there is no one orthodox interpretation of the doctrine of the atonement and no one universally agreed upon interpretation of the Eucharist.

It is widely supposed, by both Christians and non-Christians alike, that the doctrine of the atonement is the distinctive doctrine of Christianity; and Christians often speak of the value of the atonement itself as infinite, or so great as to be incommensurate with all other created goods.[1] Given

---

1.   See, for example, Alvin Plantinga, "Supralapsarianism, or 'O Felix Culpa,'" in *Christian Faith and the Problem of Evil*, ed. Peter van Inwagen (Grand Rapids: Eerdmans, 2004). For some critical commentary on the theodicy Plantinga proposes in this paper, see Marilyn McCord Adams, "Plantinga on 'Felix Culpa': Analysis and Critique," *Faith and Philosophy* 25 (2008): 123–39. I share some of her concerns about attempts at theodicy based largely or wholly on comparisons of the summed value of worlds.

that this is so, it is noteworthy that the doctrine of the atonement differs from other major Christian doctrines, such as the doctrine of the incarnation, for example, in having no formula specifying its interpretation. Although creedal or conciliar statements rule out some interpretations as unorthodox, nevertheless, for the doctrine of the atonement there is no analogue to the Chalcedonian formula for the incarnation, for example. For this reason, it is possible for there to be a variety of interpretations, all of which count as orthodox; and, in fact, in the history of Christian thought, there have been highly divergent interpretations.[2]

As for the Eucharist, the general consensus among Christians is that Christ instituted the rite of the Eucharist, that the rite involves eating bread and wine,[3] and that there is some kind of significant relation between the bread and wine on the one hand, and the body and blood of Christ on the other hand. After these basic points, there is not much agreement.

Nonetheless, even with all the divergent views about the rite, the general Christian consensus includes the conviction that something about this rite makes a powerful connection between those participating in it and the passion and death of Christ. Somehow, whatever exactly it is that atonement does, the Eucharist, whatever exactly it is, is part of that story.

And yet, even with the consensus that there is some kind of connection between the Eucharist and the passion and death of Christ, the nature of that connection is often enough neglected in discussions of the atonement. Here I want to explore that connection; but, given the great diversity of views about both the atonement and the Eucharist, I will need to sidestep the major points of controversy dividing Christians as I do so.

In order to go around the differences among the varying interpretations of the atonement, I will focus just on the salvific effects[4] of Christ's

---

2. I have discussed some of these in Eleonore Stump, "The Nature of the Atonement," in *Reason, Metaphysics, and Mind: New Essays on the Philosophy of Alvin Plantinga*, eds. Kelly Clark and Michael Rea (Oxford: Oxford University Press, 2012), 128–44, and in "Conversion, Atonement, and Love," in *Conversion*, eds. I. U. Dalferth and M. Rodgers (Tübingen: Mohr Siebeck, 2013).

3. Or grape juice. This disjunction should be understood throughout. My purposes in this paper do not require my taking a stand on whether the ritual requires that the juice of the grapes be turned into wine in order for the ritual to be valid. For ease of exposition in what follows, I will simply talk of wine.

4. In fact, traditionally, the passion and death of Christ have been thought to have not just one effect but several. Aquinas, for example, says that in addition to its redemptive effects, Christ's passion operated as a source of merit, as a sacrifice, and as satisfaction for human sins. Cf., e.g., Thomas Aquinas, *The Summa Theologica of St. Thomas Aquinas*, trans. Fathers of the English Dominican Province (Westminster, MD: Christian Classics, 1981), III.48.

passion and death.[5] I will concentrate on the impact of Christ's passion and death on human sinfulness and on the problem in the human will that makes it liable to future sin.[6] In addition, virtually all Christians agree that however Christ's atonement is understood, its effects have to be applied to a person in order for it to be efficacious for the salvation of that person.

What this application consists in is controversial, but the claim that there has to be some kind of application is not. And virtually all Christians also agree that, at least at sometimes in his life, a person can refuse whatever good it is that is offered by Christ's atonement; and the good in question will therefore not come to that person, just because he has rejected it. So for the atonement to be efficacious for a person, it has to be the case that he does not reject (tacitly or explicitly) what is offered to him in it.

With regard to the Eucharist, I will adopt a minimalist account. On this minimalist account, whether or not the rite is properly described in any richer way, it at least reminds those participating in the rite of the passion and death of Christ. At least, as the participants eat the bread, they are made mindful of the body of Christ, which they believe was broken for them; as they drink the wine,[7] they are made mindful of the blood of Christ, which they believe was shed for them. In my view, what follows in this paper is compatible with all richer interpretations of the atonement and the Eucharist. That is, what I say below is compatible with, for example, a Catholic belief in transubstantiation and the real presence of Christ in the consecrated bread and wine. But it is also compatible with the significantly different accounts of the rite found among other mainstream Christian groups.

Within these fairly severe limits which attempt to bypass divisions among Christians in regard to interpretations of the atonement and of the Eucharist, I want to try to show one significant way in which the Eucharist is part of the redemptive work of Christ's passion and death.

---

5. For some people, Christ's atonement is a matter not just of his passion and death, but of his life, passion, death, and resurrection. Nothing in this paper turns on the distinction between the longer and the shorter formulation. For ease of exposition, therefore, I will just refer to the passion and death of Christ as the atoning work of Christ; those who prefer the longer formulation should feel free to substitute it throughout.

6. And that leaves aside considerations of any other effects of Christ's passion and death. In particular, in this paper I will be omitting consideration of the way in which Christ's passion and death make satisfaction for past sin.

7. Not all participants in the rite receive the cup, and those who do sometimes drink some other grape liquid besides wine. But it is not easy to put all these qualifications into one simple description of the rite. So readers should take the qualifications as understood throughout.

ATONEMENT AND THE BEGINNING
OF SALVATION

The word *atonement* is a relative newcomer to the English language.[8] It is an invented word composed of *at* and *one* jammed together with *ment*, and it was devised to express the idea that the atonement is a making one of things that were previously not at one, namely, God and human beings. So if at-one-ment is the solution to a problem, then, it seems, the problem should be thought of as the absence of unity or oneness between God and human beings.

However exactly we are to understand closeness and union between persons, it will at least include harmony between their minds and wills.[9] Let's say a person Paula does something contrary to the will of a perfectly good God and thus introduces distance between herself and God. Understood in this way, distance between God and Paula has at least a partial source in Paula's failure to will what God wills.[10] The problem to which the atonement is the solution therefore can be thought of as having at least one main source in the human proneness to moral wrongdoing.

On orthodox Christian views, the atonement is a sufficient solution to this problem. That is, the atonement offers sufficient help for the problem to all those who do not refuse it; it makes union with God available to everyone who does not reject it.[11] Somehow,[12] the atonement brings it about that, in the end, a human being Paula who does not reject God is eventually united to God. And, in complete and full union with God, her will is internally integrated around the good that God wills.

It is important to see here that, because the problem is in the will, it is particularly intractable.

---

8.   Of course, although this word is relatively new, the thing designated by the word is old. Rituals of atonement figure prominently in the Hebrew Bible, as, for example, in the prescriptions for the Day of Atonement laid out in Leviticus.

9.   For a detailed discussion of the issue, see chapter 6 of Eleonore Stump, *Wandering in Darkness: Narrative and the Problem of Suffering* (Oxford: Oxford University Press, 2010).

10.   For discussion of the issue and arguments for this claim, see Eleonore Stump, "Atonement and the Cry of Dereliction from the Cross," *European Journal for Philosophy of Religion* 4.1 (Spring 2012): 1–17.

11.   These claims are true even for those who accept a doctrine of double predestination. On that doctrine, those who reject the salvation provided by the atonement were predestined by God to reject it. In that sense, the atonement was not intended for them, even if the value of the atonement was in itself so great that it would have sufficed for salvation for everyone.

12.   The various interpretations of the doctrine of the atonement differ in their understanding of this "somehow." There is no creedal formula that effectively distinguishes among them and privileges just one as orthodox. For some discussion of the main kinds of interpretation in the history of Christian thought, see Stump, "The Nature of Atonement."

If Paula could effectively choose of her own accord to be integrated in goodness, she would already be wholehearted in goodness, or on her way to that state. Her lack of internal integration has its source in her unwillingness to unify her will around the good. Her will is not internally integrated in the good because Paula does not *want* it to be. So, the defect in the will is such that it could be fixed by Paula only if she did not have the defect.

On the other hand, no one else can unilaterally fix Paula's will for her either, not even God. To the extent to which God fixes Paula's will by himself, he wills for Paula a certain state of Paula's will. But, then, to that extent, what is in Paula is God's will, not Paula's. If the lack of internal integration in Paula's will is an obstacle to God's being united to Paula, God's determination of Paula's will is an even greater obstacle. Mutual closeness of the sort required for union depends on an agreement between two different wills. But if God determines Paula's will, then the only will operative in Paula is God's will. In that case, there will not be two wills to bring into union with each other. There will be only one will, God's will which is in Paula as well as in God. Union between Paula's will and God's will is not established by such means; it is precluded.

It seems that the obvious solution would be for Paula to want God's help and for God to bring Paula's will into harmony with God's will in response to Paula's wanting God's help. But orthodox Christian theology is committed to eschewing Pelagianism. That is, it is committed to rejecting the view that there is anything good in a human will that is not infused into it by God's grace, and Paula's wanting God's help is a good state in her will.

Nonetheless, it is possible for grace and free will to interact in such a way as to solve the problem. The rejection of Pelagianism still leaves a person Paula with free will.

On the rejection of Pelagianism, Paula still has alternative possibilities for willing: she can refuse God's love, or she can cease refusing it. And if Paula ceases to refuse God's love, then God can give Paula grace by infusing into Paula the will to accept God's grace. And, once this will is established in Paula, then the second part of the process of salvation can occur. As long as Paula does not return to rejecting God, God can help Paula's will grow in integration around the good without violating Paula's will, because in helping Paula's will in this way, God is acting to make Paula's will be what Paula herself wants it to be.[13] This second part of the process is Paula's sanctification, and it will eventuate in Paula's complete and permanent union with God if it continues to its end.

---

13. For a discussion of the relative contributions of grace and free will, see the chapter on grace and free will in Eleonore Stump, *Aquinas: Arguments of the Philosophers* (London and New York: Routledge, 2003).

But the first part of the process of bringing Paula to union with God is one place where God is entirely dependent on what Paula does. Or, to put the point another way, if Paula were never to cease rejecting God's help, it would not be God's fault that she did not. Unless and until Paula of her own accord surrenders to God, God cannot help her, at least not by acting directly on her.

The process that is enabled by the atonement and that leads to union between God and a human person therefore begins when a person ceases to resist God; but it is up to that person, and her alone, whether to cease resisting.

ATONEMENT AND THE INDWELLING OF THE HOLY SPIRIT

It is not implausible to suppose that the passion and death of Christ can be a catalyst in bringing a person to this state of quiescence in the will as regards God. Christ's willingness to die for human beings in their post-fall condition, with all its sins and ugliness, will show Paula God's great love for her. In the passion and death of Christ, God does not manifest wrath or rejection of human beings. He does not display his regal character, his almighty power, or his role as dreadful judge. On the contrary, in the incarnate Christ God allows himself to be put to death in a painful and shaming way because of his love for human beings and his desire to bring them to himself.

If anything can help Paula to cease resisting God, it does seem that the spectacle of Christ's passion and death could do so. A display of power can prompt fear and submission, but the manifestation of deep love with great vulnerability can elicit the surrender of resistance to that love.[14]

If Paula's response to the passion and death of Christ is to give over resistance to God's love, then Paula's surrender to God will be followed by God's providing Paula the will she needs. When Paula stops rejecting God's love, then God gives Paula the will with which to ask for God's help. This is a second-order will, in which a person wills to will what God wills. Its presence in a person is compatible with a lot of willing that is not in accord with God's will. But as long as Paula has this second-order will—that is, as long as she continues to will what God wills, God can continue to give her the help she needs to integrate her will fully around the good in the process that is her sanctification.

---

14. For the distinction between submission and surrender, see Stump, *Wandering in Darkness*, ch. 8.

So in addition to whatever other effects the atonement may bring about, it has a role in eliciting in a person Paula this delicate and tricky, freely willed surrender to God, which is the necessary condition for her sanctification. That surrender is the first part of the entire redemptive process, and it results in full union with God if it persists to the end of Paula's life.

At this point, someone might suppose, with disappointment, that the account I have just given is simply an Abelard-like psychological theory of atonement that empties atonement of any real power. But this supposition would be a mistake.

That is because, on virtually all Christian accounts, a person's surrender of resistance to God is followed immediately not only by God's giving her grace but also by God's giving the Holy Spirit to dwell in her.[15] The consequence of Paula's surrender to God is therefore that Paula receives not only God's grace but also God himself. The Holy Spirit comes to dwell in her when she ceases closing God out. And however exactly it is to be understood, the indwelling of the Holy Spirit puts God within Paula's psyche in some sense and to some degree.

Science fiction is replete with stories in which malevolent nonhuman beings indwell a human mind,[16] and folklore has sometimes tended to explain certain kinds of mental illness along the same lines.[17] Stories about such cases are frightening and revulsive because the indwelling alien mind invades the mind of a human person against her will or at least without her consent. Typically too in such cases, the invader has only hatred and contempt for its human victim.

But the indwelling of the Holy Spirit requires an openness on the part of a person Paula that is dependent entirely on Paula. The Holy Spirit comes to indwell in Paula's psyche only when Paula herself ceases resisting

---

15. The indwelling Holy Spirit is a common topic of Christian theology, but it is actually not easy to specify what this indwelling comes to. We can start by saying what it is not. God's indwelling in Paula is not merely a matter of God's having direct and immediate causal and cognitive access to Paula's mind. God has this kind of access to the mind of every human being, both with regard to propositional knowledge and also with regard to mind-reading. For every person, it is possible for God to know the mind of that person with direct and unmediated cognition; it is also possible for God to communicate in a direct and unmediated way with the mind of that person. So these kinds of relation between God and human beings hold for every human person. The indwelling of the Holy Spirit, however, is found only in those people who have opened up to God. For more discussion of this issue, see Eleonore Stump, "Omnipresence, Indwelling, and the Second-Personal," *European Journal for Philosophy of Religion*, 5/4 (2013): 63–87.

16. Robert Heinlein's *The Puppetmasters* is an example.

17. If one Googles "schizophrenia and demon possession," one will find that this sort of belief is still prevalent in some communities today.

God, and it is up to Paula alone whether or not she does. The indwelling achieved by the Holy Spirit therefore is the opposite of the alien invasion of science fiction stories. And it comes with love for Paula.

For these reasons, although the Holy Spirit comes to dwell within Paula, nothing of Paula's own personhood is lost in consequence. Paula's mind remains her own, and her awareness of her mind as her own also remains. Nonetheless, when the Holy Spirit indwells her psyche, Paula has God as present as is possible within herself.

So whatever other effects the atonement has, this one effect is not lame and restricted to the psychological, in an Abelardian way, but powerful and efficacious of metaphysical change in a human person.

UNION, SECOND-PERSON EXPERIENCE, AND STORIES

Here I need to pause to say something more about union. As I have characterized it elsewhere,[18] union is a kind of mutual second-person presence; it is a kind of mutual closeness together with maximal shared attention.

Shared attention is notoriously difficult to describe in a philosophically suitable way, but it is easy to illustrate. An infant engages in shared attention when the infant looks into the eyes of its mother, who is looking back into the infant's eyes. In adults, shared attention is at least partly a matter of mutual awareness, of the sort that prompts philosophical worry about the possibility of an unstoppable infinite regress: Paula is aware of Jerome's being aware of Paula's being aware of Jerome's being aware, and so on.[19] Roughly put, then, one can say that shared attention is a kind of second-person experience between two persons who are mutually and simultaneously aware of each other.[20]

---

18. See Stump, *Wandering in Darkness*, ch. 6; and Stump, "Omnipresence."

19. Because philosophers take knowledge to be a matter of knowledge *that*, a more common philosophical formulation of mutual knowledge would be in terms of knowing *that*: Paula knows that Jerome knows that Paula knows that Jerome knows, and so on. In the case of infants, of course, shared attention cannot be a matter of knowing *that* in this way. For an interesting study of mutual knowledge in connection with joint attention, see Christopher Peacocke, "Joint Attention: Its Nature, Reflexivity, and Relation to Common Knowledge," in Naomi Eilan et al., eds. *Joint Attention: Communication and Other Minds: Issues in Philosophy and Psychology* (Oxford: Oxford University Press, 2005), 298–324.

20. Joint attention is most often mediated by vision, but it can be mediated by other senses as well. A congenitally blind child can share attention with its mother by sound or by touch, for example. In the case of an immaterial God, joint attention can occur without any mediation by the senses, provided that there is iterated mutual awareness. The senses are typically the vehicle for establishing joint attention, but they are not essential to it. For more discussion of joint attention, see chapters 4 and 6 of Stump, *Wandering in Darkness*.

In that earlier work, I also argued that second-person experience gives Paula some degree of a non-propositional knowledge of persons where Jerome is concerned. Knowledge of persons is different from ordinary knowledge *that* something or other is the case. One of the noteworthy things about the knowledge of persons is that it can be transmitted by means of stories. While a person cannot express the distinctive knowledge of his second-person experience as a matter of knowing *that*, he can do something to re-present the experience itself in such a way that he can share the second-person experience to some degree with someone else who was not part of it, so that at least some of the knowledge of persons garnered from the experience is also available to her.[21] And this is generally what we do when we tell a story.[22]

A story takes a real or imagined set of second-person experiences of one sort or another and makes it available to a wider audience to share.[23] So a story can be thought of as a report of a set of real or imagined second-person experiences that does not lose (at least does not lose entirely) the distinctively second-person character of the experiences. It does so by making it possible, to one degree or another,[24] for a person to experience some of what she would have experienced if she had been an onlooker in the second-person experience represented in the story. That is, a story gives a person some of what she would have had if she had had unmediated personal interaction with the characters in the story while they were conscious and interacting with one another.[25]

---

21. In this respect, a second-person experience differs from a first-person experience of the sort we have in perception. There is no way for me to convey to someone who has never seen colors what I know when I know what it is like to see red.

22. I am not here implying that the only function, or even the main function, of narratives (in one medium or another) is to convey real or imagined second-person experiences. My claim is just that much less is lost of a second-person experience in a narrative account than in a third-person account, *ceteris paribus*.

23. Someone might object here that any information which could be captured and conveyed by a story could also be conveyed by an expository account. I have no good argument against this claim, for the very reasons I have been urging—namely, that we cannot give an expository description of what *else* is contained in a story; but I think the claim is false. Consider, for example, some excellent and current biography of Samuel Johnson, such as Robert DeMaria's *The Life of Samuel Johnson: A Critical Biography* (Oxford: Blackwell, 1993), and compare it to the pastiche of stories in Boswell's *Life of Johnson*, and you will see the point. There is a great deal to be learned about Johnson from DeMaria's *The Life of Samuel Johnson*, but Boswell's stories give you the man as the biography cannot.

24. The degree will be a function not only of the narrative excellence of the story but also of the sensitivity and intelligence of the story-hearer or reader as well.

25. I do not mean to say that the storyteller or artist does not contribute something of her own in the narrative presentation. On the contrary, part of the importance of narrative is that its artistry enables us to see what we might well have missed without the help of the narrative, even if we had been present as bystanders in the events recounted in the narrative. It is for this reason that the quality of the artistry in a narrative makes a difference to what there is to know on the basis of it.

What is noteworthy here, then, is that, to one degree or another, a story about a person Jerome can connect another person Paula with Jerome in such a way that, although Paula is not face-to-face with Jerome, she nonetheless has a kind of second-person experience of Jerome;[26] and because of that experience gained through the story, she has some knowledge of persons with respect to Jerome.

If, after having appropriated the story, Paula actually meets Jerome and Jerome is open to Paula, then some mutual closeness, some shared attention, some union is possible between them. But in this case, any union that occurs will have had its beginning in Paula's appropriation of the story about Jerome and the knowledge of Jerome that the story gave her.

I have highlighted this point about stories because it matters for my purposes here. It is important to see that, with the exception of those few people who were present during Christ's crucifixion, everyone who responds to Christ's passion and death by surrendering resistance to the love of God has to do so in consequence of a story.

Christ is a particular person, and his passion and death are historical particulars. Information about a particular person and particular events in the life of that person, however, cannot be given in abstract and universal form. It has to be given in the form of a story for everyone who was not actually present to that person during those events. And so, for every person who was not present to Christ during Christ's passion and death, she ceases resisting and surrenders to God because of a story about Christ's passion and death through which she has come to know Christ with the kind of knowledge of persons that stories can provide. Neither the story nor the knowledge of persons she gains from it act on her will with efficient causation. Nonetheless, they can prompt in her the yielding of resistance needed to begin the process of salvation for her.

And here is the second important thing to see. When the knowledge of Christ mediated to a person through the story elicits in a person a ceasing of resistance to God, then, on Christian doctrine, she meets God in the person of the Holy Spirit, who not only comes to her but stays with her as indwelling. What was a unilateral experience on her part provided by the story becomes an actual mutual second-person experience for her in consequence of God's coming to her when she ceases to resist him.

---

26. Or an analogue to a second-person experience. Whether it is a real second-person experience or an analogue to one is a complicated matter that cannot be dealt with adequately in passing here.

The *story* of Christ's passion and death is therefore central to the work of the atonement in the process of bringing a person to union with God; this is true for all people except those who were present at Christ's passion and death. The surrender in response to the knowledge of persons with regard to Christ which is garnered from a story is the beginning of the process that results eventually in a person's complete and permanent union with God, as long as she does not return to her original rejection of God.

PERSEVERANCE

That last caveat—"as long as she does not return to her original rejection of God"—is necessary, on the view of virtually all Christians, because as long as Paula is in this life, she always retains the possibility of returning to her original resistance to God.[27] And so there are actually *three* parts to the process that brings Paula to complete and permanent union with God. There is the beginning, when Paula ceases rejecting God. There is the ongoing process of sanctification, which culminates in Paula's complete internal integration around the good. And then there is also what Augustine called "perseverance," which is the continuation of the original ceasing to resist God.

The rejection of Pelagianism implies that there cannot be any good in a person that is not put there by God. But nothing in any doctrine implies that there cannot be evil in a person put there by that person. Whatever else a human will may be capable of, on any Christian views, a person is always capable of willing what is evil, including the evil of returning to the original resisting of God. And so the process of bringing a person Paula to union with God requires Paula's original surrender to God, her sanctification, *and* her perseverance in the process.[28]

Where perseverance is concerned, then, the process of coming to union with God is like marriage in the contemporary Western version of marriage. In that version of marriage, there is a falling in love, followed by the commitment of marriage. But the commitment vowed in marriage has

---

27. Some Christians might suppose that if Paula rejects God and dies in that rejection, then it never was true of Paula that she was justified, even if it seemed as if she was. Other Christians suppose that Paula could reject God entirely even after having received justification. But this difference of view makes no difference to my point here. What everyone agrees on is that it is possible for a person who seems to be a devout Christian to reject God and die in that state of rejection. And that point is all I need for my purposes here.

28. Aquinas describes this process in a more fine-grained way, in terms of five effects of God's grace on a human soul: (1) healing of the soul, (2) desire of the good, (3) carrying out the good desired, (4) perseverance in good, and (5) attainment of eternal life. It is noteworthy that perseverance is on the list just before the last element, eternal life. See *Summa Theologica* IaIIae.111.3.

to go on day after day. And on any given day, that original commitment can be retracted. For the marriage to last, it is not enough that there was an original falling in love followed by commitment to marriage. There has to be persevering in that commitment, too.

So perseverance is crucial to the process of salvation, as it is to marriage; but a little reflection shows that perseverance is as delicate and tricky as the original surrender to God is. At one time, Augustine considered the possibility that God could give a lifetime of perseverance as one single gift of grace given at a particular time to a particular person.[29] But this way of thinking of God's part in sustaining a person in perseverance is mistaken, as Augustine himself came to think too.[30]

In explaining the beginning of the process that brings a person Paula to union with God, I said that God could not by himself alone produce the necessary state of will in Paula without destroying the possibility of the union God wants with Paula. That is because two wills are needed for union; but if God puts a state of will in Paula, then that state of will is God's and not Paula's. Then there is only one will, God's will, that is in God and in Paula. But then there also will not be two wills to unite. And that is why the beginning of the process is as tricky as it is. It has to depend on Paula, who is in no condition to will anything good of herself (given the rejection of Pelagianism). But, as I explained above, even in that condition, Paula can be so moved by the knowledge of Christ which is mediated to her by the story of Christ's passion and death that she surrenders her resistance. She just ceases to will to reject God.

So Paula has alternative possibilities: to resist God or to cease resisting God. And it is up to Paula alone which of these possibilities constitutes her will. If at a particular time her will ceases to resist God, then, in that state at that time, she can be helped by God to will the good without thereby losing her own will. But it is up to Paula alone whether or not she ceases resistance; it depends on Paula whether or not God gives her this will at this time.

It is important to see that similar considerations apply in the case of perseverance. If God were to give Paula in one fell swoop the gift of a lifetime's perseverance, as Augustine at one time wondered whether God could do, what God would be giving Paula is the inability ever to return

---

29. See, for example, his treatise *De dono perseverantiae*.
30. For a discussion of Augustine's views of grace and free will, see Eleonore Stump, "Augustine on Free Will," in *The Cambridge Companion to Augustine*, eds. Norman Kretzmann and Eleonore Stump (Cambridge: Cambridge University Press, 2001), 124–47; revised and reprinted in expanded edition of *The Cambridge Companion to Augustine* (2014).

to her original condition of resisting God. But then God would have taken away from Paula the alternative possibilities of free will that are truly her own, even on the rejection of Pelagianism, namely, the possibilities of either resisting God or ceasing to resist him. And so if God gave Paula one gift of grace that cemented her in a lifetime's perseverance, then in this case, too, there would be just one will, God's will, in Paula and in God.

Consequently, it is a mistake to think that God could give a person perpetual perseverance as one single gift of grace. The problem of perseverance is just as tricky as the problem of the original beginning of the process that brings Paula to union with God, or more so. And whether or not it occurs has to depend ultimately on Paula. God cannot give it to her as one gift of grace.

EUCHARIST AND PERSEVERANCE

It doesn't follow, of course, that God can do nothing to help a person achieve perseverance. The analogy with marriage helps illustrate the point. Married to Paula, Jerome cannot unilaterally guarantee that Paula will never divorce him, but there are many things he can do to stabilize the marriage and strengthen Paula's bond to him. In the same way, there are myriad things that God can do in his providence to help maintain a person in her commitment to him.

Traditionally, the Eucharist has been supposed to be central among those things. On views already traditional by the time of Aquinas, Christ's passion and death work their effect of saving human beings through faith from the human proclivity to sin, but the means by which this process is effected can (and ideally should) include the Eucharist.[31]

Probably the most famous line about God's love is that in the gospel of John: "God so loved the world that he gave his only begotten son that whoever believes in him should not perish but have everlasting life."[32] On Christian doctrine, the truth of that line is most manifest in Christ's passion and death. The story of Christ's passion and death shows God in the guise of one naked man being tortured to death before his mother, his friends, and his hostile, mocking enemies for the sake of saving human beings. Surely, this picture shows as poignantly as possible the love of God, and so it also has power to elicit the melting of heart, the giving up of resistance, that is the essential first step in the process of salvation.[33]

---

31. *Summa Theologica* IIIa.49.3.
32. John 3:16 NRSV.
33. *Summa Theologica* IIIa.49.1.

One way to begin thinking about the role of the Eucharist in the process of salvation effected by Christ's passion and death is to highlight the fact that bread and wine are eaten in the rite.[34] Here it is noteworthy that the words by which Christ instituted this rite identify the bread as his body and the wine as his blood and speak of them as being eaten.[35] So, for example, Christ says, "Unless you eat the flesh of the Son of man and drink his blood, you have no life in you" (John 6:53).

Even for those Christians who reject the real presence of Christ in the bread and wine of the Eucharist and who take these words of Christ to be only symbolic, there is a kind of shocking intensity about the words and so also about the rite. For a person who participates in the rite, some things that are symbolically (or really) the body and blood of the incarnate Deity are brought entirely inside that person by being eaten. Manifestly, the imagery (or the imagery and the reality) are of a union that is consummate in its energy and intimacy.

So although some incipient union with Christ in love is needed to participate in this rite appropriately, union (that is, increased union through increased love) is also the effect of this rite. In one of the few lyrical passages in his scholastic prose, Aquinas says that in the sacrament of the Eucharist a believer's soul is inebriated by the sweetness of the divine goodness.[36]

As I explained above, for virtually all people their acquaintance with the events of the passion and death of Christ has to come through a story. But because of the way in which a person Paula can come to know a person Jerome through a story, even a story can serve to produce a direct and immediate intuitive knowledge of persons of the kind characteristic of actual second-person experience. If Jerome, the person in the story, is a real person who is able to come into second-person experience of his own with Paula, then the process begun by the story can eventuate in mutual closeness and even shared attention. And this is exactly the way that the doctrine about the indwelling Holy Spirit holds that the process works for a person who comes to faith. On that doctrine, when a person appropriates the story of Christ's passion and ceases to resist God, she comes to have with Christ a closeness so powerful that the mind of God, in the person of the Holy Spirit, is actually within her, sharing attention with her in mutual love.

---

34. Aquinas says that the bread and wine of the Eucharist are nourishment for the psyche (Aquinas, *Summa Contra Gentiles*, trans. Charles J. O'Neil [Notre Dame: University of Notre Dame Press, 1989], IV.61) and that they provide growth in virtue because of the way in which the Eucharist connects a person of faith to the passion and death of Christ (*Summa Theologica* IIIa.79.1).

35. See Matt 26:26, Mark 12:22, Luke 22:19, and 1 Cor 11:23.

36. *Summa Theologica* IIIa.79.1 ad 2.

And here we should note that on every occasion on which a person participates in the Eucharist, in a forceful way she is brought back into connection with that same story about God's love in the passion and death of Christ.

It will help in this regard to sketch briefly what that forceful way is. So consider Paula as she participates in the Eucharist. However various the rite is among Christians, it almost invariably contains some reminder not only of the passion and death of Christ but also of the fact that the point of Christ's passion and death was to save people and bring them to union with God. When Paula comes to participate in the rite, then, she will have in mind her own need for help in consequence of things in herself that she herself finds hateful. But she will also have brought home to her that, however alienated she may be from herself, God is not alienated from her. God, who is perfectly good and who knows Paula intimately, does not hate her for what she is, but rather loves her so intensely that he took on humanity and endured shame and agony for her. And for what purpose? To unite her to himself in love.

The moving knowledge of persons with respect to Christ mediated by the story which originally brought Paula to second-person experience of Christ is there again for her in every instance in which Paula participates appropriately in the Eucharist. And the person about whom the story is, namely, Christ, is actually powerfully present to Paula, at least in the person of the Holy Spirit who indwells her.[37] So not only does the force of the story give Paula knowledge of persons with regard to Christ, but in addition the Holy Spirit is closer to Paula and more intimately united to her than it is possible for another human person to be.

When she participates appropriately in the Eucharist, these things will be brought vividly to the forefront of Paula's psyche. (And obviously this effect will be only stronger for those Christians who believe that in receiving the consecrated bread and wine they are receiving the very body and blood of Christ.) Insofar as Paula eats the bread (and drinks the wine) in faith, then in doing so Paula is both reconnecting with Christ's passion and death and also reenacting her original surrender and acceptance of God's love.

Furthermore, between one participation in the Eucharist and the next, Paula will have lived life as a post-fall person; that is, she will have new things in her self or her life that grieve or trouble her, so that she is tempted to give up instead of persevering. But every time she participates

---

37. See Romans 8:9 for the Holy Spirit as the Spirit of Christ.

in the rite, she will find that, however inclined she is to give up on herself or on God, God is still there, still loving her, still wanting her to come into union with himself. The result will be to elicit ever more love of God in Paula, and also joy and peace. And so, with every participation in the Eucharist, Paula will be strengthened for perseverance, in virtue of growing in love of God and in experience of God's continued love and presence to her.

So, without directly acting on the will of a person Paula, by means of the Eucharist God nonetheless provides an effective aid to Paula's perseverance. Without violating Paula's will, God strengthens it for perseverance. Through the Eucharist, Paula is vividly reconnected to the story of Christ's crucifixion and through the story (or through the story and the real presence of Christ in the bread and wine) to Christ's very passion and death.[38] In this reconnection, Paula will also reenact her original surrender to God's love—only because she is doing so *again*, with all that her history and experience bring to this repeated reenactment, she grows in her commitment to Christ as she participates in the rite. By this means, then, through the Eucharist Paula is strengthened in perseverance.

CONCLUSION

However we interpret the doctrine of the atonement, and however exactly we understand the work of Christ's passion and death in the process of bringing human beings to complete and permanent union with God, we can see that the process of salvation has three parts. There is the difficult and delicate beginning of the process that depends ultimately only on the human person in the process. There is sanctification, the extended part of the process in which a person cooperates with God to bring about her increased integration in goodness.[39] And then there is perseverance. We might call this third part the negative correlate of sanctification. It is the extended and ongoing failure to give up on sanctification and return all the way to the original rejection of God.

In both the beginning of this process and in the last part, perseverance, God cannot get what he wants by acting directly and unilaterally on the

---

38. For detailed discussion of the way in which this same process contributes to a person's growth in cooperative grace and to a person's incorporation into the mystical body of Christ, see the chapter on atonement in Stump, *Aquinas*.

39. Nothing about this description of sanctification implies Pelagianism. For more discussion of sanctification, see the chapter on grace and free will in Stump, *Aquinas*, and chapter 8 in Stump, *Wandering in Darkness*.

human will. Union would be lost, not achieved, if God did so. But the passion and death of Christ are a powerful means to elicit from a human person Paula the surrender that is the beginning of the process. By means of the story of Christ's passion and death, Paula comes to know Christ with the knowledge of persons. And when she does so and surrenders to God's love because she does so, then God himself comes to her in the indwelling Holy Spirit, so that in a way mediated by the story Paula comes into union—incipient union—with God.

When Paula participates in the Eucharist with faith, she is reconnected with the passion of Christ; and, as she is, she also reenacts her original surrender to God. This repeated psychic movement would by itself strengthen her in her commitment to God. But because the reenactment takes place within the unfolding of her own life, with its sorrow and sin, Paula's experience in the Eucharist is not strictly speaking an exact repetition of her original surrender to God. It is more nearly like the renewal of a marriage vow, which has the force it does because it takes place in the face of all those things and all that history that might tempt a person to give up.

There are no doubt many other things to be said about the role of the Eucharist in the process of salvation, and there are certainly many other things to be said about the atonement. But these reflections show that one important connection between the atonement and the Eucharist is the role of the Eucharist in strengthening a person in perseverance. This connection holds even on a minimalist interpretation of the Eucharist. It is manifestly more powerful on interpretations of the Eucharist that take Christ to be really present in the consecrated bread and wine.

Perseverance is as essential to the process of salvation as the original surrender to God is, and it is as delicate and difficult to elicit as surrender. The Eucharist has the power to elicit perseverance, time after time, throughout the life of a person in faith. In the Eucharist, a person knows Christ in his suffering for her, at least through the story and the indwelling Holy Spirit; and in knowing Christ, again, she grows in her awareness of his love of her and his presence to her. The result is that she is strengthened in love of Christ. And so, with the Eucharist, she perseveres, with love and joy and peace, even in the sorrows and sins of her life.

CHAPTER 12

ATONEMENT AND ASCENSION

MICHAEL HORTON

VIEWING THE CROSS from the perspective of the ascension allows us to take in more of the expansiveness of what Christ secured at Golgotha. The ascension not only *reveals* the success of Christ's atonement, but, like the resurrection, it is as *constitutive* of redemption as the atonement itself. Our Lord's entrance into the heavenly sanctuary was not merely a victory celebration but an essential part of the victory itself. From the atonement we learn how God has saved us *from* condemnation, death, and hell, but the ascension highlights especially what he has saved us *for*: namely, communion with the triune God in immortal glory.

This paper is more like a prolegomenon to a biblical-theological treatment of the ascension. My principal concern is constructive: namely, to explore the impact of the ascension not only on the atonement but also on our broader cosmological and metaphysical assumptions. The question is never *whether* metaphysics but *which one*. On one hand, ever since Ritschl and Harnack, modern theology has shown us that attempts to rid Christianity once and for all of metaphysics in general and Platonism in particular more often than not succeed only by ridding Christianity of itself.[1]

On the other hand, weighty programs such as the *nouvelle théologie*, Radical Orthodoxy, and the New Finnish School have attracted some

---

1.   According to Adolf von Harnack, "The account of the Ascension is quite useless to the historian." Adolf von Harnack, *New Testament Studies III: The Acts of the Apostles,* vol. 3, trans. John Richard Wilkinson (New York: G. P. Putnam's Sons, 1909), 241.

Protestant theologians to the cause of a renewed Christian Platonism over against a nominalist "extrinsicism" that led allegedly to secularism via the Reformation.[2] Modern theology has been captivated by central dogmas and reductionistic typologies, including "Eastern" versus "Western" soteriological paradigms, with *Christus Victor*, participation and *theôsis* set over against the "legalistic" ideas of original sin, penal substitution, and justification. Exploring the atonement from the perspective of the ascension, I argue that these are false choices.

TALE OF TWO ASCENSIONS

One typology seems to me to have better historical justification than others that I have mentioned: the contrasting trajectories of Origen of Alexandria (182–254) and Irenaeus of Lyons (130–202). Like most generalizations, this one is also susceptible to exaggeration. Yet the differences are profound enough to have generated distinct trajectories even into the present day, and they turn to a large extent on radically different interpretations of Christ's ascension.[3]

THE ORIGENIST TRAJECTORY

Origen wrote, "If we understand the ascent of the Son to the Father with holy insight and in a way suitable to God, we shall realize it is the ascent of mind rather than the body."[4] This thesis is generated by a cosmology that Origen delineates especially in *On First Principles*. The hierarchy that we observe in the cosmos and among human beings originates with a rebellion of rational souls prior to this world, meriting different levels of being.[5] "And when they reach the neighborhood of the earth," Origen writes, "they are enclosed in grosser bodies, and last of all are tied to human

---

2.   The nouvelle theologians include Henri de Lubac, Hans Urs von Balthasar, and Yves Congar. Explicitly indebted to the *nouvelle théologie* (especially de Lubac), John Milbank, Catherine Pickstock, and Graham Ward announced their own program in 1999 with the volume, *Radical Orthodoxy: A New Theology* (London: Routledge), followed by a stream of cultural and theological monographs. See also *Radical Orthodoxy and the Reformed Tradition: Creation, Covenant and Participation*, eds. James K. A. Smith and James H. Olthuis (Grand Rapids: Baker, 2005).

3.   In the foreword to his translation of the anthology, *Origen: Spirit and Fire*, Robert J. Daly SJ, acknowledges "the Platonizing cast of his thought" but adds that this "is, in itself, only a sign that he was a Christian thinker in the third century.... The real question is not whether Origen thinks as a Platonist, but whether in so doing he gives sufficient place to the incarnational aspects of Christianity." Robert J. Daly SJ, trans., *Origen: Spirit and Fire*, ed. Hans Urs von Balthasar (Washington, D.C.: The Catholic University of America Press, 1984), xiv. I agree entirely with his point but am less convinced that Origen's thinking meets that criterion.

4.   Origen, "On Prayer," XXIII.2, in *Origen: The Classics of Western Spirituality*, trans. Rowan A. Greer (Mahwah, NJ: Paulist Press, 1979), 126–27.

5.   Origen, *On First Principles*, 1.6.2; 1.7.1–1.8.4.

flesh."[6] Falling by their free will, these incarcerated spirits may ascend by their free will and merit higher stations; this world was created as a prison or school for winning back our wings.

Jesus' soul alone remained united fully to the Logos, and he shows the fallen souls how to return to the Father, passing from earthly to soulish and finally to spiritual existence.[7] Though less divine than the Father, the Son is the link between God and humans. The meaning of Christ's death is twofold, Origen states: "the first" is that he "has left us an example" and "the second" is that he has gained "victory over the devil...."[8] Christ's death involved no propitiatory sacrifice, since God has no wrath.[9]

The chief purpose of the incarnation was to reveal the invisible Deity to sensual creatures. Having done this, the Logos casts off his bodily carapace. Origen interpreted Jesus' resurrection allegorically, as a passing from a physical to an ethereal body.[10] The "spiritual body" of 1 Corinthians 15:44 indicates that

> in the resurrection of the just there will be nothing physical [*animale*] in those who have merited beatitude.... The spirit [*nous*], in its falling, became soul; and the soul, when formed again in virtues, will become spirit again.... It follows from this that God and these beings [rational souls of angels and humans] are in some way of the divine substance.[11]

Thus, he exhorts, "Each of you should strive to become a divider of that water which is above and which is below."[12] Indeed, "the exodus from Egypt is also a figure of the soul which leaves the darkness of this world and the blindness of bodily nature."[13]

God is a wise physician who sometimes applies strong medicine, but the fires of earthly purgation are always remedial, even for Pharaoh, Herod, and Lucifer himself.[14] The wheat and tares that are separated by Christ at his return (Matt 13:24–30, 36–42) are opinions, not persons.[15] As J. W. Trigg puts it, "To Origen this meant that, in the end, all rational

---

6. Ibid., 1.3.1.
7. Ibid., 4.4.5n.1 and 4.9.2; cf. Origen, *On Prayer*, 23.2.
8. Von Balthasar, *Origen: Spirit and Fire*, 131.
9. Joseph Wilson Trigg, *Origen: The Bible and Philosophy in the Third Century* (London: SCM Press, 2012), 101.
10. Origen, *On First Principles*, 4.2.1–4.3.7.
11. Von Balthasar, *Origen: Spirit and Fire,* 50–51
12. Ibid., 53.
13. Ibid., 65.
14. Trigg, *Origen*, 142. In fact, Origen conjectures in his *Dialogue with Candidus* (Candidus being a Gnostic leader) that the Devil will be saved.
15. Ibid., 213.

creatures will be saved and restored to their original state of contemplative union with God, 'for the end is always like the beginning.' "[16]

Origen's tripartite anthropology is all-controlling. He draws the parallel between body, soul, and spirit and the division of the faithful into simple, more perfect, and highly spiritual, as well as the historical, moral, and allegorical meanings of Scripture.[17] "One must understand the divine scripture intellectually and spiritually; for the sensible or physical way of knowing that is according to the historical meaning is not true."[18] When it comes to the "letter," he advises, "Cast all this aside like the bitter rind of a nut."[19] "[L]et us seek out not the letter but the soul.... If we can do this, we will also ascend to the spirit."[20] Furthermore, external preaching and sacraments are contrasted with the inner word, washing, and feeding.[21] The institutional church is different from the true church led by the real heirs of the prophets and apostles who are called directly by the Spirit, among whom Origen considered himself.[22] There are even two gospels: a temporal gospel concerning the Jesus of history (for the simple) and the eternal gospel that transcends the literal meaning of the New Testament (for the spiritually advanced).[23]

Although that which is "spiritual" has priority in his thinking, Origen regarded the Holy Spirit as less divine than the Son—perhaps a high angel.[24] In fact, the Holy Spirit is often identified with the human spirit, distinguished from the soul and body.[25] The ascent upward is a descent inward, into the inmost self: "[T]hat first heaven, which we have called spiritual, is our mind, which is itself spirit.... Indeed this human, made 'in the image of God,' we do not understand as bodily."[26] Origen calls believers "to remove the earth from each of you and open up your fountain. For he is within you and does not come from outside, just as 'the kingdom of God is within you.' "[27]

---

16. Ibid., 105. See Origen, *On First Principles*, 1.6.2.

17. Origen, *On First Principles*, 4.2.1–4.3.7. Origen frequently contrasts the "outer shell" (the historical, earthly, and ordinary sense of things as understood by "the many") with the "inner truth" that is mystical. See von Balthasar, *Origen: Spirit and Fire*, 44, 50, 51, 53, 55, 63, 65, 93, 102–109, 102–105, 115, 125, etc.

18. Von Balthasar, *Origen: Spirit and Fire*, 93.

19. Ibid., 103.

20. Ibid., 105.

21. Trigg, *Origen*, 191, 194.

22. Ibid., 125–26, 144–46.

23. Douglas Farrow, *Ascension Theology* (Edinburgh: T & T Clark, 2011), 20–21. See *On First Principles*, 4.3.13. n. 7. The passage in view is from Jerome's version and suggests that "the gospel which is to exist in the heavens is as far superior to our gospel as the preaching of Christ is to the rites of the old law...."

24. Origen, *On First Principles*, 1.3 (and notes 1 and 4 on page 3 in the Butterworth edition).

25. Von Balthasar, *Origen: Spirit and Fire*, 183.

26. Ibid., 55.

27. Ibid., 31.

Origen's cosmology is basically the *exitus-reditus* (exit-return) pattern of Plato's *Phaedrus*, part of a common fund for disparate groups in Alexandria: Philo, Valentinus, and Plotinus who, like Origen himself, had been a student of the Platonist philosopher Ammonius Saccas. While the Gnostics set the upper world of spirit and the lower world of matter in stark opposition, Platonism allowed Origen to see the relation as more like a ladder. The lower rungs are, well, *lower*, but they have their place in the contemplative ascent.

The Second Council of Constantinople in 553 issued fifteen anathemas against Origen's teaching, but there is probably no other figure charged with heresy who has enjoyed such enormous prestige and enduring influence in church history even among orthodox writers. Jerome led the Latin critique of Origen, replying to Origen's defender Rufinus, "What you admire so much we long ago despised when we found it in Plato."[28] Although Platonism had saved him from the stark dualism of the Manichaeans, Augustine said he found nothing in the Platonists' books that tell us that "the Word became flesh."[29] He added, "It is, I suppose, humiliating for learned people to leave the school of Plato to enter that of Christ,"[30] although the extent of his own debt to Neoplatonism remains a matter of considerable debate.

While affirming the ban on some of Origen's esoteric teachings, the metaphysical map for much of mainstream Byzantine and medieval theology was a theurgic Neoplatonism mediated especially by Pseudo-Dionysius.[31] According to Pseudo-Dionysius, "To be deified is to enable God to be born in oneself."[32] Maximus the Confessor followed a similar line, arguing "that it is no longer necessary 'that those who seek the Lord should seek him outside themselves.'"[33] "God always wishes to become incarnate in those who are worthy of it," he wrote.[34] Similar expressions are found throughout the history of Christian mysticism, including radical

---

28. Cited by G. W. Butterworth in Origen, *On First Principles*, 41 n. 1., from Jerome's *Con. Joh. Hieros.* 19.

29. Augustine, *City of God*, trans. Henry Betttenson (New York: Penguin, 2003), 10.29.

30. Ibid., 10.29.

31. A Syrian monk writing in the late fifth and early sixth centuries, Pseudo-Dionysius claimed to have been the philosopher who followed Paul after his speech in the Areopagus in Acts 17:34. This gave him enormous authority during the Middle Ages. In fact, next to Scripture, he is the author cited most by Thomas Aquinas. Only in the Renaissance-Reformation era was his pseudonymity proved.

32. Pseudo-Dionysius, *Ecclesiastical Hierarchy* II, introduction in *Patrologia Graeca*, ed. J. P. Migne, 162 vols. (Paris, 1957–1886), 3:392.

33. Quoted in Douglas Farrow, *Ascension Theology* (Bloomsbury, UK: T&T Clark, 2011), 24, from Evagrius Ponticus's *Gnostic Centuries*, 2.35; cf. 2.62.

34. Maximus the Confessor, "Questions to Thalassiust, 22 in *Patrologia Graeca*, 90:321.

forms of Protestantism where the "Christ within" replaced both the Holy Spirit and the ascended Jesus at the Father's right hand.[35]

Through Pseudo-Dionysius's influence especially, the church increasingly replaced Christ as the ladder of salvation. As Douglas Farrow summarizes, throughout the Middle Ages the ascension of Christ goes through successive waves of "internalization and marginalization" in favor of "the ancient Hellenic quest for the *visio dei*.... That was a worldview naturally resistant to the hard edge of biblical eschatology, but quite comfortable with a hidden Christ who is always ascending and a Mary who is always bringing him down again; with an endless liturgical rhythm in which the *parousia* (not unlike the philosophers' stone) is always within reach yet forever receding."[36]

With the Renaissance came a resurgence of Neoplatonism, often in less "Christianized" forms, as in Pico della Mirandola, who also presumed to lift the ban on Origen. Erasmus recommended the Platonists as the height of philosophy and Origen as the best of the Christian authors — of far greater spiritual value than Augustine, he said.[37] J. B. Payne observes, "The starting point for Erasmus's sacramental thought, as indeed for his whole theology, is the Platonic conception of the contrast between flesh and spirit."[38] And it was Erasmus, Farrow relates, "who in his attack on late medieval superstition repeats the point that 'it was the flesh of Christ which stood in the way' of an authentic spiritual faith among the apostles; that 'the physical presence of Christ is of no profit for salvation.' "[39]

THE IRENAEAN TRAJECTORY

Irenaeus's *Against Heresies* predated Origen's work by a half-century and described the Gnostic consensus in terms that could include Origen's basic scheme: "This, then, is the true redemption ... that their inner man may ascend on high in an invisible manner, as if their body were left among created things, while their soul is sent forward to the Demiurge."[40] However, Irenaeus said that Christ did bodily "ascend to the height above, offering and commending to His Father that human nature which had been found,

---

35. Douglas Farrow's *Ascension and Ecclesia: On the Significance of the Doctrine of the Ascension for Ecclesiology and Christian Cosmology* (Grand Rapids: Eerdmans, 2009) provides a useful genealogy leading through various modern theologians and philosophers.

36. Farrow, *Ascension Theology*, 24, 163.

37. Trigg, *Origen*, 255.

38. J. B. Payne, *Erasmus: His Theology of the Sacraments* (Richmond: John Knox Press, 1969), 35.

39. Farrow, *Ascension Theology*, 23, quoted from *The Handbook of the Christian Soldier*, Fifth Rule (*The Erasmus Reader*, ed. E. Rummel), 146.

40. Irenaeus, *Against Heresies* in *Ante-Nicene Fathers*, vol. 1, trans. Alexander Roberts, ed. James Donaldson (Grand Rapids: Eerdmans, 2001), 1.21.5. (Hereafter *AH*.)

making in His own person the first-fruits of the resurrection of man."[41] He said, "For by the hands of the Father, that is, by the Son and the Holy Spirit, man, *and not a part of man*, was made in the likeness of God."[42] Tertullian added in the same vein, Christ "carried it [our flesh] with him into heaven as a pledge of that complete entirety which is one day to be restored to it. Be not disquieted, O flesh and blood, with any care; in Christ you have acquired both heaven and the kingdom of God."[43]

The Reformation was not a wholesale rejection of the long conversation between Jerusalem and Athens, but it was critical of the more Origenist trajectory evident especially in more radical forms of medieval mysticism that also shaped the thinking of Anabaptist leaders. In his debate with Erasmus, Luther claimed to have put Origen back under the ban and said, "I think that Denys [Pseudo-Dionysius] Platonizes more than he Christianizes."[44] In fact, it was this "ascent of mind" that the German reformer had in mind when he contrasted "theologians of glory" with "theologians of the cross."[45]

Calvin's dependence on Irenaeus should not be exaggerated; there were many patristic influences, especially Augustine and Chrysostom.[46] Plato at least realized that the aim of humanity is union with "God," Calvin says, yet "he could not even dimly sense its nature" apart from union with Christ. Only those "who raise their minds to the resurrection" have an accurate conception of the beatific vision.[47] The reformer's references to Origen are negative, and he described Pseudo-Dionysius's *Celestial Hierarchy* as impressive at first but turning out to be "nothing but talk." "If you read that book, you would think a man fallen from heaven recounted, not what he had learned, but what he had seen with his own eyes."[48]

---

41. Ibid., 3.19.3.

42. Ibid., 5.6.1 (emphasis added).

43. Tertullian, *Resurrection*, para. 51 in *Ante-Nicene Fathers*, vol. 3, trans. Alexander Roberts, ed. James Donaldson (Grand Rapids: Eerdmans, 1995), 545–94.

44. Quoted from Luther's *The Babylonian Captivity of the Church*, by Farrow, *Ascension and Ecclesia*, 133.

45. See Walther von Loewenich, *Luther's Theology of the Cross* (Minneapolis: Augsburg, 1976).

46. Irena Backus, "Calvin and the Greek Fathers" in *Continuity and Change: The Harvest of Later Medieval and Reformation History*, eds. Robert J. Bast and Andrew C. Gow (Leiden: Brill, 2000); Johannes Van Oort, "John Calvin and the Church Fathers," in *The Reception of the Church Fathers in the West: From the Carolingians to the Maurists*, ed. Irena Backus (Leiden: Brill, 1997); A. N. S. Lane, *John Calvin: Student of the Church Fathers* (Edinburgh: T&T Clark, 1991); Richard Muller, *Calvin in Context* (New York: Oxford University Press, 2010), esp. 120–55 and 235–62. Augustine ranks first, although Calvin criticized Augustine on occasion for being too Platonist. See *Comm. on Jn.* 1.3 in *Calvini opera* 59 vols. In *Corpus Reformatorum*, eds. C. G. Bretschneider, H. E. Bindseil, et al., vols. 29–87 (New York: Johnson, repr. 1964), 47–48.

47. Calvin, *Institutes of the Christian Religion*, 2 vols., trans. Ford Lewis Battles, ed. John T. McNeill (Philadelphia: Westminster Press, 1960), 3.25.2; cf. 1.5.11.

48. Ibid.,1.14.4.

Hans Urs von Balthasar charged that Irenaeus's "basic attitude cannot be assimilated by true Protestantism."[49] Locating Reformed theology within the more "Irenaean" stream, the balance of this paper challenges Balthasar's judgment, highlighting the role of the ascension in defining this trajectory.

RECAPITULATION: THE TWO ADAMS

The christological emphases that emerged in Reformed circles reflect an Irenaean concern to highlight the saving significance of Christ's humanity. The Word became flesh not simply to reveal God's love, nor to blaze the trail for our educative ascent of mind, nor only to offer his body as a sacrifice, but to fulfill the covenantal role that Adam abandoned. This is most evident in Irenaeus's doctrine of recapitulation.

RECAPITULATION AND ACTIVE OBEDIENCE

Irenaeus describes recapitulation this way: The eternal Son was sent by the Father to be "united to his workmanship, ... so that what we had lost in Adam—namely, to be according to the image and likeness of God—that we might recover in Christ Jesus."[50] Irenaeus even refers to a "first covenant" made with Adam as the head of the human race, a "covenant of law" distinguished from "the gospel covenant."[51] Adam and Eve were created in true righteousness and holiness, but like children they were not yet mature or confirmed in immortal glory.[52] Thus, the consummation can never be a return to the beginning, but rather, entrance into a state of glory that no human being has ever known. This story of the "two Adams" is not an allegory about something else but a historical reality that forms the plight-solution and promise-fulfillment pattern of Christian hope.

Defining recapitulation directly, Calvin says that it is the Son's union with us and our union with him: the marvelous exchange. "Our Lord came forth as true man and took the person and name of Adam," he says, "in order to take Adam's place in obeying the Father."[53] "How has Christ abolished sin? He achieved this for us by the whole course of his obedience." "In short," he adds, "from the time when he took on the form of a

---

49. Hans Urs von Balthasar, *The Glory of the Lord: A Theological Aesthetics*, vol. 2, *Studies in Theological Style: Clerical Styles*, trans. Andrew Louth, Francis McDonagh, and Brian McNeil CRV, ed. John Riches (Edinburgh/San Francisco: T&T Clark with Ignatius Press, 1984), 80.

50. Irenaeus, *AH*, 3.18.1.

51. Ibid., 1.10.3. Cf. 4.16.1 and 4.16.3 and 5.16.3.

52. Ibid., 4.11.1–2.

53. Calvin, *Institutes*, 2.12.3.

servant, he began to pay the price of liberation in order to redeem us."[54] Christ not only bears our guilt, but by his meritorious obedience as the faithful Son of Man wins for us the right finally to eat from the Tree of Life. In the same vein, John Owen writes, "There is no contemplation of the glory of Christ that ought more to affect the hearts of them that do believe with delight and joy than this, of the recapitulation of all things in him."[55] Even more glorious than the first creation, "this new relation of the creation unto the Son of God" is "more beautiful than it was before."[56]

Sin, Calvin says, springs not from "a lower appetite" or "sensuality," but

> unspeakable impiety occupied the very citadel of his [man's] mind and pride penetrated to the depths of his heart. Thus it is pointless and foolish to restrict the corruption that arises thence only to what are called the impulses of the senses; or to call [these senses] the "kindling wood" [of sin].[57]

What Adam lost was communion with God, from which flowed all of the blessings of life, righteousness, and dignity.[58] And grace is not a medicinal substance infused into the soul to elevate it toward the super-natural, as medieval theologians had argued.[59] Rather, it is the favor and gift of the Father, in the Son, and by the Holy Spirit. As incarnate, the Son "is near us, indeed touches us, since he is our flesh."[60] It is not just in his divinity that Christ is life-giving, Calvin says. As the eschatological first-fruits, his humanity is "pervaded with fullness of life to be transmitted to us," and this is why "it is rightly called 'life-giving.' "[61]

The contrasting trajectories become clearer. First, while Origenism is concerned centrally with the ascent of the soul or mind away from our bodily history, Irenaeus and his heirs focus on God's descent to us and his ascent to the Father in our flesh, taking our history with him into the age to come. Calvin says, "Christ aggregated to his body that which was alien-ated from the hope of life: the world which was lost and history itself."[62] Elsewhere he writes,

54. Ibid., 2.16.5.
55. John Owen, "The Person of Christ: His Mediatorial Office in Heaven," in *Works of John Owen*, vol. 1, ed. William H. Goold (London: Banner of Truth Trust, 1965), 1:372.
56. Ibid., 1:373.
57. Calvin, *Institutes*, 2.1.9; cf. 2.1.4.
58. Ibid., 2.1.5–6.
59. Thomas Aquinas, *Summa Theologia*, trans. Fathers of the English Dominican Province (Westminster, MD: Christian Classics, 1981), II-II, 23, 2; I-II, 110, 2.
60. Calvin, *Institutes*, 2.12.1.
61. Ibid., 4.17.9.
62. Calvin, *Corpus Reformatorum*, 101 vols., eds. K. G. Bretschneider et al. (Berlin: Schwetchike, 1834–1900), 55:219.

In this sense Irenaeus writes that the Father, himself infinite, becomes finite in the Son, for he has accommodated himself to our little measure lest our minds be overwhelmed by the immensity of his glory.... Actually, it means nothing else than that God is comprehended in Christ alone.[63]

Jesus came not merely to *show* us the way, but to *be* the Way.

Second, and related to the first point, everything that happened to Jesus will happen to those who are united to him. While for Origen the end is a return to the beginning, for the Irenaean trajectory the end is far greater than the beginning, with the Last Adam entering the everlasting Sabbath as our victor.

Third, by his ascension Christ has opened up a space within our history for the descent of the Spirit who brings the powers of the age to come into this present age. In fact, Owen observes of the ascended Christ,

He it is in whom *our nature*, which was debased as low as hell by apostasy from God, *is exalted* above the whole creation.... In him the relation of our nature unto God is eternally secured.... Heaven and earth may pass away, but there shall never be a dissolution of the union between God and our nature any more.[64]

These redemptive-historical events cannot be mapped onto a preexisting cosmology. Rather, they *are* the map.

RECAPITULATION AND ATONEMENT

In his great prayer recorded in John 17, Jesus has in view one dramatic movement from Golgotha to glory. His cross will secure eternal life for his people, and in his glorification those who are united to him will be brought into the intimacy of the Father-Son relationship (esp. vv. 1, 21–22).

Rather than treat recapitulation as one aspect of the atonement, I suggest that the atonement should be seen as a central aspect of recapitulation that is realized in the whole life and ministry of Christ from the incarnation to his return in glory. Christ's threefold office is a recapitulation of the original commission given to humanity in Adam: as prophet, he is the true and faithful witness; as priest, the mediator who reconciles sinners to God; as king, the conqueror who brings the frightful disorder of the fallen world into a glory beyond even that of its original creation.

---

63. Calvin, *Institutes*, 2.6.4.
64. John Owen, "Preface to the Reader" in "The Person of Christ," 1:276–77, 281.

There is no basis therefore for any antithesis between *Christus Victor* and *Agnus Dei*, the atonement as victory over evil powers and as a propitiatory sacrifice. In fact, the key *Christus Victor* passages indicate that Christ's conquest over the powers of Satan, death, and hell is based on his having satisfied the claims of God's law and having borne its curse in our place (Heb 9:22; 1 Cor 15:55–57; Rom 8:1–23; Col 2:14–15).[65] The legal aspect of our union with Christ is the basis for the mystical and organic aspects, just as the legal aspect of marriage or adoption is the basis for a secure and intimate relationship. Calvin affirmed Christ's royal victory already in his atoning death, but he also underscored the real transition from the state of humiliation to exaltation.[66]

ASCENSION AND EUCHARIST

It was in the Eucharistic controversies of the Reformation era where differing views of the ascension engendered differing Christological emphases. Some Anabaptist leaders returned directly to Origen's principal ideas. Among the magisterial reformers, though, there was still considerable debate. Zwingli maintained a friendship with Erasmus, sharing a fondness for Platonist philosophy and, at least early on, for Origen.[67] W. P. Stephens notes that the Zurich reformer's emphasis fell on "Christ as God rather than Christ as man."[68] He heartily emphasized Christ's bodily ascension, but like Erasmus he argued that Christ's physical absence from us is of little consequence, since he is omnipresent in his deity.[69] Zwingli wrote, "Christ is our salvation by virtue of that part of his nature by which he came down from heaven, not of that by which he was born of an immaculate virgin, though he had to suffer and die by this part."[70]

It is hardly surprising that Luther heard such statements as Nestorian, as did Calvin. Most basically for Calvin, Zwingli struck at the very heart of our union with Christ—the whole person, including his saving humanity.

---

65. I explore the integral nature of *Christus Victor* and propitiation in Michael S. Horton, *Lord and Servant: A Covenant Christology* (Louisville: Westminster John Knox, 2005), 178–260.

66. A superb treatment of the subject is Jeremy Treat's recently published *The Crucified King: Atonement and Kingdom in Biblical and Systematic Theology* (Grand Rapids: Zondervan, 2014).

67. W. P. Stephens, *The Theology of Huldrych Zwingli* (Oxford: Clarendon Press, 1986), 9–17. W. P. Stephens relates that Zwingli's marginal notes on Romans "points to the overwhelming, but independent, use of Origen by Zwingli, although Augustine's teaching on grace became steadily more dominant" (see Stephens, 18–19).

68. Ibid., 121. Stephens adds, "The Augustinian and Neoplatonist contribution is evident in the whole of Zwingli's theology, and especially in his understanding of the sacraments" (254).

69. For a fair interpretation of Zwingli's Christology, see W. P. Stephens, *The Theology of Huldrych Zwingli*, 108–128.

70. Zwingli, *Commentary on True and False Religion*, eds. Samuel Macauley Jackson and Clarence Nevin Heller (Durham, NC: The Labyrinth Press, 1981), 204.

"For in his flesh was accomplished man's redemption," he argues.[71] Calvin said, "It would be extreme madness to recognize no communion of believers with the flesh and blood of the Lord.... The flesh of Christ is like a rich and inexhaustible fountain that pours into us the life springing forth from the Godhead into itself."[72] When we receive the bread and the wine, says Calvin, "let us no less surely trust that the body itself is also given to us."[73] The signs are "guarantees of a present reality: the believer's feeding on the body and blood of Christ."[74] Otherwise, faith becomes a "mere imagining" of Christ's presence—an ascent of mind that he attributed to Zwingli.[75] The Lord's Supper not only assures our minds but also "secures the immortality of our flesh" which is "even now quickened by his immortal flesh."[76]

Calvin appeals explicitly to Irenaeus for his view of the Supper in several places.[77] With Irenaeus, he insists that it is not enough that the Son united himself to our humanity; we must be united to him now in order to be saved. Hence, according to the Belgic Confession, although by his resurrection Jesus has "given immortality" to the humanity he assumed, "nevertheless he has not changed the reality of his human nature; forasmuch as our salvation and resurrection also depend on the reality of his body" (Article 19).

However, for just that reason, Lutheran Christology raised the specter of Eutychianism by positing that Christ's divine attributes (such as omnipresence) were communicated to his human nature. According to this position, Christ is omnipresent even in his humanity, though invisibly, and this genus of majesty was his already at his incarnation.[78] "Hence at his exaltation," Bavinck summarizes, "Christ received nothing he did not already have.... Immediately at the moment of his incarnation, Christ *is* that which he could *become*."[79] I should mention in passing that at least on this point Karl Barth takes the Lutheran side in the controversy when he

---

71. Calvin, *The Gospel According to John*, vol 1:1–10, trans. T. H. L. Parker; Calvin's New Testament Commentaries 4, eds. David W. Torrance and Thomas F. Torrance (Grand Rapids: Eerdmans, 1959–72), 167.

72. Calvin, *Institutes*, 4.17.9.

73. Ibid., 4.17.10.

74. B. A. Gerrish, *Grace and Gratitude: The Eucharistic Theology of John Calvin* (Minneapolis: Augsburg Fortress, 1993), 165.

75. Calvin, *Institutes*, 4.17.5–6.

76. Ibid., 4.17.32.

77. Julie Canlis, *Calvin's Ladder: A Spiritual Theology of Ascent and the Ascension* (Grand Rapids: Eerdmans, 2010), 159.

78. Bavinck provides a good summary of the Lutheran view from a Reformed perspective in *Reformed Dogmatics*, vol. 3, *Sin and Salvation in Christ*, ed. John Bolt, trans. John Vriend (Grand Rapids: Baker, 2006), 428–29, citing J. Gerhard, J. A. Quenstedt, J. Buddeus, F. A. Philippi.

79. Bavinck, *Reformed Dogmatics*, 3:428–29, citing Quendstedt.

says that Christ's exaltation "is completed already" in his humiliation.[80] In fact, "His being as such (if we may be permitted this abstraction for a moment) was and is the end of the old and the beginning of the new form of this world even without his resurrection and ascension."[81]

As Bavinck summarizes, "The Reformed view is that Christ is the mediator in accordance with both natures." "The divine and human participate in both states in the one person.... His exaltation is thus a real change, a state gained as a reward of his obedience. The preposition διὸ ('therefore') in Philippians 2 as well as the Letter to the Hebrews points to Christ earning his exaltation through obedience."[82] Consequently, in the exaltation of "his humanity," observes Bavinck, "our humanity was exalted beyond all prior dignity ... so that same person is the subject of the exaltation in both his natures."[83] At the same time, the Reformed reject the Socinian view that this exaltation changed the divine nature as such, as if he were now divine in a way that he had not been previously.[84]

Calvin had no interest speculating about the whereabouts of the heavenly throne on which Christ is seated. "But what is the manner of the ascension itself?" he asks. Apart from the ascension in the flesh, the continuity between Christ's earthly and heavenly existence becomes questionable — along with our continuity with him in our future resurrection. Indeed, Paul writes that Christ "ascended far above all the heavens, that he might fill all things" (Eph 4:10 ESV). "But if to fill all things in an invisible manner is numbered among the gifts of his glorified body," says Calvin, "it is plain that the substance of the body is wiped out and that no difference between deity and human nature is left." By Christ's own testimony, "he can be touched and seen," Calvin adds. "Take these away and flesh now ceases to be." A docetic ascension negates Paul's assurance that "'we await from heaven a Savior, ... who will change our lowly body to be like his glorious body' [Phil 3:20–21]." We do not hope for "an invisible and infinite body," but our glorified humanity together with our exalted Head. Yet Christ remains in heaven "until the time of restoration" (Acts 3:21).[85]

80. Karl Barth, *Church Dogmatics*, eds. G. W. Bromiley and T. F. Torrance, trans. G. W. Bromiley (Edinburgh: T&T Clark, 1956–75), IV/2:250.
81. Barth, *CD* IV/2,132–133; also see my chapter, Michael S. Horton, "Covenant, Election, and Incarnation: Evaluating Barth's Actualist Christology," in *Karl Barth and American Evangelicalism*, eds. Bruce McCormack and Clifford Anderso (Grand Rapids: Eerdmans, 2011), 112–47.
82. Bavinck, *Reformed Dogmatics*, 3:418–19.
83. Ibid., 3:432, 435.
84. Ibid., 3:435.
85. Calvin, *Institutes* 4.17.27, 29.

Explaining away Christ's ascension in the flesh inevitably leads to a muting of the significance of Pentecost. Jesus said, "It is to your advantage that I go away." However, where for Zwingli this was because it revealed his omnipresent deity, Calvin emphasized Jesus' own explanation: "For if I do not go away, the Helper will not come to you. But if I go, I will send him to you" (Jn 16:7 ESV).

The whole thrust of this farewell discourse is his ascension and the sending of the Spirit. Calvin says, "I willingly confess that Christ is ascended that he may fill all things; but I say that he is spread abroad everywhere by his Spirit, not by the substance of his flesh."[86] Calvin complains of his critics, "For thus they leave nothing to the secret working of the Spirit, which unites Christ himself to us. To them Christ does not seem present unless he comes down to us. As though, if he should lift us to himself, we should not just as much enjoy his presence!"[87] Similarly, Irenaeus said that the Gnostics "do, in fact, set the Spirit aside altogether."[88]

Rather than pursue dubious Christological solutions, Calvin — like Irenaeus — pointed to the Holy Spirit.[89] Douglas Farrow suggests that Calvin, like Irenaeus, "found it necessary to reckon more bravely than the other reformers with the absence of Christ as a genuine problem for the church. It is *we* who require eucharistic relocation."[90] Instead of moving from Eucharist to ascension, Calvin moved in the other direction, and this led him to stress "the particularity of Jesus without sacrificing sacramental realism." This "forced him to seek a *pneumatological solution* to the problem of the presence and the absence."[91]

Calvin was hardly alone in the development of this view.[92] Nevertheless, I share Julie Canlis's judgment:

---

86. Calvin, *Comm. Acts* 1:9; cf. *Inst.* 4.6.10 and 2.16.4.
87. Calvin, *Institutes*, 4.17.31.
88. See Canlis, *Calvin's Ladder*, 230–31, quoting Irenaeus, *AH* III.17.4, in Mary Ann Donovan, *One Right Reading? A Guide to Irenaeus* (Collegeville, MN: Liturgical Press, 1997).
89. Calvin, *Institutes*, 4.17.10.
90. Farrow, *Ascension and Ecclesia*, 176–77.
91. Ibid., 177–78, emphasis added. Even after his reception into the Roman Catholic Church, Farrow maintains that Calvin stands out as an early modern representative of this Irenaean trajectory against Origen and Pelagianism. See *Ascension Theology*, 40–41, citing Calvin, *Institutes* 4.17.27 and his commentary on Hebrews.
92. Without downplaying Calvin's genius for clear formulations, he was indebted to Reformed colleagues like Martin Bucer and Philipp Melanchthon. Calvin said that the view he defended "received its finishing touches from Peter Martyr [Vermigli], who left nothing more to be done." Cited John Patrick Donelly SJ, in his introduction to Peter Martyr Vermigli, *Dialogue on the Two Natures of Christ*, trans. and ed. John Patrick Donelly SJ, vol. 21 of *Sixteenth-Century Essays and Studies* (Kirksville, MO: Thomas Jefferson University Press and Sixteenth Century Journal Publishers, 1995), xiii.

The radical—even watershed—role that Calvin gave to the Spirit in the Lord's Supper cannot be overstated. As had not been done since perhaps the patristic writers, Calvin attempted to take seriously the pneumatological dimensions of presence: the Spirit is not the Pentecostal replacement *for* Christ but the way *to* him.[93]

Calvin says, "In sum, God comes down to us so that then we might go up to him. That is why the sacraments are compared to the steps of a ladder."[94] Canlis observes, "The problem with medieval sacramentalism, in Calvin's opinion, is that it reversed the direction of the ladder."[95] She adds,

> If human life has been brought 'up' into God without change or confusion and our 'partaking' of his very humanity is raising us up into God's triune *koinônia*, then we see just how essential the Eucharist is as a confirmation of Calvin's doctrine of participation.[96]

ASCENSION AND DEIFICATION

Propitiation and victory underscore the danger that Christ's death has overcome for us. Yet to be delivered *from* sin's curse, and therefore from the kingdom of Satan, is not yet to be *united to* God. The atonement needs the ascension and Pentecost.

Athanasius famously stated, "He indeed assumed humanity that we might become God."[97] Given the consensus of the Eastern fathers on the distinction between God's essence and energies, though, deification could never include any ontic overlap (univocity) between divine and creaturely being. In fact, Athanasius insists that we will be deified only in the Son, "without losing our own proper substance."[98] Irenaeus had made the same point: "Neither is the substance nor the essence of the creation annihilated."[99] The Son "became what we are, that He might bring us to be even what He is Himself," says Irenaeus.[100] A little further, he stipulates that this consummate union "will render us like unto [Christ]."[101]

---

93. Canlis, *Calvin's Ladder*, 239.
94. Ibid., 160, quoting Calvin, *Serm. 2 Sam.* 6:1–7.
95. Ibid., 159.
96. Ibid., 160.
97. St. Athanasius, "On the Incarnation," in *Nicene and Post-Nicene Fathers*, ed. Philip Schaff et al., 2nd series (Grand Rapids: Eerdmans, repr. 1982), 4:65.
98. Athanasius, *De Decretis* in NPNF2, vol. 4, trans. John Henry Newman, ed. Philip Schaff and Henry Wace (Grand Rapids: Eerdmans, repr. 1982), 3.14; cf. *Against the Arians*, in the same volume, 1.39.
99. Irenaeus, *AH* 5.36.1.
100. Ibid., preface to Book 5.
101. Ibid., 5.8.1.

All of these qualifications guard against Origen's version of deification. Where Irenaeus sees Christ as passing through different stages of our human-historical existence (humiliation and exaltation), recovering what was lost in Adam, Origen sees Christ as passing from fleshly, to soulish, and finally to spiritual existence, as our example. At the cross, says Origen, "the dispensation of the flesh was ended." Consequently, the Son is now indistinguishable from the Holy Spirit.[102] We must no longer think of Christ as a human being circumscribed by space. "For it is not a man who is 'wherever two or three are gathered in' his 'name' (Mt 18:20); nor is a man 'with' us 'always, to the close of the age' (Mt 28:20); and when the faithful are gathered everywhere, what is present is not a man but the divine power that was in Jesus."[103] Similarly, Origen counsels, the soul that will "climb to the heights of heaven shall no longer be a man, but according to his word, will be 'like an angel of God'" or perhaps divine; but in either case, "he shall certainly no longer be a man."[104]

DEIFICATION IN IRENAEUS

In Irenaeus and other patristic writers, deification is the full realization of the gifts of immortality, complete restoration of the image of God, adoption, and the vision of God in Christ. For Irenaeus everything in deification turns on the activity of the three divine persons in the economy rather than on the believer's ascent to God.[105] The Spirit lifts us up into the eschatological life of Jesus Christ, presenting us to the Father. Irenaeus says that this occurs not by a "casting away of the flesh, but by the imparting of the Spirit."[106] Glorification is our true humanization: "The glory of God," he says, "is a human fully alive."[107] Farrow notes that for Irenaeus,

> The ascension of Jesus Christ is not the return of God to God. It is the ascension of the God-man to his rightful place, the place of glory that Adam and Eve never knew, but are yet destined to know.... We will be deified by the Spirit, knowing God by way of God.[108]

102. Von Balthasar, *Origen: Spirit and Fire,* 135.
103. Ibid., 136–38.
104. Ibid., 358.
105. Julie Canlis makes this point in *Calvin's Ladder,* 177, from Mary Ann Donovan, *One Right Reading? A Guide to Irenaeus* (Collegeville, MN: Liturgical Press, 1997), 118.
106. Canlis, *Calvin's Ladder,* 183–84, quoting Irenaeus, *AH,* 581.
107. Irenaeus, *AH,* 4.20.7.
108. Farrow, *Ascension Theology,* 144, 150.

REFORMED INTERPRETATIONS OF DEIFICATION

If Calvin and other Reformed writers define recapitulation as a synonym for union with Christ, as I have shown, then it should not surprise us that they affirm deification (or glorification) as the consummation of that union.[109]

First, like Irenaeus, Calvin interprets descent and ascent in thoroughly Trinitarian terms. Calvin shared Luther's emphasis on the downward descent of God in the flesh. "All who, leaving Christ, attempt to rise to heaven after the manner of the giants, are destitute," Calvin warns in his comment on John 8:19. Herman Selderhuis notes from the reformer's *Commentary on the Psalms* that "God does not command us to ascend into heaven, but, because of our weakness, he descends to us."[110] And yet, focusing merely on the descent was bound to limit—and did limit—the eschatological and pneumatological significance of Christ's ascension for us. To Luther's emphasis on the downward descent of Christ to us, Calvin adds the equally Pauline emphasis on the Spirit's work of seating us with Christ in heavenly places. Calvin says that there is "a manner of descent by which he lifts us up to himself," which Philip Walker Butin explains as follows:

> Not only does Christ (in the Spirit) condescend to manifest himself to believers by means of visible, tangible, created elements; at the same time by the Spirit, the worshiping church is drawn into the heavenly worship of the Father though the mediation of the ascended Christ, who is seated with the Father in the heavenlies. For Calvin, this accentuates, rather than diminishes, the true humanity of Christ.[111]

It is this double movement—the descent of the Son in our humanity and the Spirit's raising us up with Christ eschatologically—that gives Calvin's doctrine of union a distinctively Irenaean flavor.

For both Irenaeus and Calvin, the believer's ascent with Christ is a trinitarian operation. According to Irenaeus, Christ "has also poured out the Spirit of the Father for the union and communion of God and man, imparting indeed God to men by means of the Spirit, and, on the other hand, attaching men to God by His own incarnation, and bestowing upon

---

109. See J. Todd Billings, "United to God through Christ: Assessing Calvin on the Question of Deification," *Harvard Theological Journal* 98, no. 3 (2005): 315–34. For a more thorough treatment, see J. Todd Billings, *Calvin, Participation and the Gift: The Activity of Believers in Union with Christ* (New York and Oxford: Oxford University Press, 2008).
110. Herman Selderhuis, *Calvin's Theology of the Psalms* (Grand Rapids: Baker, 2007), 203, referring to Calvin's comments on Psalms 42:2 and 24:7.
111. Philip Walker Butin, *Revelation, Redemption and Response: Calvin's Trinitarian Understanding of the Divine-Human Relationship* (New York: Oxford University Press, 1995), 118.

us at His coming immortality durably and truly, by means of communion with God."[112] Similarly, Calvin says that "for this reason Christ descended to us, to bear us up to the Father, and at the same time to bear us up to himself, inasmuch as he is one with the Father."[113]

It is therefore not our ascent to a spiritual realm but Christ's humiliation and exaltation and the Holy Spirit's act of uniting us to him that is saving. The Father "raised us up with him and seated us with him in the heavenly places in Christ Jesus" (Eph 2:6). On Colossians 3:1 Calvin writes, "Ascension follows resurrection: hence if we are members of Christ we must ascend into Heaven, because He, on being raised up from the dead was received up into Heaven that He might draw us with Him."[114]

Second, deification is the realization of our humanity, not our inner divinity. Created in God's image, our likeness to God in his moral attributes is intrinsic to our human nature. Therefore, to be made consummately like God — as far as a creature can be — is not to be less human but more fully so. Like Irenaeus, Calvin observes that Christ is Son by nature; we are sons by adoption.[115] Calvin quotes Irenaeus (*AH* 5.2.3): "By nature we are mortal, and God alone immortal."[116] Expounding 2 Peter 1:4, he writes, "... that God, then, should make himself ours, so that all his things should in a manner become our things ... The end of the gospel is, to render us eventually conformable to God, and, if we may so speak, to deify us." He explains:

> But the word *nature* is not here essence but *quality*.... There are also at this day fanatics who imagine that we thus pass over into the nature of God, so that his swallows up our nature. Thus they explain what Paul says, that God will be all in all (1 Corinthians 15:28) and in the same sense they take this passage. But such a delirium as this never entered the minds of the holy Apostles; they only intended to say that when divested of all the vices of the flesh, we shall be partakers of divine and blessed immortality and glory, so as to be as it were one with God as far as our capacities will allow.... But we, disregarding empty speculations, ought to be satisfied with this one thing — that the image of God in holiness and righteousness is restored to us for this end, that we may at length be partakers of eternal life and glory as far as it will be necessary for our complete felicity.[117]

---

112. Irenaeus, *AH*, 5.1.1.
113. Calvin, *Institutes*, 1.13.26.
114. Calvin, *Commentary on the Epistles of Paul to the Philippians, Colossians, and Thessalonians*, trans. John King (Grand Rapids: Eerdmans, 1983), on Colossians 3:1.
115. Calvin, *Institutes*, 2.14.5.
116. Calvin, "Psychopannychia," in *Tracts and Treatises*, trans. Henry Beveridge, ed. T. F. Torrance (Grand Rapids: Eerdmans, 1958), 3:478.
117. Calvin, *Commentary on the Catholic Epistles*, trans. and ed. John Owen (Grand Rapids: Baker, repr. 1996), 371.

Calvin's explanation is virtually identical to that of John of Damascus, who teaches, "For these words do not mean any change in nature."[118] Believers will be "deified in the way of participation in the divine glory and not in that of a change into the divine being."[119]

In the *Institutes*, Calvin observes, "Peter declares that believers are called to become partakers of the divine nature.... If the Lord will share his glory, power, and righteousness with the elect—nay, will give himself to be enjoyed by them and, what is more excellent, will somehow make them to become one with himself, let us remember that every sort of happiness is included under this benefit."[120] He asks, "What is the goal of our adoption which we attain through him, if it is not, as Peter declares, finally to be partakers of the divine nature (2 Pet. 1:4)?"[121] Immortality is not the spirit's native origin but the prize that Christ has won for us.[122] Creation in God's image is "participation in God," but justification and recreation in Christ by grace is a joy beyond words.[123]

It is striking that even after his deep criticisms of Osiander's more Origenist view of union, Calvin nevertheless maintained that deification is "that 'than which nothing more outstanding can be imagined.' "[124] Nevertheless, "we are one with the Son of God not because he conveys his substance to us, but because, by the power of his Spirit, he imparts to us his life and all the blessings which he has received from the Father."[125] He says that the "fanatics" imagine that at death "we shall revert back to our original state," erroneously conceived as absorption into deity.[126]

The same affirmations and qualifications of deification that we observed in Athanasius, Ireaneus, and Calvin are repeated frequently in formative Reformed systems. For example, Zacharius Ursinus points out that Christ is still present with us, not only by his divinity but also "by union with his human nature" through the same Spirit who united the Son to our human-

---

118. John of Damascus, "Exposition of the Orthodox Faith" in NPNF2, 9:65–66. Compare also with Calvin's formulation in his *Commentary on John 6:51*.

119. Ibid., 9:31.

120. Calvin, *Institutes*, 3.25.10.

121. Calvin, *CO* 9.351, cited in Joseph Tylenda, "The Controversy of Christ the Mediator: Calvin's Second Reply to Stancaro," *Calvin Theological Journal* 8 (1973): 148.

122. Calvin, *Institutes*, 2.1.1.

123. Ibid.

124. Carl Mosser, "The Greatest Possible Blessing: Calvinism and Deification," *Scottish Journal of Theology* 55:1 (2002): 40, comment on 2 Pet 1:4 (*quo nihil praestantius cogitari potest*) from *CO* 55.446: "... a kind of deification [*quasi deificari*]."

125. Calvin on John 17:21 in *Commentary on the Gospel According to John*, trans. William Pringle (Edinburgh: T&T Clark, 1840, repr. Grand Rapids: Baker, 1996), 170–83.

126. Calvin, *Commentary on the Catholic Epistles*, 330; cf. *Institutes*, 1.15.5.

ity. "Our glorification results from Christ's ascension into heaven."[127] This consummate conformity to Christ, then, is not a matter of becoming less creaturely but more truly human than we have ever been.[128]

Turretin affirms that "we will—in body as well as soul . . . be transformed into [Christ] by a participation of the divine nature," made one in love with God and each other.[129] And yet, he disagrees with Thomas Aquinas's stipulation that "When . . . a created intellect sees God in his essence, the divine essence becomes the intelligible form of that intellect."[130] The real question is this: To what extent will we allow a union of creatures *as creatures* with God? "Believers are said to be partakers of the divine nature," writes Turretin, "not univocally (by a formal participation of the divine essence), but only analogically."[131] Quoting John of Damascus, Turretin maintains that we will behold God not in his essence but in the face of Christ.[132] Sharing Job's hope (Job 19:25), we will behold the invisible God with our physical eyes—"that is, of the sight of the incarnate Son of God with respect to his human nature."[133]

Similarly, Owen affirms that while God's essence will forever remain "incomprehensible to our minds, . . . the blessed and blessing sight which we shall have of God will always be 'in the face of Jesus Christ.'"[134]

For this intimate and eschatological conception of union, Calvin was fond of the organic image of ingrafting.[135] The gospel "testifies that we shall be partakers of the divine nature, for when we shall see God face to face, we shall be like him (II Pet. 1:4; I John 3:2)."[136] Elsewhere he adds,

> This is the wonderful exchange which, out of his measureless benevolence, he has made with us; that, by his descent to earth, he has prepared an ascent to heaven for us; that, by taking on our mortality, he has conferred his immortality upon us; that, accepting our weakness, he has strengthened us by his power; that, receiving our poverty unto himself, he has

127. Zacharius Ursinus, *Commentary on the Heidelberg Catechism*, trans. G. W. Williard (Phillipsburg, NJ: Presbyterian and Reformed Publishing, repr. of 1852 ed.), 249, 252.

128. Canlis, *Calvin's Ladder*, 114.

129. Francis Turretin, *Institutes of Elenctic Theology*, trans. G. M. Giger, ed. J. T. Dennison Jr. (Phillipsburg, NJ: P&R Publishing, 1992), 3:611.

130. Thomas Aquinas, *Summa Theologica* I.12.5, trans. Fathers of the English Dominican Province (repr. Westminster, MD: Christian Classics, 1948).

131. Turretin, *Institutes of Elenctic Theology*, 1:190.

132. Ibid., 3:611.

133. Ibid., 3:610.

134. John Owen, "The Person of Christ," 1:292.

135. Calvin, *The Epistles of Paul the Apostle to the Romans and to the Thessalonians*, trans. Ross Mackenzie (Grand Rapids: Eerdmans, 1960), 124.

136. Ibid., 105.

transferred his wealth to us; that, taking the weight of our iniquity upon himself (which oppressed us), he has clothed us with his righteousness.[137]

Third, and closely related to the previous point, to be united to Christ is to be in communion with his body. It is not the ascent of the lonely soul, Plotinus's "flight of the alone to the Alone."[138] As the true humanizing of believers, recapitulation is also the true socializing of the anti-covenantal "disengaged self."[139]

The mystical union is so real that Calvin can say,

> This is the highest honour of the Church, that, until He is united to us, the Son of God reckons himself in some measure imperfect. What consolation is it for us to learn, that, not until we are along with him, does he possess all his parts, or wish to be regarded as complete! Hence, in the First Epistle to the Corinthians, when the apostle discusses largely the metaphor of a human body, he includes under the single name of Christ the whole Church.[140]

Augustine coined the term *totus Christus* ("whole Christ") to refer to Christ as head and the church as his body. A Dionysian interpretation of the church's union with Christ, revived in our day, is mapped onto a Platonist anthropology. De Lubac writes, "The Christ, it has been said, needs the Church as a *pneuma* needs a *sôma*."[141] Jesus Christ becomes the invisible soul of the visible church. More radical (and less orthodox) is Graham Ward's formulation of *totus Christus*. Calvin cannot have a robust view of the church's participation in Christ, says Ward, because he is so fixated on the body of the "gendered Jew." Ward's own solution is to regard this body as infinitely expanded—"transcorporeal"—so that he "returns" in and as the church.[142] This spiritual body is *"more real than any physical body."*[143] Suspicions are little dispelled by his protest, "This is not Origen's 'ascent of mind.'"[144]

---

137. Calvin, *Institutes*, 4.17.2.
138. Plotinus, translation in Andrew Louth, *The Origins of the Christian Mystical Tradition from Plato to Denys* (Oxford: Clarendon Paperbacks, 1983; repr. 1992), 51.
139. I borrow this phrase from Charles Taylor, *Sources of the Self: The Making of the Modern Identity* (Cambridge: Harvard University Press, 1992).
140. John Calvin on Eph 1:23 in *Commentaries on the Epistles of Paul to the Galatians and Ephesians*, trans. William Pringle (Grand Rapids: Eerdmans, 1957), 218.
141. Henri de Lubac, quoted by Boersma, *Nouvelle Théologie* (New York: Oxford University Press, 2009), 266. See also Henri De Lubac, *Catholicism: Christ and the Common Destiny of Man* (London: Burns, Oates & Washbourne, 1950), 29; Yves Congar, *I Believe in the Holy Spirit*, trans. David Smith, 3 vols. (New York: Seabury Press, 1983), 2:19–20.
142. Graham Ward, *Cities of God* (New York and London: Routledge, 2000), 154–72.
143. Ibid., 180.
144. Ibid.

No less real, the mystical union according to Calvin is eschatological, with Christ as the first-fruits. It is not the relation of one's soul and body but of Vine and branches, Head and members, husband and wife.[145] There remains an eschatological tension between the "already" and the "not-yet" that affects Christ and his happiness as well as us and ours. This interpretation clashes not only with more Platonist views, but with a Zwinglian logic that renders questionable a real union with God through Christ's glorified humanity. Here I have in mind especially Karl Barth, whose reticence to identify God's Word directly with anything creaturely, not to mention his lament concerning the triumph of "Calvin's sacramentalism" over Zwingli in the Reformed confessions,[146] represents a radical departure from Reformed teaching on union with Christ.

Fourth, justification is the legal basis for, rather than the alternative to, sanctification and glorification. Attempts to interpret Calvin as substituting union with Christ, much less deification, for justification are no more successful than the Finnish interpretation of Luther.

Like the contrived opposition between propitiation and *Christus Victor*, "justification *or* deification" is yet another false choice unknown to the apostle Paul, who announced, "Those whom he predestined he also called, and those whom he called he also justified, and those whom he justified he also glorified" (Rom 8:30–31).[147] From the security of the "once-and-for-all" aspects of this union (viz., election, justification, regeneration and adoption) there arises the "more-and-more" aspects. One cannot be united to Christ for justification without also receiving in him sanctification and glorification. "With a wonderful communion day by day, he grows more and more into one body with us, until he becomes completely one with us."[148] Through the Word and sacraments the Spirit works "to lead us little by little to a firm union with God."[149]

In Calvin's view, "Paul not only exhorts us to follow Christ, but also takes hold of something far higher, namely, that through baptism Christ

---

145. Augustine coined the phrase *totus Christus* to refer to the "whole Christ" as Head and members. In the Middle Ages, this idea was increasingly interpreted within the Neoplatonism of Pseudo-Dionysius, as the church (in effect) replacing the absent body of the historical Jesus. Michael Horton, *People and Place: A Covenant Ecclesiology* (Louisville: Westminster John Knox, 2008), 155–90.

146. Karl Barth, *CD* IV/4:88, 128–30; cf. *The Word of God and the Word of Man*, trans. Douglas Horton (New York: Harper Torchbooks, 1957), 114.

147. The seventeenth-century Reformed divine William Ames observed, "Glorification is nothing other but the carrying out of the sentence of justification.... In glorification the life that results from the pronouncement and award given to us we now have in actual possession." William Ames, *The Marrow of Theology*, trans. John D. Eusden (Durham, NC: Labyrinth Press, 1983), 172.

148. Calvin, *Institutes*, 3.2.24.

149. Ibid,, 2.15.5.

makes us sharers in his death, that we may be engrafted in it."[150] Participation, not imitation, is the root.[151] Just as Calvin added to Luther's emphasis on Christ's descent the equally Pauline emphasis on ascent with Christ, he added to Luther's "once-and-for-all" emphasis the "more-and-more" aspect of our union.

Fifth, like Calvin, the most formative Reformed theologians identified glorification and the beatific vision with the resurrection of the dead as one event that glorifies us in body as well as soul.[152] As noted above, Calvin observes that where Plato's beatific vision is a flight away from our body, union with Christ raises our contemplation to the resurrection. John Owen observes that "Plato's contemplations about the immortality of the soul" work against the hope of resurrection. He adds that this is the problem "in all contemplations of future glory when things are proposed to it whereof in this life it hath neither foretaste, sense, experience, nor evidence." He stipulates, "No man ought to look for anything in heaven but what one way or other he hath some experience of in this life."[153] Turretin emphasized that grace does not annihilate nature.[154] Our bodies are raised, not replaced.[155] For us, time is not left behind, but fulfilled and perpetually renewed. It is *"this* time" defined by sin and death that is disappearing.[156]

These emphases suggest the closest affinity with the Second Council of Constantinople, whose eleventh anathema against Origen reads, "If anyone shall say that the future judgment signifies the destruction of the world and that the end of the story will be an immaterial *physis*, and that thereafter there will no longer be any body matter, but only *nous*, let him be anathema."[157]

---

150. Ibid., 4.15.5.

151. Ibid., 3.3.9.

152. Turretin, *Institutes of Elenctic Theology*, 3:609, 612. As the Belgic Confession (Art. 37) concludes, "And for a gracious reward, the Lord will cause [his elect] to possess such a glory as never entered the heart of man to conceive." From the ascension we are assured, according to the Heidelberg Catechism, "first, that Christ is our advocate in the presence of his Father in heaven; second, that he as the head, will also take us, his members, up to himself; third, that he sends us his Spirit as an earnest, by whose power we seek those things which are above, where Christ sits at the right hand of God, and not the things on the earth" (Heidelberg Catechism, LD 18, Q. 49). When Christ returns in the flesh, the Westminster Confession adds (32.3), "the bodies of the unjust shall, by the power of Christ, be raised to dishonor: the bodies of the just, by His Spirit, unto honor; and be made conformable to His own glorious body."

153. John Owen, "The Person of Christ," 1:290.

154. Turretin, *Institutes of Elenctic Theology*, 3:618–19.

155. Ibid., 3:596, 618–19.

156. Ibid., 3:596.

157. "The Seven Ecumenical Councils" in *NPNF2*, vol. 14, 316ff.

Over against the Neoplatonism that has frequently infected theology, writes Bavinck, "in Reformation theology" the antithesis to grace is not nature but sin.[158] Grace is not simply "an aid to humans in their pursuit of deification"; it is "the beginning, the middle, and the end of the entire work of salvation: it is totally devoid of human merit. Like creation and redemption, so also sanctification is a work of God. It is of him, and through him, and therefore also leads to him."[159]

CONCLUSION

I hope to have assisted in disproving Hans Urs von Balthasar's charge that Irenaeus's "basic attitude cannot be assimilated by true Protestantism." If there are good reasons to reject the Kantian—ostensibly "post-metaphysical"—projects of Ritschl, Harnack, and their heirs, there are good reasons to resist the lure of a revived Christian Platonism (indeed, an explicit Origenism) with its sweeping narrative of nominalism mediated through the Reformation and its allegedly "extrincisist" view of the God-world relation.

Irenaeus had focused on the historical economy of creation, fall, redemption, and consummation, and he upbraided the Gnostics for raising purely speculative questions. However, Origen could not suffer this response. While Scripture and church teaching were a good first step for the simple, he wrote, "what existed before this world, or what will exist after it, has not yet been made known openly to the many, for no clear statement on this point is set forth in the Church teaching." This left plenty of room for speculation, and Platonism provided the advanced course in metaphysics.[160]

The ascension especially forces us to lay our metaphysical cards on the table. Does the biblical drama yield its own doctrine of participation? Can eschatology transform ontology? Does the story of Israel culminating in Jesus generate its own cosmology, or is the gospel a wonderful symbol or illustration of a truth that, as "Greeks," we have always known deep down?

Biblical eschatology opens up the closed Platonist circle into a historical line. It is the movement from type to reality, promise to fulfillment within history, not from the lower world of matter to the upper world of spirit. At the same time, history itself cannot generate a single seed of

---

158. Bavinck, *Reformed Dogmatics*, 3:578.
159. Ibid., 3:579.
160. Origen, *On First Principles*, preface, 7.

its redemption; God must rend the heavens and descend to us. Even in Hebrews, the categories of earthly and heavenly have become transformed into the eschatological division between "this age" and "the age to come." The old covenant belongs to "this present age," while the new covenant inaugurates "the age to come."

The ascension occurs not within the Gnostic drama or Platonist/Neoplatonist myth of *exitus-reditus* (exit-return), but as the fulfillment of a greater exodus that Jesus accomplished in Jerusalem (Luke 9:31) and a greater conquest of the whole earth by his Word and Spirit. "Thus," Calvin concludes, "we look to our Head Who is already in heaven, and say, 'Although I am weak, there is Jesus Christ who is my strength. Although I am full of all miseries, Jesus Christ is in immortal glory and what He has will some time be given to me and I shall partake of *all* his benefits."[161] With the ascension, Immanuel is not only God With Us, and God For Us, but Us With God.

---

161. Calvin, *Serm. Acts* 1:6–8 (*CO* 48.619), emphasis added.

SUBJECT INDEX

AUTHOR INDEX